Molly Ivins

Molly Ivins

A REBEL LIFE

Bill Minutaglio
&
W. Michael Smith

PUBLICAFFAIRS
New York

Published in the United States by PublicAffairs™, a member of the Perseus Books Group.

Printed in the United States of America.

PublicAffairs books are available at special discounts for bulk purchases in the U.S. by corporations, institutions, and other organizations. For more information, please contact the Special Markets Department at the Perseus Books Group, 2300 Chestnut Street, Suite 200, Philadelphia, PA 19103, call (800) 810-4145, ext. 5000, or e-mail special.markets@perseusbooks.com.

Book Design by Timm Bryson

Library of Congress Cataloging-in-Publication Data
Minutaglio, Bill.
Molly Ivins : a rebel life / Bill Minutaglio & W. Michael Smith.—1st ed.
p. cm.
Includes bibliographical references and index.
ISBN 978-1-58648-717-1 (hardcover)
1. Ivins, Molly. 2. Women journalists—United States—Biography. I. Smith, W. Michael. II. Title.
PN4874.I92M56 2009
070.92–dc22
[B]
2009023034

First Edition
10 9 8 7 6 5 4 3 2 1

To Tess Minutaglio,

A STRONG AND LOVING SOUL

CONTENTS

PREFACE

After examining thousands of personal documents she continuously donated to public archives in Texas—and after interviewing more than 100 of her relatives, close acquaintances, co-workers, and bosses—one thing was clear: Molly Ivins was many things. As her collaborator Lou Dubose once put it, she was trilingual. She spoke private-school French, erudite Smith College English, and ribald Texan. She was also, arguably, one of the best-known and most influential journalists in American history. Three of her books were national bestsellers, her columns appeared in over 300 newspapers, and she was pursued by the most powerful kingmakers and rainmakers—they wanted her to run for office, they wanted her to be on national TV, they wanted to know if she could help them win the presidency and if they could make a movie about her life.

Yet beyond her prolific work and the demands on her celebrity, there was something else. She was an extraordinarily fastidious self-chronicler. She stored everything, including items that people wished she had never saved. Copies of letters she had sent out to friends and family and colleagues. Reporters' notebooks. White House invitations. Letters from statesmen, world leaders, senators. She kept her grade-school report cards, memos to and from her bosses, pay stubs, publishing contracts, postcards from France, Bolivia, and Mexico. She kept her itineraries and programs from Broadway shows. She kept phone logs, car bills, and grocery shopping lists. Medical records. Scribbled messages about her medications. Countless intimate letters from her mother, her domineering father, her supportive brother and sister. Letters from lovers. If someone sent something to her and she deemed it important, she kept it.

And then, at the height of her career, she decided to begin giving it all to the Dolph Briscoe Center for American History at the University of Texas at Austin. A close friend of hers said that "she wanted all of this to be seen"—as a nod, her friend surmised, to transparency in the historical record, an open accounting. But as the friend went on to say, it was also her way of finally showing that in real life she was far more complex than the public persona familiar to millions of readers.

Among many of these readers she had achieved a one-name status (*Molly!*), a latter-day Mark Twain-meets-Will Rogers. She was the wisecracking social commentator who gleefully teed up on anyone whose boot heels clicked across the marble floors in the House of Power. Her column and her books were always anchored by a photo of her wide-open, inviting face—and she always seemed on the verge of a booming laugh. She crisscrossed the country, drew huge crowds, made innumerable national TV appearances, and was given honorary degrees, and all the while, powerful Hollywood producers were trying to decide whether to create a television series based on her—or to go all the way and put her life on the big screen.

The many interviews with her closest friends and supporters pointed to a life that few of her many loyal readers were aware of. Entirely apart from her politics, she faced wicked physical and mental challenges for long stretches of her life—a life often characterized by breathtaking twists and turns and an aching poignancy. Through it all she maintained an almost compulsively generous touch. She had a difficult time saying no to people who came to her seeking something—her money, her time, her celebrity. She gave thousands of dollars to close friends and to people she barely knew. She gave plane tickets, frequent-flier miles, and hotel rooms. She made public appearances and spoke for free even when she was in danger of dying. When she found out that someone had been tossed out of work—or, in other cases, had lost their income and insurance when their husbands died—she figured out a way to put them on her payroll. When friends were sick, she would come to their house, make the bed, clean, and cook. When someone admired a book at her home, she pressed it into that person's hands. After dining at a really good restaurant in New Orleans, she paid the entire bill for the large gathering at her table. When acquaintances needed a place to crash in Paris, she made some calls and found them one. And when a reporter from *Rolling Stone* came to Austin to learn about, say, George W. Bush, she patiently walked him through things he would otherwise never have been able to comprehend. She had circles of friends, and then even more circles of friends, throughout all those moments when she faced death and a seemingly endless series of narrative rollercoaster rides. Her powerful New York friends. Her Washington insider friends. Her liberal Dallas friends. Her loyal Austin friends—of which there were many. Her West Coast friends. As her fame grew, and with it her outsized influence, she rarely turned any of them down if they needed a blurb for their book, a letter of recommendation, a glance at their new screenplay, a place for their children to spend a week with "Aunt Molly." She bought books for the children and quizzed them on history and life. She seemed not to question the motivations of the people who wanted a piece of her time or needed something from her—she just gave it to them. She threw famous parties at her house in South Austin and it was an apt metaphor that the door was always open to any stranger who wandered in (as happened frequently). For years, her home phone number was listed in the public directory. There was the sense that she was almost always available—and frustration prospered among the many famous people who wondered why she was too busy to instantly return their calls. And why, when they called her, they got this message:

"You've reached Molly Ivins. I'm not able to come to the phone right now. You might try my office number, which is 445–7172, or my Ace Assistant Betsy Moon, who almost always knows where I am."

As was also apparent from her friends, she had a gift for leaving people with the impression that she was letting them in on an intimacy, usually underscored with the impression that she was sharing a joke with you. At her private high school, the most refined one in Texas, her laughter would echo in the hallways. At Smith College, the door to her room would be open and you could hear her chuckling all the way down the hall. In Austin, at the madcap, smoky campouts with future governors and hippie musicians frolicking alongside a gin-clear river, her laughter would rise from under the canopy of ancient live oak trees. In New York, at the somber *New York Times*, she smiled as she padded barefoot in the newsroom and talked about her front-page stories on Elvis or Son of Sam. She seemed perfectly willing to share a laugh with people whose politics were diametrically opposed to hers.

Her laughter was also there when she was dying and people traveled from around the world to be at her bedside. Maybe not as booming or as hearty as before, but it was there more often than not.

This book is an attempt to outline Molly Ivins's roots and show the path that led to her singular American presence. She was often the only woman in the room, in the middle of the action, going blow-for-blow with the Texas and Washington potentates. A careful decision was made not to stud this book with endless quotes from her work. (Her columns and articles are readily available in several collections.) The idea was to illustrate how her upbringing and background led to her being a public figure.

One of the authors worked for Molly Ivins for six years in the 1990s as a researcher, reporter, and all-around-aide (from placing calls to the White House to making the runs for cigarettes). The other author was mentioned in a column she wrote lauding his work on the subject of poverty in the Rio Grande Valley (he also attended the Columbia Graduate School of Journalism a decade after she had). In the spirit of a review by her excellent friend David Broder about a book one of us had written—an unauthorized biography of George W. Bush, wherein Broder said he could discern no evident bias—our method in this work was to rely on her own papers and the words of her friends.

Ivins was acutely aware, some of those friends said, that she had become a public figure. She did a stint on the highest rated TV show in America. Sit-com characters were based on her. And she was also aware that she was operating from a base, in Texas, where it was almost unheard of for women to succeed the way she did. She talked with Bill Clinton . . . and Hunter Thompson. She was revered by Willie Nelson, Paul Krugman, Ann Richards, Maya Angelou, Calvin Trillin, Dan Rather, and Garrison Keillor.

Love her or hate her (and there were thousands who hated her, including the people who sent her death threats), she was compared to Rogers, Twain, Ambrose Bierce, H. L. Mencken, Rabelais, Lenny Bruce, and even the prophet Jeremiah (all of them, of course, men).

Toward the end of her rollicking life, she kept pushing, maybe harder and harder, the longer she lingered with breast cancer—the seemingly endless years of mastectomies, failed breast reconstructions, chemotherapies, radiation sessions, the loss of her wild red mane. There was a blues lyric she liked, one that suggested how hard it was: "There's so much shit in Texas, you're bound to step in some." Her many admirers knew she was working as a woman in a ballsy, unforgiving environment. It was lonely, even dangerous, for women who wanted to speak their minds—let alone wave a razor-edged middle finger at the powers-that-be. The kindest critics called her "a hairy-legged liberal." The darker ones, those who ominously moved in the shadows, said she was better being a "dead cunt." She laughed about it all, but she was always, always on her guard: One day she was in downtown Dallas and had just walked out of a dark, hole-in-the-wall bar. It was a place filled with grifters, one-legged rodeo cowboys, aged strippers caked with dollops of hopeful rouge, and booze-addled newspaper people who'd gathered to drink hard while trying to avoid walking into the stone pillars that held the place up. She had on a sparkling, tight dress and as she walked outside the bar, she felt an insistent hand on her ass. She turned, leaned back for leverage, formed a fist, and swung hard. Her hand thudded into the shocked face of the man she assumed had touched her. His teeth and blood sprayed on the streets of Dallas.

She increasingly applied that muscle to the things she believed in. She had embraced subjectivity very early in her journalism career. And as her influence grew, she was able to literally shift national policy—her phone rang and it was Clinton, or John McCain, or Tom Daschle, or Dan Rather, or some other media/political kingpin on the other end of the line. The pols would delay putting out bills and legislation until they knew exactly when she was going to write something. In terms of being the barometer for the outside-the-Beltway, populist, liberal, progressive constituency, then Ivins was the one. Her aides even quietly began referring to her millions of readers as "Molly's constituency." Some of them secretly hoped she really would run for office.

At a banquet in New York, she was introduced by Maya Angelou. The poet had never met her. Ivins bounded on stage, walked up to Angelou, wrapped her in a bear hug, and then told the audience: "Maya Angelou and I are identical twins, we were separated at birth." Angelou, like everyone else, laughed. It was outrageous. Angelou would say: "Whoever separated us at birth must know it didn't work."

When Ivins died, Angelou wrote a poem about her that read, in part:

Up to the walls of Jericho
She marched with a spear in her hand

Research for this book extended into New York, Washington, D.C., Minnesota, California, Colorado, Florida. There was an exploration of Ivins's time in France. Much of this work was filtered through continuous immersion in the often-unfathomable state where she was raised and continued to live. She left Texas at various times in her life, but it always went with her. And, arguably, it brought her back. She found Texas, especially Austin, to be the right place to endure the fame. One time, over some margaritas at a downtown Mexican restaurant in Austin, she said to one of the authors: "You have to roll with it." She was talking about all the hype, the hustle, that she had experienced in the glare of the public spotlight.

After she died there were memorial services—large ones in Austin and in New York, and smaller homespun vigils and remembrances and gatherings around the nation. There were condolences from Clinton and Bush. It was an affirmation of her success and influence that, months after her death, people continued to wonder what she would say about various political events, and to discuss who would play her in the movie about her life.

In Austin there were signs that read "WWMS"—"What Would Molly Say?" Friends said she would have kept laughing. At her home, she had used all of her fancy national journalism awards as trivets. One friend interviewed for this book said that "she was stronger than most people knew."

Bill Minutaglio &
W. Michael Smith
Austin, August 2009

CHAPTER ONE

General Jim

Things haven't changed all that much where George W. Bush comes from. Houston is a cruel and crazy town on a filthy river in East Texas with no zoning laws and a culture of sex, money and violence.

—HUNTER THOMPSON[1]

In late September of 1959, a twenty-one-year-old University of Southern California student—good-natured Dick Swanson—was commanded to a buffet table. Before him were hunks of raw, oil-soaked liver, each "about the size of a club sandwich." It was close to midnight, the ritual candles were burning, and Swanson—Pledge Number Seven—was being told to swallow a greased plank of liver without chewing it. The dental-school freshman tried to ingest the squishy meat three times. He gagged, reached in his mouth to extract it, and tried again, again, again. On his last attempt, the blue-eyed boy from Hollywood began choking. He lurched forward, staggering, panic washing over him as he fought to catch a breath. He flailed toward a door as if desperately searching for something, and then thrashed hard to the ground. The fraternity brothers watched him collapse. Swanson was already dead when he arrived, at 1:48 A.M., at Los Angeles Central Receiving Hospital.

James E. Ivins—destined to become president of one of the most powerful oil-and-gas companies in the world—took note of the spreading news about Swanson's death. He decided to write a letter. He wanted, *needed*, to write a letter to *Time* in the fall of 1959. Someone reading the magazine's piece about the boy's death at the USC chapter might not understand the full story.

Ivins had three children of his own, including a daughter who was already planning for college. She was at St. John's, the finest private school in Texas; among her classmates were the children of the most powerful barons of the international oil kingdom. She loved France, cats, gum, and apricots. Her family decided one day to call her "the mole in the hole"—because she was always up in her room over the garage, writing note after note, reading God knows what, staring at the sketches on her pad, worrying about her weight, wondering if the rains were ever going to blanket perpetually humid Houston.

Her father was The Worthy Grand Master of the 80,000-member Kappa Sigma fraternity. He had taken his children to the Grand Conclave in Denver. He composed his letter to *Time:*

> . . . [T]o condemn the fraternity system out of hand is to disregard the useful and objective functions it performs as an adjunct of higher education; nor is it fair to imply that what obviously was an act of hazing constitutes part of a formal initiation procedure.
>
> JAMES E. IVINS,
> Worthy Grand Master of the Kappa Sigma Fraternity,
> Houston[2]

As a child she often heard people referring to him as "The General" or "The Admiral." One acquaintance said he was like Captain Ahab—resolute and disciplined to the point of obsession. He had suffered hearing loss during World War II, and family members and others sometimes began to feel obliged to bark out their questions and answers to him, an act that only reinforced their vision of Jim Ivins. Finally, he was tall, six-foot-six, almost always in sinewy shape. When he walked into a room, solemn-faced and straining to listen, he filled the doorway with a coiled presence. The neighborhood children watched him guardedly; one remembered him as "ramrod straight. Piercing blue eyes. And a commanding voice . . . we always knew he was serious."[3]

The family, with relatives in Indiana, Wisconsin, and Illinois, had "Scottish-Irish roots" (she would later say with a laugh that its background might explain her father's stoic nature).[4] Jim Ivins was precise, controlled, and he considered it good breeding to write all manner of letters to family members, colleagues, and friends. He was firm in his speaking manner, coolly polite to women he had just met. He enjoyed reading—especially stories about the sea. He perused the *Houston Chronicle* and *The New Yorker.* His children watched as his hair faded to gray by the age of thirty and then to "snow-white," even though "he always weighed exactly what he did when he was on the [rowing] crew at the University of Wisconsin."[5]

His own father, who had worked on and off for the Miller Brewing Company in Wisconsin, had been erratic in his earning habits and family lore suggested that Jim Ivins was determined not to turn out that way. When his father was debilitated by a stroke late in life, the event registered deeply with the son. He wrote, in a never-published memoir, about his father's death: "I always felt that life short-changed him."[6] From an early age, he gravitated toward solidity and predictability. His mother told family members that Jim Ivins had become "the man" of the household when he was just five years old.[7]

⟹

Twelve pounds at birth, he was raised in the greater Chicago area in a less-than-prominent family and educated at Nicholas Senn High School in North Chicago. The classical inclinations of the school, which was founded in 1913 on former farmland, had a distinct influence on him. He developed a bent for Shakespeare. The other books he treasured—works by James Fenimore Cooper, Sir Walter Scott, Robert Louis Stevenson, Herman Melville—were the ones he gave his children in the 1940s and 1950s. His daughter Mary, the second child of three, would remember that many of the tomes he made available were defined by themes of chivalry, duty, devotion, and honor.[8] On the other hand, she would say, "he was proud that he had gone to school with, as he said, micks, wops, kikes and blacks."[9]

Jim Ivins was drawn to an idealized notion of another age, a time when ambiguity was discouraged, when self-discipline was valued above most things. His self-challenging regimen extended especially to the water. He rowed at the University of Wisconsin in the mid-1930s in a program influenced by coaches who had served at Yale and Harvard. His involvement with rowing, which would last a lifetime, into his eighties, ranged from coaching teenagers to slipping out on his own into a lake or river in his single shell. He had developed, as his daughter noted, the deep love of sailing that seems to possess some Midwesterners—and would spend decades of his life on a bay, the Great Lakes, a river, or an ocean, navigating for sailboat crews in trans-Atlantic races, serving on Coast Guard vessels, pleasure-sailing to the Bahamas—or just rowing, alone, for hour after hour.

He worked to put himself through college as a crew coach during the Great Depression. But his college funding was also aided by family members, including his uncle, the Right Reverend Benjamin Franklin Price Ivins, the seventh bishop to oversee the Episcopal Diocese in Milwaukee. The bishop, serving from 1933 to 1953, was among the most prominent members of the Ivins family: He attended Columbia University, was a "settlement worker" during the heyday of the Settlement House Movement's attempts to address the problems of the disenfranchised, and served as an army chaplain in World War I. One newspaper account also mentions his work with the I.W.W.—presumably the Industrial Workers of the World: "During the war, he concentrated on organization work and was sent to the state of Washington to do special work among the I.W.W."[10] But if he had any acute links to I.W.W. leftist philosophies, he certainly didn't transmit them to his nephew James, who would become a resolute capitalist deep in the heart of the most conservative corners of Texas.

For part of his time in Wisconsin, Jim Ivins lived for free in the basement of an Episcopal church. He attended law school at Wisconsin, continued his commitment to the Kappa Sigma fraternity, and saved $150 from his coaching duties to buy *Slowpoke,* the first of several sailboats he would own in his lifetime. And as the United States was moving toward war, he married Margaret Robbie Milne, a vivacious woman from a well-to-do manufacturing family whose roots were in Canada but had settled in Chicago. The newlyweds moved to St. Louis, where he went to work as an investigating attorney for the relatively new Securities and Exchange Commission, created by President Roosevelt as part of his extended New Deal effort to corral the U.S. economy. Their first child, blond and blue-eyed Sara, was born in St. Louis.

As war escalated, he repeatedly lobbied to join the Coast Guard. He was finally assigned to the USS *Gallup,* an escort vessel scheduled to sail from San Diego for the Pacific theater on June 1, 1944. He moved his young family to California and in Monterey on August 30, 1944, Mary Tyler Ivins was born. He picked the name and when his wife complained that "Mary" was too common, he said, "Well, if it's good enough for the mother of God, it's good enough for my daughter." The "Tyler" was added in honor of his stepmother. Relatives wondered if Mary would be tall, like her father. They wondered if she would be as extemporaneous—as unfiltered—as her mother.

⟻⟼

Margaret Robbie Milne's father, a manufacturer from Canada, had "made and lost a couple of fortunes"[11] through the first decades of the twentieth century. The family eventually settled in Illinois. Close to the time of the great stock market collapse of 1929, her Smith College–educated mother succumbed to the latest surge of flu epidemic. Margaret was sixteen. "I don't think she ever recovered from that sense of abandonment. She tried to comfort her grieving father and to mother her two much-younger siblings, but it was too much for her."[12]

Her father was wiped out by the Great Depression but then dutifully began reassembling his wealth. Margaret, with eyes set wide across a slightly long face, was enrolled in private schools. But the onus of being sixteen years old and a surrogate parent to her siblings apparently took its toll. A teacher at the exclusive all-girls Roycemore School in Evanston, Illinois, noticed her looking overworked and drowsy in class. Concerned about her health, the teacher alerted her father at the family home on Orrington Avenue. Margaret, who credited the teacher with "[saving] my life,"[13] left Roycemore in 1929. She moved to the prestigious Walnut Hill School in Natick, Massachusetts, and followed her late mother's path to Smith, where she studied the classics, majored in psychology, and developed a lifelong affinity for theater. Her college career was interrupted in her junior year when her father's business suffered yet again. Unable to pay for Smith, her father pulled her from school and sent her to live with cousins in Missoula, Montana. She told people she lived as "a broad in Montana" and joined a local branch of the Kappa Kappa Gamma sorority.[14] She ultimately graduated from Smith in 1934, and her devotion to the school would last a lifetime. Being a Smith graduate defined her, and she would regularly attend class reunions and alumni excursions.

She was known to people as someone who laughed easily and who occasionally blurted out the seeming non sequitur, some unusual observation about another person or herself that was so unguarded as to be either refreshing or rude. Friends and family knew her to be a light-hearted, easy-to-tease soul—her daughter would later call her "ditzy"[15]—but there were moments when she lingered, with utmost seriousness and something approaching gravity, on her memories of Smith. It was as if there was something dormant in her, some spark still glowing from her Smith education that had never really ignited. As she approached her thirties, she found herself married to a young, exacting lawyer named James Ivins and with a growing family. Smith had become an idealized place that she hoped one of her daughters might attend. She was not a psychologist, didn't have a paying job, and hardly had time to read. Her husband was constantly traveling, working late. But she liked to be in touch with Smith, to know the news about it, to occasionally remind people that she had gone there well before she had followed her husband around the country and up the corporate rungs.

The USS *Gallup* performed antisubmarine patrols, escorted battleships, shelled Biak Island, provided cover for troop landings as part of the New

Guinea offensive, and flanked the task force that led to General Douglas MacArthur's return to the Philippines. James Ivins, a gunnery officer at the time, developed close friendships with a small handful of his Coast Guard mates, and years later the common reference point was still their work firing on the beaches of New Guinea and sweeping the stormy channels during the massive Battle of Leyte Gulf, sometimes considered the largest naval battle not just of World War II but of any war. The *Gallup* arrived in San Francisco on Christmas Day in 1944 and then spent the next six months patrolling the North Pacific, off the Aleutians.

For years, Mary Ivins had thought her father spent the war years mundanely ferrying supplies and hadn't been anywhere near serious combat. In time, she learned that his hearing loss was a result of his having stood next to the *Gallup*'s roaring guns for two days straight during the battle at Leyte Gulf. What she also learned much later, after taking possession of her father's personal letters, was that her father was often single-minded about the task at hand—and about the way society, mankind, was ordered.

On March 23, 1945, he wrote in a letter home about his second child, Mary Tyler, or "Ty" as he sometimes liked to call her: "I'll bet the kids are cute as bugs and run you nuts between the two of them. So Ty is starting to sit up, isn't it rather early for that? I sort of forgot. I don't know for sure when she was born. I know it was in late August, how about wising me up?"[16]

April 11: "I think Mary is going to be your favorite daughter."[17]

April 13: "I think your new stationery is solid, but how about a picture of you lately? I think you have a complex about your looks. When you put your mind on it you are one hell of an attractive girl. No woman looks good unless she worked on it and you don't work on it enough. I want you to be a stunner, babe, and you can be. . . . The Chinese woman of the upper classes, they say, has only one aim in life—to make herself attractive to her husband. Not a bad idea, hey?"[18]

April 22: "I think one more offspring, boy or girl, will about complete our family."[19]

April 25: "The black gal to clean sounds like a fine deal if you can swing it. Bet you still wish we had Shanghaied Jessie when we departed St. Louis, she would probably be welding ships in Oakland for $60 per week by now if we had. I'm rapidly losing what I once considered a broad tolerance on the race question. These damn niggers we have on here for steward's mates—two of 'em anyway—are so uppity that I'm getting narrow-minded about the whole thing. I sincerely believe we've leaned over backward on this ship to avoid creating even an impression of prejudice to our colored brethren. It's a fact you can't tell them to do things the way you do the white boys—you have to be much more 'tender' to them. And do they appreciate it? Not one whit. They seize every opportunity they can to push themselves in further taking liberties and privileges. . . . They keep on repeating the same lazy slipshod errors so much so that we have corrected them repeatedly, and on top of it all, they are the most tarnation confounded, infernal shiftless lot I ever laid eyes on."[20]

Later on, as his second child came to know him better, it was clear that his time at sea—his exposure to different circumstances and people—had shaped him in indelible ways. "My father always said of WWII: 'To have a job worth doing, and to do it well, is the greatest satisfaction in life.'"[21] She felt his experiences in WWII were the best times of his life. But, in the end, there was an overt trait of his that she linked to the war—and that came to terrify her:

"Perhaps it was connected to the deafness, but my father's one great failing was his temper. The one emotion he was good at expressing was anger. He could erupt like Vesuvius. He never hit anyone in the family, but my God, he was terrifying.

"I believe that all the strength I have comes from learning how to stand up to him."[22]

After leaving the Coast Guard at the end of the war, he apparently flirted with the idea of following his father and working for the Miller Brewing Company—this time, running beer distributorships north of San Francisco. (Margaret, who had grown up in Chicago during Prohibition, thought that anyone who sold alcohol was a hoodlum.) But he decided to stay in the legal profession and the family moved briefly to the Chicago area.[23] Through his Kappa Sigma connections, he met Gardiner Symonds, a Harvard-educated Chicago native who was busy building what would become one of the most powerful multinational corporations in history. Symonds was going back and forth between Illinois and Texas, overseeing the Chicago Corporation's oil interests along the Gulf Coast. The Chicago Corporation acquired the Tennessee Gas & Transmission Company in 1943, to help ship fuel across the country during WWII. After the war ended, the Chicago Corporation divested Tennessee Gas & Transmission Company and it became an independent firm, with Symonds as its president. Tenneco, as it was eventually called, grew into a multibillion-dollar behemoth, developing thousands of miles of pipeline spread like far-flung steel cobwebs under and above whole chunks of the United States. There were endless legal tangles over federal regulations, including government attempts to oversee how much fuel Tenneco was shipping, and Symonds needed someone trustworthy not only to unravel the knots but also to find the loopholes. Symonds was from the Chicago area, just like Jim Ivins. He was a Kappa Sigma stalwart, just like Jim. As he thought about ways to build Tenneco, to grow it on Wall Street and get the financing he needed to build and acquire more pipelines (and eventually to take over several iconic, independent Texas oil exploration companies), he wanted an attorney who knew his way around the possibly thorny Securities and Exchange Commission. James Ivins was a perfect fit. In 1949, the family was moving to Texas, where he would help run Tenneco's billion-dollar empire.

Postwar Houston was hurtling with a mad mix of wildcatters, foreign investors, racist police, the nouveau riche, big-time swindlers, and the on-the-ground representatives of powerful names in Washington and on Wall Street. The region around Houston was exploding with industrial development and commerce, some of it tied to the Marshall Plan to rehabilitate ravaged portions of Europe and keep them free of Soviet influence. A necromancer's brew of chemicals was being created in the yawning refineries and factories branching out from Houston to the bleak Gulf of Mexico. There was often an acidy stench in the concrete-colored sky; some people laughed and called it "the stink of money."[24]

Howard Hughes was slipping into small barbecue joints off Lockwood Drive after driving home mega-deals on Texas Avenue downtown. Humble Oil, later to be called Exxon, had moved into Houston and was growing into a mega-corporation. Jesse Jones, the former secretary of commerce and chairman of the Reconstruction Finance Corporation, had returned to Houston—where he owned almost 100 buildings, published the *Houston Chronicle*, and listened to a pissed-off Lyndon Johnson refer to him as "Jesus H. Jones." The Bush family, which had dispatched George Herbert Walker Bush from the Northeast to Midland, Texas, was planning to move its Texas base of operations to Houston.

Glenn McCarthy, the man who inspired the character of Jett Rink in the novel and movie *Giant*, was also in Houston. McCarthy was a bourbon-swilling wildcatter humored by heaven's thumbprint, someone who seemed able to spark oil gushers just by tapping his eel-skin boot heel on the ground. He had a dizzying string of discoveries in sometimes unlikely parts of Texas, considered himself as lucky as a four-leaf clover, and decided to spend $21 million to build the ostentatious Shamrock Hotel in the oil-and-gas capital of the United States. He ordered it painted in sixty-three hues of green and then spent more than $1 million on the opening bacchanalia on St. Patrick's Day in 1949. The Shamrock had the world's largest swimming pool, and McCarthy imported boats and water skiers to put on shows in it. He invited Errol Flynn and Howard Hughes (from whom he'd just bought a plane), offered tastes of his own "Wildcatter" brand of bourbon, and generally worked hard to dent his $200 million fortune. For years, the hotel was the scene of riotous parties, with Frank Sinatra, Robert Mitchum, Dorothy Lamour, politicians, and oilmen making scenes and backroom deals and sweating in a fevered conga line that reinforced for non-Texans the stereotype that Houston was an unleashed, uncouth city of Caligula on the Texas coast. A bow-tied Frank Lloyd Wright once toured the building with a budding architect. Wright pointed at some details on the ceiling: "Young man, that's the effect of venereal disease on architecture."[25] He wasn't alone in seeing the place as the Lone Star Circus Maximus, a house where unhealthy things flourished and were celebrated.

The Ivins family moved, in the late 1940s, down the street from the electric Shamrock, the building that for many people had become a symbol not only of the city but of Texas itself, a state bursting with hyper-exaggerated, boozy tendencies, as if all that oil, all that money, had uncorked some orgy of wretched excess on the underbelly of the American nation. From the bedroom windows in the Ivins house, you could see the green, money-colored lights glittering atop the hotel. Not far away, in the Third Ward, it was a different world. Some of the most original roots musicians in America were writing their blues poetry, capturing details that the *Houston Chronicle* was not. Throughout her teens, Mary Ivins was always aware that there were other layers of reality in heavily segregated Houston. She talked about those layers with friends, wondering exactly what was beyond her world at the insouciant hem of the naughty Shamrock Hotel.

In the Third Ward, Sam "Lightnin'" Hopkins, revered overseas though often overlooked in the United States, was throwing dice in alleys off of Dowling Street and trying to decide if he should get an ass-pocket bottle of Old Heaven Hill. The quintessential bluesman had achieved a street-Zen sense of how to survive—to "done get over" in Houston, Texas, as his blues buddy Hop Wilson sang it. Lightnin' put it this way: "You know a rich man ain't got a chance to go to heaven, and a poor man got a hard way to go." Another singer, Weldon "Juke Boy" Bonner, once said that Houston was "an action town."

It was the largest city in Texas, and in the South overall, and the areas where the black and Latino residents lived were neatly defined but also surprisingly close to the most affluent neighborhoods. The poverty, the lack of city services, the absence of clean running water were staggering; for some newcomers to Houston, it was like the chaos of mid-nineteenth-century New York, with its thickening layers of closely held power, its transient confidence men, its Wall Street bankers, and its self-proclaimed clergymen and scheming neighborhood bosses, all of them working the waterfront, the courthouses, the bank vaults, and the election booths. And every day, men with callused hands—Hispanic migrant workers from the Rio Grande Valley and black field hands from the Piney Woods—would jump off the backs of incoming trucks and buses and ask who was hiring that day in the hot city.

As Houston gorged on unbridled growth and a disregard for zoning, as if that latter notion was tantamount to asking a man to brand his cattle, the disparity between the wealthier families and the chronically poor became almost feudal. The city, like New York, was filled with immigrants—some from other parts of the country, some from overseas. And there was ample room for bitterness and achingly unrequited dreams. People were moving to Houston but few of them were going to be as affluent as the people tied to the oil-and-gas industry. "Back in the scuffling city at the end of the Freeway, a hundred thousand wheels of fortune are spinning. A million individual dreams are down and wagered," as Sigman Byrd, an overlooked genius from Houston, once wrote.[26] It was, in the end, a place where a skeptic might conclude that the American Dream came far easier to some than to others.

⟻⟼

Houston was always fiercely segregated along racial lines and the first few decades of the twentieth century there were marked by massive KKK rallies, race riots, lynchings, and violently rebuffed attempts to end desegregation. In the 1920s, movie theaters were prohibited from screening films starring Jack Johnson because he acted in them with whites; in the 1960s, crosses were burned at the homes of black residents brave enough to sit on the school board. In the black and Latino communities, the police were feared and reviled for their persistent, merciless brutality. The separation, the apartheid, was only underscored and exacerbated by the city's phenomenal economic surge.

The Ivins family initially lived in a pleasant, middle-to-upper-class pocket populated by strivers and young families. The last child in the family, Andy, had been born in 1949, and as he grew, he liked to walk to the corner with his sister Mary. Her father and brother had been the first to call her "the mole in the hole," but during her teens, the rest of the family also began calling her "The Mole." When they wrote her letters and notes and postcards—to the historic camp where she spent her summers, to her boarding school in France, to her boarding school in the Northeast—they would call her "The Mole." She really was always burrowing, collecting, hoarding. (The Mexican maids in Houston might have understood it as Mexican *mole,* the spicy Oaxacan dish whose name descended from the Aztec word *molli,* meaning complex concoction.) By the time she was thirteen, going on fourteen, "Mary" was increasingly calling herself "Molly" and everyone followed suit.

At the corner of their street were decorative four-foot-by-four-foot cement street markers. The children would sit on the markers and wait for their father to come home from his job downtown. Sometimes, after brisk hellos, he would drive them back to the two-story house and immediately begin to wash his Lincoln. "He was very disciplined. My mother was very loving but my father was a real hard worker. Molly picked that up from my father. Molly was a real hard worker . . . you know she was disciplined."[27] On weekends, he could be more relaxed; he would often take everyone sailing. His wife would make chicken á la king, the parents would get the bunks, and the kids would sleep in the cockpit. There were laughs; the kids would swim and jump into Galveston Bay.

It was also a period punctuated by arguments between the parents, with Molly breaking in at an equal volume, remembers Andy:

> You know sometimes my mother and father would get in a fight. It seems like they had a regular, normal marriage, but sometimes they would get to screaming at each other and I was wondering if Molly was interceding to keep that from happening. Or just protect my mother maybe . . . or protect my father. It was probably to protect my mother. You know they had cocktail hour. And after a couple of cocktails, they got shitfaced. She would be interceding when my mother was being yelled at . . . she would get pissed and yell right back at him. But we would have some extreme fucking fights at dinner.[28]

She had decided to move to the un-air-conditioned attic, so she didn't have to share a room with her sister. Her father had rigged up a cheap, plastic intercom that never seemed to work. Sometimes he would wake the kids up by singing the "Star Spangled Banner." She'd be in the hot attic, overhearing the screaming matches with the parents below, and would come down and challenge her father. "I've always had trouble with male authority figures because my father was such a martinet," she later said.[29] Her brother believed the dividing lines were clear: "If there was ever a contention whether something was black or white, it was between Molly and our father."[30] The differences were so stark and intense that "she was going to be anything he wasn't."[31]

The three children were close growing up. Andy seemed inclined to bond with Molly, but the sisters shared a number of things. Their father loved boats and he taught the girls how to sail: "Our boat was called *The Two Belles,* and that was supposed to be Sara and Molly."[32] The girls loved being at the coast, chasing each other along the beach. They would stand on the shore, throw sticks in the water, and pretend the sticks were horses having a race. Back at home, the parents insisted on that same togetherness at family gatherings, on weekend car trips, at church. At Easter, Andy would don a little white suit jacket, his sisters would giggle and wear new dresses, and everyone would pose for pictures. The Ivinses attended Palmer Memorial Episcopal church every Sunday and Andy served as an altar boy, but there was never any sense that religion dominated the household. "One of the things that Molly was famous for was pulling out the Bible and reading. She didn't listen, or sing or do anything else. She was reading, in church. She was doing whatever she wanted to do."[33] And there were times in church when her father simply leaned over and rapped her on the head with his knuckles.

She grew extremely fond of Ann Holland, who lived on the same street as the Ivinses. Holland was Molly's first true friend, and they would remain devoted to each other for decades. Holland felt an outsider's kinship with her—the sense that they were iconoclasts dutifully living in the moment on McClendon Street and in their Houston circles while at the same time hovering above it all. Holland studied the sisters: "Sara was very outgoing, optimistic, gregarious, blue eyes, blond hair. We were very different—Molly and I were both not popular. We were weird. We both loved to read books. We were drawn to each other because nobody else wanted to hang out with us. We did a lot of hiding—hiding in attics and whispering ghost stories."[34]

At Holland's house, the two built a small fort behind the garage. They would hide in it for hours, until they heard voices calling them to dinner. They made plans, secret plans, "adventuring plans." And "nobody really knew our identity. It was sort of a Batman scenario. Like society would be plunged into darkness or there would be some kind of menace. Who would have thought that Ann Holland and Molly Ivins would come out of this little fort behind the garage and save the world and amaze everybody? Who would have thought that? We'd spin our little self-heroic dreams in this little fort behind the garage. We were both hiders . . . and I know Molly did her share of hiding in her house."[35]

It was often so damned hot in Houston—Bombay on the Buffalo Bayou—so humid that people would say it seemed to be raining from the ground up. People would say that the whole fevered place was on the same latitude as New Delhi—that the rain was rising instead of falling. Molly would watch the way the skies would sometimes open and the water instantly would collect in mosquito-laden ditches, and she could see people swarming the neighborhood, sweeping water, splashing it from one side of the walk to the other. Children would stare out their windows as men would come and spray a fog of DDT to make the clouds of mosquitoes disappear.

The family moved in step with the rhythm of the near-west side of postwar Houston, a place where the WASPs aspired to join the country clubs, to be affiliated with the private schools, the arts, and the civic outlets. Thousands of people were relocating to Houston, many of them drawn by the promises of the oil-and-gas sector. The Republican Party was also denting the Southern Democrat strongholds, inspired by the presence of so many East Coast businessmen who had been assigned to work and live in Houston. There was a circle of affluence, a pattern to follow for anyone who aspired to the upper reaches of the social orbit. Many people chose to live near Rice University, near the Shamrock, near the private schools, near the Museum of Fine Arts and as close as possible to one of the most exclusive neighborhoods in America, River Oaks—the neighborhood that Molly's father had decided they should pursue. Meanwhile, her parents also enjoyed traveling together: In 1953 they stayed at the Hotel Sevilla in Havana, where they stopped in at the gift shop to pick up postcards to mail to her. They also went to New York, stayed at the Pierre, saw Broadway shows and brought her the programs.

She attended Oran M. Roberts (named after an ardent Confederate who became Texas governor) from first through sixth grades. She spent her seventh and eighth grades at Sidney B. Lanier Junior High. By the end of the 1950s, the family had moved to River Oaks; their house was on Chevy Chase Drive, not far from the velvet lawns at the River Oaks Country

Club—where blacks, Hispanics, and Jews had long been excluded through a soi-disant "gentleman's agreement," and where the members of the George Herbert Walker Bush family were courting oil money and Republican votes. That club was where George W. Bush would later mingle with the other members of his National Guard unit—a "Champagne Unit" filled with the sons of senators, cabinet secretaries, and energy titans.

In her pink-walled room above the garage at her new home, Molly sometimes drew pictures of herself and of people she found amusing. Her parents would peek in on her and see her with her long legs folded, knees aimed at her chin, as she pressed pencils to paper. Before becoming a teenager she was already six feet tall, and was adopting a certain breathy way of talking—putting the emphasis on the first syllables and mixing in a sort of East Coast boarding school, Katharine Hepburn–like formality. In her inch-high self-portraits, she was bug-eyed with hair firing into the air as though each strand was magnetized.

In the summer, her parents sent her to camps in the rolling Texas Hill Country, where the affluent families of Dallas, Houston, and Mexico City regularly sent their children. In the three-page-long letters she wrote home, she was very clear about what she liked and what she disliked—and also what she wanted: raisins, daisies, comic books, and "you know that wonderful feeling you get just before a storm."[36] After some initial resistance, she eventually grew to like being away from home at Camp Mystic, a private Christian camp where Lyndon Johnson had also sent his daughter, Luci Baines Johnson. Ivins was eleven at the time; in her cabin, surrounded by live oak trees, not far from the cypress-lined, blue-green Guadalupe River, she was writing a letter every day:

> Dear Mom: I was so glad to get your phone call. I'm having more fun. It isn't like home where you tell me to set the table and I yell at you to shut up. . . . Love, Mary[37]

When she was back home in River Oaks, the neighborhood sometimes seemed hushed. It was more Southern than Western. It wasn't what a lot of people thought of when they thought of Houston—or Texas. There were palms, magnolias, bougainvillea, and azaleas, all of them supple from the blanketing humidity, many of them hand-nurtured by Mexican gardeners whose battered Resistol hats barely lived up to the promise of "resisting" the sweat, of preventing the moisture from stinging their eyes. In River Oaks, it seemed as if everything flowed from a twenty-eight-room mansion—a plantation, as some of the black maids called it, named Bayou Bend. Mary knew about its owner, the "First Lady of Texas," the soft-voiced daughter of the governor, the one whose father had announced when the improbably named Ima Hogg was born: "Our cup of joy is now overflowing! We have a daughter of as fine proportions and of as angelic mien as ever gracious nature favor a man with."

She knew the story: how the genteel oil heiress had turned her life to classical music, to fine art, to exquisite things, to refined sensibilities, as if the turmoil in the desperately poor Fourth Ward, dotted with shacks with no running water, was a thousand miles away instead of just one or two. It was as if it had slipped by unnoticed and her mansion, and all the homes at its hem, including the ones on Chevy Chase Drive, had settled into a languid, soigné ensemble. Houston was the richest city in Texas, the one obviously fueled by so much oil money, and where the residents of River Oaks helped fund the major museums, opera, ballet, and orchestras. That fact wouldn't change for decades, even long after she had moved from River Oaks and other people—including President George H.W. Bush's secretary of commerce Robert Mosbacher and Enron's doomed Jeff Skilling and Andrew Fastow—had settled into the community that was among the wealthiest zip codes in America.[38]

But over the years she would insist again and again that she had grown up in East Texas, not Houston:

> I grew up in East Texas. I played basketball all over East Texas. We used to play in a town called Bed. It was a big joke, going to play in Bed. And let me tell you, the East Texas women are some of the meanest women on the face of the earth. We used to play in these small towns; the guards were almost invariably named after flowers—there would be Lily, Rose and Violet. The forwards were always jewels—Ruby, Pearl and Opal. But it was East Texas, so everybody had two names, you know, like Ruby Jo or Pearl Ann. And they always wore pink plastic curlers in their hair during games so they'd look good at the dance afterwards. Meanest women I ever met.[39]

If one wanted, it was possible to pin down Houston geographically as part of East Texas—but for many people East Texas was something else entirely. Some understood the term "East Texas" as a reference to the rural, black-dirt side of the state with the looming pine trees and rivers the color of dull pennies. There were African-American communities dotted with flimsy shacks. There were Confederate memorials on the downtown squares in small, almost hidden, towns. There were Pentecostal churches made from tarpaper and clapboard. The sour smell from a pulp mill. Feathers flying off trucks rumbling away from the chicken farms. Monster-sized catfish heads hung on fence posts. And a dead coyote sometimes strung up on the same stretch of fence as some sort of warning and maybe even a boast.

If you were black, East Texas was not a place to wander back roads with abandon. People knew the stories about the hanging tree buried deep in the woods, near where the Navasota River curled away from the town of Mexia. They knew about the black man castrated by the citizens of Pittsburg, Texas, in 1941—a hidden nightmare playing out at the exact moment the nation was transfixed by the events at Pearl Harbor. They knew the hidden patches of woods where blacks would be tied to the sturdy trees and beaten. In East Texas, a man could easily be lost, swallowed in a place called The Big Thicket. And in places like Egypt, Texas, some people dreamed of going west to California, the way people in Panther Burn, Mississippi, dreamed of going to Chicago or Detroit. Some knew they would never make it that far, so they settled for leaving rural East Texas and going to the big city of Houston. There were jobs in the refineries, in the hotel laundry rooms, in the rice mills, in the country clubs, in the homes in River Oaks. That was where the real East Texas met the real Houston. Maybe, just maybe, Houston was less backbreaking and ominous than what happened in the cotton fields, in the woods, off the dirt roads, down by the snake-laden Navasota where people learned to turn away as if they hadn't seen the bloated body in the water. But, truth be told, many poor people in Houston were already wishing they had never come there; some were planning to leave, maybe following a path to California—where people were writing back to Texas about how you could find fruit strewn on the lush earth.

There were some other wickedly specific ties from teeming, overheated Houston to the real East Texas rural outposts. In the heart of Houston, if you cared to hear the story, there was also a hanging tree—a towering, thick oak—outside the gates of the cemetery where the city founders and leaders were buried. Follow the curve of the bayou, from the Bayou Bend mansion, and you would come close to that tree. Study the murky bayou that helped to define River Oaks—that was the body of water that the businessmen employed to coax a city from what was, more or less, a swamp at sea level—and you would learn that people disappeared in it as easily as they did in the woods. Rogue police and murderers would bludgeon men and shove them into Buffalo Bayou. (No one knows, of course, how often it happened, but it did—and it came to full, awful transparency in the 1970s when a twenty-three-year-old Vietnam veteran named Jose Campos Torres was handcuffed, beaten, and thrown into the fetid stream, where his body was found floating two days later.)

In the South, in all it implied and meant, some said Houston had no equal, that it was the most brutally brazen. And it was filled with strangers, newcomers, who had been delivered to a world where old mores were still as embedded as the ancient pains. At night, on Elysian Street, black residents in Houston would watch the lights downtown, the way they reflected on the highway construction crews rolling over the "freedman's towns"—knocking down the old homes where freed slaves had been allowed to live, paving over the cemeteries where freed slaves were buried. Houston was urban and blatant, the sooty, citified manifestation of things, ideas, that flowed from the old slave markets in East Texas or that slave trader Jean Lafitte oversaw just down the Texas coast in Galveston. In 1860, 30 percent of the people in Texas were slaves. Texas heroes, including Jim Bowie, the men whom Texas students were required to study, were unrelenting slave traders. And if you were prone to believe that the history of the place had never been adequately exhumed and taught to young people, you might begin to think that it was hell on earth—where the nouveau riche and the Big Oil gods they worshiped had turned a deaf ear to the sighs that echoed in the tombstone rubble of the desperately poor Fourth Ward, the Fifth Ward, and all the areas of Houston where blacks had been exiled in plain sight.

Growing up, Molly didn't often travel off prescribed paths in Houston—onto Lyons Avenue and into the area that some people would call The Bloody Nickel. She didn't go to Telephone Road, Denver Harbor, Segundo

Barrio, or other areas on the east side where the smokestacks, refineries, and petrochemical labyrinths filled up the horizon, the bayous gurgled unnaturally, urine-colored bubbles lifted off the water, and the air had a perpetual chemical tang like the taste of an old coin in your mouth. She could see some of the ghettoes from her car window as her father drove downtown. For some visitors to Houston, it was like an urban archipelago, like a set piece from another era, like something from a Russell Lee photograph. Driving by, you might think it seemed staged, almost intentionally sad to the point of being unreal.

As postwar Houston was growing, as the layers were becoming more complex, she sometimes liked being alone in her room. She liked to think about that summer camp her parents were going to send her to. It wasn't Houston, thank God, with all those rich fraternity boys at home from Yale and Princeton—acting like they hated the Northeast and were glad to be back on the west side of the city drinking Pearl beer and pissing off the back porches of the estates in River Oaks.

St. John's was within walking distance of Chevy Chase Drive. It was, some said, the finest private high school in Texas. And it was here that the Bush family desperately wanted to send its first, obstreperous son. George W. Bush was never admitted; he was destined for the other gilded prep school in Houston, Kinkaid. (Miffed at the way it all unraveled, the Bushes had even bigger designs for the family scion. After some time at Kinkaid, he was going to Philips Andover Academy in Massachusetts. That's where Bush's father and grandfather had gone.)

The Ivins family had designs for their daughter as well, a similar path in a way: After St. John's she was supposed to be shipped off to the East, to Smith College, because that's where her mother and her grandmother had gone. Her father believed in an orderly progression of events and circumstances—for others, for his children, for himself. He did love The Mole, even if he snapped at her about her weight, her hair, her clothing—and maybe he didn't see how these flashes of brutality revealed his own inconsistencies, his unsteady hand. He loved her but he made it hard, she always said.

People from Houston who knew both families tried to draw parallels between the Bush and Ivins households. George W. Bush's father would occasionally offer something to the people who listened to him when he sank into those uncomfortably revealing moments at the country club—"the club," as many people in the neighborhood called it. Bush's old man would hold a martini in his hand, smooth the wrinkles in his Bermuda shorts, and talk about his method: "I promise to love George W. unconditionally—even when he screws up." People who knew the Bushes but wouldn't speak against them said that there were, in fact, conditions—or, rather, preconditions. These were never stated; they just hung out there like invisible, but still towering, commandments. Follow the path the family has charted for you. Don't veer. Don't disappoint your parents. And in the Ivins household, it was really the same thing. The Mole's old man was more than clear about what he wanted from her. She would be erudite, destined for some stellar career as an educator, researcher. And, without question, she would be conservative, affluent, married, the mother to his grandchildren. Grandsons would be good. He could take them to one of his favorite haunts, the Houston Yacht Club, just down the seemingly perpetually bleached, raggedy stretch of Texas coast where the wealthiest families—including Ross Sterling, the co-founder of Humble Oil—congregated. Her father wanted to be elected "Commodore" of the Yacht Club and was bitterly disappointed when he lost.

The Ivinses could see that Sterling had built a sprawling mansion right next door to the Yacht Club, on the bay. It was modeled after the White House and was said to be the largest home in Texas. It had ten Ionic columns, twelve-inch-thick Texas limestone walls, and solid-bronze plumbing. It was easy for The Mole to study it, taking the full measure of what power meant to her father. He once told her that if they were ever caught in a squall she had to drop the sail and throw the anchor out—and one day when a storm suddenly began rocking the sailboat, she dutifully followed his instructions but forgot to tie the anchor to the boat. She laughed, forever, about the way her father sputtered with fury. But when she entered various yachting contests, she made sure to let him know, right away, how she had performed: "I've been in Fort Worth representing the yacht club in the Texas Junior Championship . . . it was really a ball, we drove the chaperone insane and had the time of our lives."[40]

⊰⊱

When she was sent to summer camp her parents dutifully boxed up presents for her and shipped them out. In the summer of 1955, she wrote from Camp Mystic—advising her parents that she had been accepted into one of the two "Indian tribes," and that she was doing "tribe training" and "tribe cheers." She was a Tonkawa, not a Kiowa.

She also went to camp—and, later, to school—with Quintana Symonds, the daughter of the man who ran Tenneco. Her best friend, Ann Holland, was assigned to her cabin. Holland's father was an influential assistant secretary of state—a Houston lawyer assigned to work with the CIA and to brief President Eisenhower on communist movements in Central America.

She watched camp counselors shoot water moccasins, she saw deer darting toward the pecan trees, and she floated in the cool river under the branches of the towering cypress trees. Her camp records revealed that she was a "high intermediate swimmer, intermediate diver, and beginner in tennis." She wrote to her parents: "I am also taking charm and arts and crafts."[41] She did English riding, tried to follow the direction of Lulu, her diving coach, and landed the role of Betsy Ross during "stunt night." She also got into trouble, receiving an "unsatisfactory" on her "Tribe Sheet" for bumping heads with a girl named Lucy: "Lucy seems to think I have a superiority complex or don't respect her or something. I had a talk with her and I thought everything was straightened out, but Lucy doesn't seem to think so. I'll probably get another 'unsatisfactory' on my next Tribe Sheet."

The girls listened to Elvis records, talked about their father's offices in Houston, watched *Captain Horatio Hornblower* and *Strange Lady in Town,* did can-can shows while wearing ruffled dresses, and played kickball against the Kiowas. She wrote a letter, every day, to her parents. She asked them to water her daisies and feed her cats. She demanded letters in return and she admonished her parents for not filling up her mailbox on Thursdays, which was mail day. And she insisted that her parents send her a surprise: "If you don't have anything to send, send an empty box. *But I want a surprise.*"[42]

Between her problems with Lucy and those with other campers, her letters clearly show a voice emerging. She was sizing people up, bucking rules, committing it all to paper. "On my left is a horrid girl named Pamela. . . . We all went up on Tribe Hill last night and learned about tribe training and some tribe cheers. . . . It's raining cats and dogs now. Someone must have stepped on Indian Joe's grave."[43]

She had a huge, rolling laugh, one that some people said was husky, or that made her sound older. Later, when her eyesight started slipping, she developed a habit of cocking her head back an inch or two and looking down at something or someone. People would say she was measuring, like a tailor with a bar of chalk. She would eventually draw more little faces, little men with beards and piercing eyes pinched into weird caricatures of anger. And she wrote more letters, more notes and poems and diary entries. Just before her twelfth birthday, she tried an experiment with one of her letters:

> Hey Stupid! Don't Read This. Look. Didn't I just get through telling you not to read this. What are you doing? You're just wasting your time. You think I'm going to say something important. Well I'm not. You think you should come to the news right now. But you're not going to. See! Anyone who has gone this far is either crazy or has nothing better to do. Now here you are at the end and what have you found out? Nothing!
>
> Don't you agree with me that you're stupid?
>
> —Mary[44]

CHAPTER TWO

River Oaks

I'd like to get away from earth awhile and then come back to it and begin over.

—ROBERT FROST, "BIRCHES"

Bob Moore was pushing across the campus of St. John's in his purposeful gait, and the uniformed students—girls in pinafore dresses hemmed below the knee, white socks pulled up the calves—watched as the English teacher ate up the space. He had gone to Reed College, in Oregon, a school that fostered a certain kind of heartland liberalism, intellectual rigor, and what would later become known as an anti-academic-establishment ethos that nurtured Beat Generation poets Gary Snyder, Lew Welch, and Philip Whalen.

St. John's was founded in 1946 by a few of the most powerful and wealthy families in the world: William Farish, who had co-founded Humble-Exxon and become the chairman of Standard Oil; the Blaffers, who co-founded Humble-Exxon; and the Cullens, who had made their fortune in oil. They imported Alan Lake Chidsey, the Harvard-educated assistant dean of students at the University of Chicago, as the first headmaster. He was classically inclined and the author of a trio of books published in the 1930s: *Romulus: Builder of Rome*, *Rustam: Lion of Persia*, and *Odysseus: Sage of Greece*. On Wednesday mornings, Molly Ivins would troop to chapel with the other uniformed students and listen to Chidsey preach Episcopal morality, love for your country, and love for your school.[1]

Given that St. John's was effectively created as a gateway for children of the most prominent families in Texas—among its other founders was a Texas state supreme court justice—Moore was something beyond an anomaly. He taught the poetry of Robert Frost and could quote favored lines to his students, including Frost's line about getting away from the earth. He talked about Ernest Hemingway and the American transcendentalists. He lectured on voting rights, organized food drives, and he also did something that truly put him at odds with the ultra-conservative, even anti-Catholic quarters of Houston: He supported the presidential candidacy of John F. Kennedy. He even appreciated Elvis and *Mad* magazine, and generally offered up a daily antidote to the buttoned-down aura that the headmaster had created. He was what some people carefully called a "free thinker" and he became the first major adult male counterbalance in Ivins's life. On campus, Moore openly relished the underdogs, the outsiders, those he believed had some sort of inner poetry. Anytime her father was rigid, Moore suggested possibilities—even within the confines of the most exclusive school in the state, even in a small setting, like St. John's, where there were only fifty-two students in her grade. "He never lost connection with the sheer intensity of teenagers. . . . He loved the big, pimply kind, especially," she said.[2] Ivins revered Moore and would dedicate her first book, in 1991, "To Robert P. Moore, the best teacher."[3]

Some students had been enrolled at St. John's since kindergarten. Those who transferred in were labeled "newcomers" and sometimes had to work hard to fit in. Ivins was big-bodied and acutely aware of her height when she joined the ninth-grade students at St. John's in 1959—not just a "newcomer" but one who was a head taller than most of the boys. In Houston, there was another "newcomer," George W. Bush, trying to find his way at that other private school, Kinkaid. Through her father's orbit, through the oil-and-politics networks that swirled around River Oaks and connected the two exclusive schools, she occasionally bumped into Bush. They knew each other enough to say hello, to chit-chat. Ivins said, "He hung out with friends of mine and dated some girls I knew. I knew him to say hi."[4] Ivins's mother liked the Bushes. She would eventually work for George H.W. Bush's political campaigns, carrying around a little "Bush Bag" with the candidate's name crocheted on the side.

At St. John's, Ivins was clearly not political. She read, she studied, she wrote essays and poetry. Reflecting on her early teenage years, Ivins would choose variations on a theme to describe how she fit in, or didn't: "I should confess that I've always been more of an observer than a participant in Texas Womanhood: the spirit was willing but I was declared ineligible on grounds of size early. You can't be six feet tall and cute, both. . . . I spent my girlhood as a Clydesdale among thoroughbreds." She also framed it this way: "I was the Too Tall Jones of my time. I grew up a St. Bernard among greyhounds. It's hard to be cute when you're six feet tall."[5] Her eyesight was also in decline. She saw an ophthalmologist for the first time when she was eight. Her myopia rapidly progressed over the next year—and the doctor informed her that "this proves one thing—either that you were a progressively heavy reader and student or that you inherited your myopia." She got her first pair of contact lenses in 1962, the year she graduated from St. John's. [6]

As a palliative to whatever awkwardness she might have felt, Moore's door was always open to Ivins, as was his house. He and his wife, also from Reed College, regularly invited students to hang out and talk, enthusiastically, about music, Kennedy, and the French existentialists. "He was definitely an inspiration for a lot of us. And Molly was really close to him. He was progressive politically and he was kind of our mentor and guide. We would go over to his house and smoke cigarettes and talk. We had a little study group about existentialism. He would let us pursue adult activities," remembers her friend Margaret Sher. "We got along, or we were all suffering together."[7]

Other close friends said that, based on her height, people assumed Ivins was playing some sport, most likely basketball—and that she would succeed at it. She dutifully played basketball for the junior varsity but rarely shone in the games against the small-town schools in Nederland and Pasadena. Her coach, Doug Osburn, who would later spend twenty years as the head baseball coach at Rice, barked at her to "pick your shots, pick your shots," and she would later say that she found it useful advice as a journalist.[8] "We were quite slow, we never made the varsity. We peaked in 11th grade. Girl's basketball was different back then. You had half court. We were not shining lights but we tried hard," remembers Sher.[9]

"Molly was never athletic," says Anne Kelsey, another classmate. It was clear that she was interested in reading, maybe as a way of skirting whatever expectations were placed on her at school and even by her parents. "Molly was so cerebral and loved books, but I don't think she was comfortable in her own home. I think she retreated into books quite a bit and read and read and read. I think she adored her siblings. . . . I always felt that Molly was kind of isolated as a young person. She was so tall and unusual. My feeling about this comes from stories she directly told me."[10]

Other classmates, people who would count themselves as good friends for the rest of her life, say much the same thing: Upon meeting her they were instantly struck by her height, by the fact that everyone in the Ivins household seemed tall. And that there seemed to be some underlying strain between Molly Ivins and her father. And that her mother, perpetually cheerful, seemed to be acting somewhat like Lucille Ball. As a friend put it: "She had mixed feelings about her father as a child. He was a very 'within' kind of person. He was sort of a square-jawed, steely hero type. Very handsome. Tall man. Gray hair. Very sort of your remote Marlboro man. Mary's mother was very, very different. Very approachable and very warm. . . . Mary put her father on a very remote pedestal."[11] (Though she was calling herself Molly by the time she was at St. John's, some childhood friends still called her Mary.)

One day, Ann Holland watched and listened as her mother and Ivins's mother stood outside and talked about their trip, earlier in the day, to the hair stylist. "Betty," Margaret Ivins asked, "do I look like a Panda bear?" And Holland laughed, thinking to herself that it was just the kind of loony question that her friend Molly might have asked.[12]

Ivins knew that her mother had been educated at the finest schools available to women in the '20s and '30s and that she was inherently smart, yet also that she insistently leaned toward a comic daffiness that all but erased the intellectual underpinnings she surely had cultivated at

Smith. She was a good mother, and Ivins's friends felt that she was always there for her children. She was really, on a day-to-day basis, only doing what the other '50s-era women in their circle were doing. One friend said: "I always thought her mother was delightful. She was a little bit ditzy, kind of scattered but really supportive of her kids, both of our moms were. Nobody worked. They participated in kid activities and volunteer activities."[13]

Her mother was also proud of the fact that her daughter attended the best school in Houston, and she regularly checked on her progress. At home Molly was popping with opinions about her teachers and the other students. It was clear, early on, that she was good at English, terrible at math. She wrote stories for the student newspaper, and she wrote a poem titled "Nausea" for the literary magazine:

> *As it slithers into the room, the familiar, sick terror rushes upward, but I stifle the scream of horror in my throat. The ugly thing slimes into the corner and leaves its fetid stench in the air . . . it springs, pounces on my face, its monstrous distorted countenance rips away the last shreds of my sleepy defense. Hideous, unmistakable—another day.*

"She was a bookworm compared to the rest of us," says Marcia Carter, a classmate who lived down the block from Ivins. "Our nickname for her for a few years was Mature Mother Molly. We called her the Triple M, because she was always so disgusted with our stupid shenanigans as high students. She would always go, 'How can they be such children?' She was very different than how she was as an adult. She was very serious." Some of Ivins's friends were kicked out of the library for being unruly or were cited for school uniform violations, but she almost never broke the rules. Latin teacher Basil Fairweather once told the class, in his broad English accent, that he was leaving the room and the students were on the honor system as they took their exams. Ivins watched as some people opened up their textbooks in search of the answers. She found Fairweather and turned in the cheaters. As Carter explains: "She was making every effort to be an intellectual at a time when the rest of us were making every effort to fit into something. It didn't seem to bother Molly that she didn't fit, but it bothered the rest of us that we didn't, because she was busy thinking about things, and we were just busy being stupid adolescents."[14]

As the perpetual antidote, there was Robert P. Moore—arguably the first bona fide progressive that any of the young people in her inner circle had met. "Bob was the first liberal that all of us knew. He was a very witty man, he loved teaching, and he loved the students. We all hung out at his house all of the time. He was also a truly literary person. He loved books, and good writing, and really encouraged it in his classes, and Molly's bent for that was evident to him. And he was the one that really encouraged her in that direction," says Carter.[15] After a few of her friends traveled with Moore and his wife on a summer trip to Europe—during their several weeks in a Volkswagen van "they let us drink and do all the things that our parents wouldn't do"[16]—Ivins seemed to change her mind about some of her classmates. She felt, one said, that the group had grown up somewhat. They were a bit more adult, able to connect with Moore at a deeper level and, maybe, to take the St. John's credo—"faith and virtue"—more seriously. Carter says:

> Most of the people there were from stodgy, well-to-do families. But I think that everybody was just so bored with this whole trip that was laid on you if you were a girl, about how to be a lady, and how to just grow up and be a wife. And we were all out there doing political things, and once again influenced by teachers at St. John's. Mr. Moore was, by far, the most liberal. There was never any question that he knew his stuff and imparted it well, but was definitely kind of a political animal who didn't mind telling rich people that you need to do more. But our class was considered kind of a bad class. We were considered kind of the dregs. The class of '62 was not one of their stellar classes, we were told regularly. They [the administrators] did not like us as a group. We were way too . . . we didn't like the rules. We were always trying to change the rules. We would mimic the teachers, or do things that were rude to the teachers. Molly didn't really like any of that.[17]

What she did want was to be famous. One day when she was young, she carefully wrote down a resolution on a piece of paper and tucked it away in her wallet: If she turned the age of twenty-five and hadn't been famous yet—she would commit suicide.[18]

Through an affinity for literature and journalism—and for the yearbook called "The Rebel"—Ivins grew closer to classmate Margaret Sher, whose parents avidly read the small progressive magazine *The Texas Observer*. Edited by Willie Morris, it was one of the true crusading publications in the nation, routinely pursuing stories that the large city dailies turned their backs on. It was fiercely liberal; the fact that the *Observer* even acknowledged the existence of blacks and Hispanics in Texas set it apart from those lumbering, reactionary dailies. It was, in its way, an adjunct to the historic "race newspapers"—the *Dallas Express*, the *Houston Informer*, and the *Texas Freeman*—that for decades served readers who felt excluded from mainstream coverage. To call the publication iconoclastic was an understatement, especially in a state that tended to behave as though it was still a separate nation. And reading it, let alone working there, clearly defined an individual as more than just a healthy skeptic. For someone like Molly Ivins, whose father was building his reputation as the most powerful lawyer at Tenneco, reading it was a bit like carrying *Das Kapital* around town.

Sher's father, a surgeon, had roots in the New York era "when a lot of people were radical . . . involved in a radical, artsy crowd."[19] He befriended poets and writers. The Shers also lived outside River Oaks, and, in a sense, outside what River Oaks stood for. "My parents subscribed to every magazine in the world—they were from New York. So they had a whole bunch to read and we also subscribed to *The Texas Observer*. So we used to sit outside, smoking and discussing *The Texas Observer* when we were in high school."[20] Ivins and Sher would crack each other up, talking about the stuffed-shirts they knew, about how they wanted to move away, to see Houston fading in the rearview mirror.

There was another attraction at the Sher household. Margaret's mother seemed inclined to be political, to talk politics, and it was something that Ivins hadn't really done before. "Molly ascribed to my mother [the sense] that women could have political views and stake out positions. Molly modeled herself after my mother. You see, she was heavily involved in the League of Women Voters and various political policy activities and she showed us that it was OK to do that. It was in River Oaks, and you didn't find it that much."[21] Ivins grew closer to Sher when she learned her friend was an ardent Kennedy supporter—and that the Sher household was also supporting the Texas populist and civil libertarian Senator Ralph Yarborough. "I think that's why she hung out with me. We were big Kennedy supporters and we were definitely in the minority at St. John's. One of our teachers said that if Kennedy won, he would get on his knees and beg forgiveness."[22]

There was a sense among her best friends that Ivins was straddling things, trying to find her own path but still adhering to her parent's designs. Her parents wanted her to learn the violin and she dutifully tried, but her father eventually wound up making her practice outdoors, behind the garage. She concentrated on the things she really liked: She doted on her cats, one of whom was seemingly always pregnant, never having been spayed. Her friends came to the house to swim in the pool. She entered sailing competitions at the Houston Yacht Club. And she began to immerse herself in French at St. John's, standing out among the five girls taking the language, able to carry on conversations with the teacher.

The school was small and the social circles seemed to favor the thoroughbreds, the gamines, not the Clydesdales. In high school, she didn't date anyone seriously, though she was often at the crackling, funny dress-up parties that the River Oaks children invited each other to attend. "She wasn't exactly the dating, popular girl. That was always a struggle because of her height."[23] At the soirees and proms, there was always a mad, last-minute swirl, the "oh my God, who are we going to go with at the last second . . . that was always torture, but we all went."[24]

Her friends knew that she had cut stories out of the Houston newspapers about extraordinarily wealthy girls who had been "introduced" at their debutante balls—including the daughter of the man Jim Ivins worked for at Tenneco.[25] She would later tell a friend that her parents sometimes forced her to go to the dances, that she felt incredibly awkward being taller than most of the boys. Sometimes she would slip away, hide in the bathroom, and read a book.

⋘⟷⋙

In the summers, her parents were traveling to New York, London, or Paris. Sometimes they would sail in the Bahamas. Ivins was participating in the Texas Junior Yachting Championship, teaching sailing, and going to private camps inside and outside Texas. After a trip to Fort Worth for the yachting championship she sent a letter to her parents: "We really shook up Fort Worth. Our crew had a second place until the last race. . . . Mother, don't drop dead but I'm getting my hair cut. Yup, the mop is chopped. I finally got up the nerve and now I'm very depressed. Think I'll go shoot myself."[26] Her mother arranged for her to spend a few weeks in the summer of 1960 as a camper and assistant counselor at L'Ecole Champlain, a place Ivins would later describe as "a fancy French language camp for genteel young ladies which resides on a particularly sheltered corner of Lake Champlain." [27] Her job was to teach canoeing and sailing and also to continue her own education in French. "My job is too choice for words. We have a new group of kids now, as it is the second term of camp. I have a very nice spastic in my class now. I know that sounds like a cruel joke," she wrote to her parents, who were traveling in France. "I just realized that this is going to reach you in Paris. Good heavens. You must go outside and look around and just be impressed to pieces for me, The Mole."[28]

Meanwhile, her father was moving closer to the presidency of Tenneco. His view of his role suggested a certain bitterness that his history sculpting Tenneco had been overlooked. One day he turned to Andy and tried to explain what he did for a living: He found the legal justifications for anything the founder of Tenneco could invent or devise. "What he would do was make what Gardiner [Symonds, the founder of Tenneco] did legal. Gardiner would go forward and Gardiner was going to do whatever he was going to do, because, shit, he was a balls-out businessman and took Tenneco from a tiny little nothing to the twenty-first largest corporation in the United States. So, anyway, Daddy was the legal mind behind everything."[29]

General Jim was clearly concentrating on his career, occasionally exploding in anger, sometimes drinking too much, amazing his children and friends with his fortitude at sea. He participated in several dangerous yachting races, including the 3,000-mile Transatlantic Race from Newport,

Rhode Island, to England's Eddystone Light, where he helped navigate the *Ondine* in record time through stormy oceans and brutal winds, and on to a victory that merited toasts at the Island Sailing Club in Cowes—as well as a spread in *Sports Illustrated* that featured a large photograph of Jim Ivins at the helm, his tongue sticking out of his mouth as he is blasted by sea spray.[30]

Molly was watching him, listening to his calls, and overhearing his meetings in the living room. When oil men would come by, the children would be shooed away and the men's voices would dip down. Years later, she would tell one of her best friends that she could overhear her father talking about controlling oil prices, steering the markets to drive Tenneco's profits.[31]

Her mother had settled into a cycle, attending church functions, society functions, various school events for the children. Sara was off to the University of Texas, where she joined a sorority, and Margaret harbored hopes that her other daughter would go to Smith. She knew to anticipate that her husband would announce he was off to pursue a yachting adventure, that he might be gone for weeks, sometimes to sail, sometimes to do Tenneco business in New York or Delaware, where the company had incorporated. Sometimes Margaret would join her husband in New York. In January 1960, she sent "Mary" a postcard saying that "your Christmas present to me was two tickets to 'A Man for All Seasons.'"[32] There would be moments when the family was firmly together, and sometimes it would circle directly around her husband's interests—a "big, long road trip to Disneyland, Grand Canyon, Carlsbad Caverns, Teton, Yellowstone" with a stop in Denver for the "Grand Conclave" of the Kappa Sigma fraternity that Jim Ivins served as Worthy Grand Master.

Molly began to grow closer to Andy, and they would walk home together from St. John's. She was always striding, moving fast, telling stories, trying to make him laugh.

One day he turned to her: "Why do you walk so fast?"

She replied: "Well, you look up at the horizon and it makes you go quicker."

Meanwhile, other guests were arriving at the house on Chevy Chase, men on the front lines of molding the Republican Party in Texas, and building it with oil money and support from East Coast GOP kingmakers.

One of them had particular ties to Jim Ivins: Kappa Sigma "Brother" John Tower was the first Republican sent to the Senate from Texas since 1870 and he was selected as the Kappa Sigma Man of the Year in 1961. He would eventually assume the same title as Jim Ivins—Worthy Grand Master. (Today, the fraternity awards the annual John Tower Distinguished Alumnus Award.) Ivins had gotten his position at Tenneco through his connections at Kappa Sigma and he knew enough to welcome John Tower into his home.

That same year, 1961, discussions were turning into debates, and then arguments, at the dinner table. Andy says: "Molly was obviously taking a different side than my father. I don't know if she was doing that on purpose or if he was trying to antagonize her or what. I mean he was conservative . . . but politics wasn't necessarily his forte. But arguing was. He was an attorney—so she and he would get after it. I think there were a lot of political things to talk about."[33]

In the summer she traveled to France on the cruise ship *Nieuw Amsterdam*, once considered the Dutch equivalent of the *Queen Mary.* She had two roommates on board and was escorted by chaperones as part of an academic and cultural immersion program at L'École Montcel in Jouy-en-Josas. She and the other young women were required to wear formal dress for dinner, to speak French at all times, to abide by rules of decorum. The Château du Montcel had been home to "delightful programs in France" since the 1920s, and Philips Andover and other elite private schools in America sent students there for several weeks each summer. Occupied by the Nazis during the war, the château was a grand, rambling complex dating back to the seventeenth century and Louis XIV. From her first days in France, in July, Ivins was sending letters to her parents, often on stationery she had taken from the ship: "I keep thinking it is some make believe place like Disneyland. I am going to live in France after college. I think all of France is a movie set. Oh, it's so French! P.s. I have rediscovered morning. It is a glorious time. I'll never sleep late again. We saw a wedding procession and an elopement, complete with ladder."[34]

The grounds at the Château were extraordinary. A long driveway cut through carefully manicured lawns, and there were tennis courts, a pool, soccer fields, and basketball and volleyball courts. At the back of the house a slope led to winding paths lined by ferns, wild strawberries, weeping willows, and ancient bridges. Her room was painted yellow and exposed to the sun. As she had done at the age of eleven at the private camps in the Texas Hill Country, she wrote a letter home almost every day. These letters were longer, though—sometimes five or six pages—and often punctuated with a sketch of something that had caught her eye. They were signed by "The Mole." She was turning seventeen and her writing showed a mixture of skepticism, frantic humor, spiked irreverence, and judgmentally inclined observations: Her roommate "is a bit strange, but we change every two weeks."[35]

With other girls she took day trips to Jouy, exploring markets, tasting something unusual called "yoghurt," drinking café au lait, eating sole, mushrooms, and omelets. After a week she also thought she was losing her mind over a classmate: "[She] is driving me insane. I never met such a masculine, unsophisticated girl. I am very careful not to offend her but she has no such scruples. Oh well, it's reasonably easy to avoid her."[36]

She told her parents that she was afraid she'd be viewed as a stubborn "goat" and not a "sheep." She was, as always, the tallest woman in group photographs, the ones where demure-looking young women sit straight and stare at the camera. In chat sessions in the salon, she conversed in French about the country's educational system or the history of the Comédie-Française. On outings, she visited Napoleon's tomb, the Eiffel Tower, the Arc de Triomphe. She also told her parents that the Hotel des Invalides "carries the echoes of ancient anguish."[37] Farmers carrying baguettes looked like they had "guns in their baskets." And it seemed as if half the women in Brittany rode motorcycles, something she couldn't imagine in Houston. From the windows of her bus, she noticed something else she hadn't seen in Houston: "We saw some really gross and pity [sic] types on the Left Bank. There were couples necking on park benches, as a matter of fact, there were couples necking just about everywhere. The owner of the patisserie in Jouy thinks I look like Jackie!" She drew a little picture of herself as Jacqueline Kennedy on the bottom of the letter, next to a drawing of a man who looked like a hairy gnome, some horny beast with bug eyes and wild hair. She labeled the drawing of herself "The Mole Comme Jackie." She labeled the gnome "A Parisian Intellectual."[38]

Her time in France was making some indelible impressions. In the château chamber one day, a violinist and pianist played Beethoven so exquisitely that she felt genuinely moved. She saw Moliere's *Le Bourgeois Gentilhomme* at the Comédie. She boated on the Seine, had tea in small cafés above small shops, attended the ballet at Place du Trocadero, heard *La Bohéme*, and made plans to attend a bullfight on the Riviera. She decided her favorite street was Avenue Franklin Roosevelt and that she enjoyed dining at Colombe d'Or, visiting Monte Carlo, Arles, and Avignon, and going to Sanremo for lunch. In Monaco, there was Aristotle Onassis's yacht *Christina*, sometimes regarded as the finest yacht in the world. She wrote to her family that in Arles she endured the bullfight at the Course de Toro and cried when the second bull was killed. The matador was arrogant and she was glad she had read *The Brave Bulls*, by the Texas artist and writer Tom Lea. On the way to Avignon she went past the Bouvier house and learned that Jackie was there that day. And she was excited to see the house in which George Sand had lived and written many of her most famous works. She visited Victor Hugo's house and then Rodin's residence, which resonated with her because she had just been thinking about arts, artists, and reading *The Agony and the Ecstasy* by Irving Stone. "I've decided that Brittany is better than Isle de France, Provence is better than Brittany, the Riviera is better than Provence, and Paris is still best of all, and France is the best country in the world."[39]

She was still groaning, at times, about the girls who were insisting on talking about their love lives, real and imagined. "The girls are a very interesting group. There are no smoothies but lots of natural charmers. They're quite unsophisticated . . . they are often more concerned over their own comforts, likes and dislikes, than the glories of an ancient France or the benefits and idiosyncrasies of a new civilization. No perspective." She signs the letter: "Vive La France, I got pinched on the Metro. The Mole."[40]

At times, she would retreat to her yellow-walled room and, with her long red hair covering her startlingly blue eyes, she would raise her face from the latest letter she was writing—about the very girls who were spying on her: "Girls are great except for three drips and my roomie . . . all are hell bent on getting into Eastern colleges. I thought they were all a bit immature. Let's face it, I'm just superior to everyone. It seems that I am almost French now." At the bottom she had sketched a stick figure towering over small people and labeled "Superior One."[41]

Her trip to France, her first real journey away from home, affirmed the possibilities that the Shers and Robert Moore had introduced. It was one thing to talk Sartre with Moore and his wife Maxine, learning to blow cigarette smoke instead of swallowing it, cackling and slipping in some funny words in French. But being there, being in France, was something else entirely: Women on motorcycles. George Sand. Women necking in public. Jackie. Women at bullfights. Women wearing whatever the hell they wanted, instead of long St. John's dresses with white socks and saddle shoes. By mid-August she was packing her things, ready to have them carted off and loaded onto the *Nieuw Amsterdam* for the trip to the States. She was turning seventeen in two weeks. "I miss sailing a lot. But it hasn't been so bad since we left the Riviera and I couldn't see any boats. Yesterday we went to Dior's and believe me, there is nothing quite so haute as the world of haute couture. There were quite a few celebs there, passing verdicts in well-bred tones. I had my shoes off under the chair, and my girdle pinched, but I passed verdicts with the best of them."[42]

Back in Houston, during her senior year at St. John's, there was a perfunctory note from her father, referencing some "bad" news about Smith College, perhaps suggesting that she had applied there and not gotten in—or implying disappointment that she had turned her back on Smith:

> Mole, too bad about Smith. But you've got 3 top notch colleges to choose from. There are TV dinners in the icebox. See you Sat. nite, Love D.[43]

Ivins women from two earlier generations had gone to Smith. Even Margaret Sher's mother had gone to Smith. "Both my mother and grandmother had gone to Smith. Of course, contrarian that I am, that made me determined not to go there," Ivins once said.[44] With her family, she visited and settled on Scripps College, a small liberal arts college in California founded in 1926 by Ellen Browning Scripps, who had been active in the women's suffrage movement and the expanding Scripps newspaper empire. It shared facilities with Pomona College, where Margaret Sher was headed.

In Houston, there were some goodbye parties. Ivins was still catching sight of George W. Bush on the periphery of her scene. He didn't seem particularly intellectual, or like someone really worth knowing; he was just another face in the wink-and-nod crowd at the country club. She and Sher made home-brewed beer in Sher's garage, something they planned to unleash at the end of football season, and they laughed at how serious everyone seemed to be as school came to a close. "We definitely smoked and drank. . . . What we used to do our senior year was a lot of drinking. That was part of our MO."[45]

In 1962, she seemed to spend more time at Sher's one-story bungalow. Kennedy's election had been, her friend says, a defining moment for Ivins. So was the escalating intensity of the civil rights movement; the Freedom Riders had spread into the South, and even the large Texas newspapers Ivins was reading were forced to take note of the violent reactions directed at civil rights supporters. Increasingly, the issue of race relations became a focus for Ivins, but it was something she only talked about: "We were very impassioned about civil rights . . . coming at it from an intellectual rather than an experiential place."[46]

But at the time she became one of the fifty-two graduates in St. John's class of 1962, she had begun thinking about doing something beyond working at the school newspaper or yearbook: "I had started out, in my very precocious, aspiring junior intellectual from East Texas way, to be a great author. But I figured out fairly early that there were a whole lot of other people who were also planning to write the great American novel—which meant that some of us were not going to make it."[47]

⟷

She entered Scripps in the fall of 1962 and it was quickly a big drag. The school felt isolated and immersed in the arts to a degree that she found unappealing. She studied experimental psychology and was given a Skinner Box and a rat:

> My rat was supposed to learn that if he pressed the bar, he would get a food pellet. He was a bright rat—he learned in no time flat. Then, he had to learn that he had to press the bar twice in order to get a food pellet. But, my rat had committed something called over-learning, which can be plotted on a Bell Curve. And what happened was, he would press once and not get his food pellet, and instead of trying again, my rat developed something called neurotic ritual. It would turn around three times to the left, tossing its little ratty head, and then kind of fall over backwards in frustration. I ruined a perfectly good rat, and felt guilty about it for years and never saw any use in it. And then one day, shortly after the fall of the Berlin Wall, I had occasion to visit the State Department, and particularly those who had served on the Soviet desk, and realized as I watched them all turning to the left three times and kind of throwing their heads around that they had all committed over-learning and I then understood their problem and this was really good. All right, that's the value of a liberal arts education.[48]

She was in Susan Miller Dorsey Hall, named after the former superintendent of schools in Los Angeles. The campus was one of the prettiest in the nation, carefully landscaped with rare plants and gardens. Her dormitory had French doors, paintings on the walls, and a "browsing room" for reading. The women called themselves "Scrippsies." The so-called Claremont Colleges, which included Scripps and Pomona, shared various facilities but also maintained separate identities, not unlike the relationship among some schools in the East, including Barnard and Columbia. Browning's vision, some said, was to have something akin to a West Coast–California version of the Ivy League and Seven Sisters. But the mission and the pleasant Mediterranean climate, the perfumed air, didn't convince Ivins that she should stay. It might have been too abrupt a transition from the mongrel mess in roiling Houston or the international existentialism she had sampled in France. California, Scripps, seemed too dreamy and, in their way, stultifying at a time when she was just months removed from

Paris, from smoking and debating issues with her progressive mentors, from leafing through Willie Morris's latest, seemingly seditious edition of *The Texas Observer*.

She told people at Scripps she was from East Texas and some people wanted to hear tales about Texas. She was reluctant to tell her parents that she loathed Scripps and she tried, in a way, to give a willing nod to Scripps's reputation as a bastion of arts. She signed up for a modern dance class even though she was still less than graceful. She struggled through the course and debated how to approach her final test, which was to choreograph a piece for five classmates. Mulling over her options, which included the fact that the other women were also stumble-footed, she went for some humor. She called her work "A Cluster of Grapes Being Eaten by a Bear." Set to Stravinsky's *Rite of Spring*, Ivins's work featured her playing the bear and the five other dancers playing the grapes. The audience was mute. There was no laughter. When the last strains faded and the dancers froze, the crowd erupted with thunderous clapping. "I can tell you have a true feeling for the dance," her professor told her. Nobody got the joke. By that time, she was leaning heavily toward leaving the university.[49]

She began filling out the paperwork that might lead to a transfer to Smith or, in case she couldn't get there, Reed. She was nineteen and going to Reed would close a loop, maybe put her closer to what Reed-alumnus Robert Moore stood for, believed in, preached. Reed had a reputation for literature, for poetry. She hoped, though, that Smith would let her in. "She didn't like the California thing at all. I think the scene had an emphasis on social things and it wasn't intellectually challenging for her. There was just something about the California lifestyle. I think she just really wanted to be in the East."[50]

She simply said that being at Scripps was never going to work out. The place wasn't fun, or funny, for her: "I was definitely a misfit there."[51]

She was admitted to Smith in 1963 and lived in Gardiner, one of ten "houses" on the Quadrangle. One of the largest at the college, it was built in 1926, had four residential floors, and featured a bucolic path to campus that led students past Paradise Pond. Ivins told friends she felt at home at

Smith, almost instantly. She sensed that there were more people like her at Smith, people who saw what was happening overseas, who cared about what was happening in the South, who wanted to be intellectuals too. Smith's mission statement suggested that the school was designed to promote "the powers of womanhood" so that a woman's "influence in reforming the evils of society will be greatly increased."

She studied Smith's history. And given that everyone again assumed she was a basketball player, a gazelle on the hard courts, Smith's historical connection to the game struck her as especially ironic. The first collegiate women's basketball game was played at Smith in 1893 but few people saw it: Men were banned from watching since the whole affair was considered a breach of social etiquette. That first game, which ended in a score of 5 to 4, was played by women in bloomers and long-sleeved blouses. The players had to remain frozen in their zones and were allowed only one bounce of the ball. Despite this glacier-like pace, one of the Smith players somehow managed to dislocate her shoulder. Ivins marveled at the story, wondering about the historical context and even how the hell somebody could sustain such an injury.

Betty Friedan had graduated from Smith in 1942 with a degree in psychology, the same field Ivins's mother had pursued and abandoned; Gloria Steinem graduated in 1956. Barbara Bush, Nancy Reagan, Julia Child, Margaret Mitchell, and Sylvia Plath were students there as well. Ivins described her first encounter with the school this way: "Smith, like many of the seven sisters colleges at that time, was sort of very preppy. You know, I can remember exactly the uniform: It was knee socks, Bass Weejun loafers, kilts, blouses with a circle pin on the collar, and a certain type of sweater . . . to me they all looked exactly alike."[52]

The uniform was hideous enough, but Ivins also worried about her "face full of zits" and the Texas accent that would come gushing out if she had a drink. She immersed herself in her classes, and she studied history, politics, philosophy, and French. She stayed up late smoking cigarettes, drinking some more, and debating her friends about politics—often volunteering to be the "informed" witness from the South. When Friedan came to campus, just before *The Feminine Mystique* was published in 1963, Ivins was one of only five students to hear her talk. The swirl and hum of the welling feminist movement, the way Friedan rejected girliness and all the prescribed decorum, appealed to Ivins. She liked being around women who talked politics, who had career ambitions, who said they weren't at school to prepare for life as a homemaker. Other students, those who gravitated toward her, agreed that she certainly was different from the girls who were hoping to meet a husband at the college dances. She liked the process of school, she liked the classes, and she liked to make fun of the bowtie-wearing fuddy-duddies, the men and women who acted like Mr. Chips and Mr. Magoo. Her laughter struck some of her friends as more than just a healthy irreverence. "She was tough. I mean the thing that really hit me about her is that so many of the women were soft and soft-spoken. Kind of very, very genteel in the sense of 'don't speak too loudly.' Always be understated, in everything. But Molly was out there. She was flat out there. She spoke her mind. 'Make a path, I'm coming through.' And always that cigarette, and now that I think about it, a drink in her hand," says Anne Seifert, one of her closest, oldest friends. Seifert, who would go on to earn a doctorate in epidemiology, do research at Harvard, and write several books, was studying experimental psychology at Smith.[53]

Ivins majored in history, earned more B's than A's, and held a job working as a reader for Cara Walker, class of 1898, who lived in Northampton. She would visit Walker once a week and read *National Geographic* and updates from the Smith alumni magazines, especially about the class of 1898. She wondered if the old lady would be depressed each time she told her another story about yet another student having either died or suffered some terrible loss: "I'm sorry to tell you Miss Walker, but Laura Pebble's husband passed on in California." The elderly woman replied: "Good, I never liked her anyway."[54]

That fall, she was extremely cognizant of how people on campus were reacting to the news that Kennedy had been murdered in her home state. "In the shock and horror of its aftermath, Texans were not popular in the Northeast. That was when I learned to speak without an accent."[55] And she felt ostracized. "You try going to Smith from Texas after November 1963. Being a Texan was not a treat."[56]

After she muted her accent, people on campus were surprised to hear that she was from Texas. She sounded, to some, like a student from a boarding school on the Upper East Coast. But as people got to know her, they'd insist that she tell them stories about Texas, as if it was an exotic outpost. She would oblige. One close friend at Smith had grown up in middle-class areas of Long Island and to her it was like being introduced to another world, one that seemed funny as hell: "She would go back to Texas and come back to Smith and then she would go on about the holy rollers on the radio: 'I turned on the station! I'm saving you!'" And her friends would roar with laughter, roar at her "irreverence" and ask for more. "She was so good at it and she was so funny. I couldn't believe people like this existed. When she would tell me about these religious people on these stations and would do it with this drawl, I was mesmerized. It was so foreign to me. She just did it so well."[57]

Patterns were emerging, paralleling each other: She held court and spun sagas about Texas, she exaggerated them out of all proportion, searching for just the right funny high notes. She used outrageous premises to invent cartoon paradigms, and she turned "Texan" to underscore each caricature, to confirm someone's worst fears or most exotic expectations. She would do voices she had heard on the Baptist radio stations, those of Texas football coaches barking out military commands, bloviating Senator Foghorn Leghorn send-ups on the Texas politicians—and people would howl. She was dispensing bits of cultural anthropology, as if they were boisterous dispatches, and sometimes they were about places she hadn't really experienced, or that really didn't exist. Like "Bed, Texas," with its mean girls scrambling on the courts in plastic hair curlers.

Some students magnetically popped to attention when her voice emerged from another cumulus of cigarette smoke. She was holding another beer, reading French poetry out loud, listening to the Beatles. "She was freer, happier. She was laughing all the time. She always had a spin on something. She was not apologetic for who she was. It was like 'this is who I am, this is what I think, this is what I'm going to do. The rest of you do whatever you want. I've got my trench coat and I'm going.'"[58] And she really did wear a trench coat on campus, to cover the "social gala dress" that was usually required for high-end campus functions. Friends suggested she did it to be irreverent, to be cool, to make sure that people could see the mane of red hair set against the less-than-girly coat. That year after

Kennedy was assassinated in Dallas, and the drawling, lop-eared Lyndon Baines Johnson took his place in the Oval Office, some students turned to Ivins to explain Texas again—to interpret "the place that had killed my president," as David Halberstam once put it.

Her ability to objectify Texas, already manifesting itself through the candy-colored circus prism of Glenn McCarthy and his ilk, was catapulted to a far more fierce, complex dimension in the wake of what happened in Dallas in 1963. It was enlightened self-interest to let people know that you were able to hover above Texas even though you were from there, that you were able to judge it and certainly condemn it when necessary. As one of her best friends said: "I just didn't realize that there was this part of the country that I was very unfamiliar with."[59]

Ivins was, in a sense, in demand. And there was something else: She was stunning, and men and women were noticing her. "Molly was just gorgeous. I don't think that people who knew her later in life had any idea how beautiful she was. I mean she would take your breath away. She had a figure to die for, probably because of all the smoking. I mean she didn't eat very much. She was really, really slim. She had hair that was gorgeous and it was red, red. And her eyes were the bluest of the blue color I'd ever seen. She was a knockout."[60]

She was constantly on the phone, putting letters in the mailbox, arranging visits to New York, Massachusetts, Vermont, and other places where her school friends and relatives had homes. She stayed in close contact with her oldest best friend, Ann Holland—and, increasingly, with Ann's brother, Henry "Hank" Holland, Jr. Aside from her father and Robert Moore, Hank Holland was the most important male figure in her life. He was also someone whose senseless, wickedly violent demise helped her untangle a Gordian knot of leaden expectations and assumptions. And if he had lived, there most likely would never have been a public Molly Ivins.

"The love of my life," she called him.[61]

CHAPTER THREE

Ghost

They had believed in literature, had believed in Beauty and in personal expression as an absolute end. When they lost this belief, they lost everything.

—NATHANAEL WEST, *Miss Lonelyhearts*

Yale student Hank Holland took the one-armed statue of Pan—stole it, really—from his parents' massive stone estate at the end of the gravel driveway in Greenwich, Connecticut, close to the thoroughbred neighborhoods where the East Coast editions of the Bush family had settled (George H.W. Bush met his wife Barbara at the local country club).

Holland had attended the same private school in Greenwich as George H.W. Bush, but he behaved in a far more unhinged manner than anyone in the Bush orbit—and he took the stolen statue of Pan back to Yale, to a toga party, and put it on display. His mother called the police in Greenwich and asked them to issue an all-points-bulletin for Pan. Hank Holland was pleased. It was the kind of orchestrated chaos that he loved.

His father, recruited by the CIA from the powerhouse Baker Botts law firm, had had an intense forty-nine years on earth. He was quietly involved in blackballing Germans who had moved to South America—and, more publicly, he served as the very powerful assistant secretary of state for Inter-American affairs in the Eisenhower administration, from 1954 to 1957. One of Hank Holland's predecessors in that post was Nelson Rockefeller. Historians maintain that Holland was exceedingly instrumental in making sure—during his tenure in the State Department and after he left to become a Wall Street lawyer—that countries south of the United States remained prime sources for U.S. business interests, including the major American fruit companies that controlled parts of Central America. He was an ardent "apostle of 'free enterprise,'" as Arthur Schlesinger, Jr. would call him.[1] He was truly "our man in Central and South America," drawing people into his confidence over languorous lunches in Bogotá and Mexico City. He would relay information on communist tendencies directly to the CIA and, if necessary, President Eisenhower. It was assumed by some Washington observers that Holland, who left his State Department work in the late '50s, would one day become secretary of state in a future Republican administration, maybe for Richard Nixon. He had spent time traveling in Central and South America on high-profile trips with then–Vice President Nixon—the news stories about Holland's relationship with Nixon reverberated in just the right circles in Houston.

Henry Holland was the whole package (a "good man," as the Bushes liked to say), and when he was at the country club in Greenwich, people would come off the golf course—just to watch him dive in the swimming pool. He was, everyone said, an amazing diver. And as his son Hank grew up, it was assumed that he would follow his father into extremely high-level work in a Republican White House and at least a job with his father's law firm, Baker Botts—where the family of Bush loyalist James Baker III had its interests. Over several summers, Hank Holland's father would place him in different countries so he could get a ground-level idea of America's corporate interests. One year Hank lived in Mexico City with members of the Goodrich family. Another year he lived on a sugar plantation in Cali, Colombia. And on Hank Holland went—to Venezuela and other countries—and in each location, he mastered the local culture and dialects. "My father really saw Hank as the generational realization of himself," says Holland's sister.[2]

The parallels to the Bush family were acute: the ties to Greenwich, the sense that the first son was going to be defined by everything his father had accumulated. Ivins knew, though, that there was a radical difference between Hank Holland and a River Oaks player like George W. Bush. Growing up, Ivins was close to the Holland family and always aware of her friend Ann's tall brother, but it wasn't until she was at Smith that he registered in deeper ways. When Hank Holland went to Yale, Ivins's mother suggested she reach out to him, stay in touch. Her daughter hadn't dated in high school; it would be good for her to see an old friend, someone at Yale, just a little more than an hour away. In time, Molly and Hank were so close that some suspected they would marry.

He was slim but muscled, six-foot-four and obsessed with being a perfect physical specimen. When he asked her to go to a Harvard-Yale football game—along with Anne Seifert and her date Dan Davis, a Yalie and heir to the Weyerhaeuser forest products fortune—she instantly said yes. Their relationship developed quickly. They dated, smoked, drank, and were eventually inseparable. She learned more about him: Holland had also gone to the exclusive Landon School in Washington, D.C. and the Deerfield Academy in Massachusetts. Deerfield was where Horatio Alger had once been headmaster and various members of the Rockefeller family had been enrolled. He had thought about going to Philips Andover, where his cousin was in the same class as George W. Bush. At Yale, he lived at the Eero Saarinen–designed Morse College, spoke seven languages, was a deejay on a Spanish-language station in New Haven, studied hypnotism, and had a prized parrot he'd brought back from South America and taught to sing opera. He rode an Italian motorcycle, reminded people that he was a near-death "blue baby" born when the Paricutin volcano erupted in Mexico, said that he was planning to do advanced studies in Germany, could beat the hell out of most people on the tennis court, and had become an argumentative atheist. Holland was wired, gurgling with news, tripping from one topic to another, caffeinated in a way that left people either breathless or annoyed. He devoured books, ideas. He latched onto philosophies and foisted them on acquaintances. And in the company of Ivins's female friends, he could also suddenly be suave, attentive, and even deferential.

His hero was the nineteenth-century archeologist, adventurer, and linguist Heinrich Schliemann, who had traveled the world in search of major antiquities, ancient Troy, and Priam's Treasure. Schliemann reputedly spoke twenty-two languages and Holland wanted to do the same. At night, he would slip out of the house and walk to the Greenwich storefronts and stare at the window displays—he was trying to name the products in each of seven languages.

Holland's father was diagnosed with cancer in 1961 and his children watched him waste away for a year straight. Once, Hank sat with his sister and talked about how their father would look better with a clown wig on his head. His father died in the summer of 1962 but it really didn't stop the son. He totaled several cars, scared the hell out of the rich people driving by in Greenwich, stayed up all night long, acted in summer stock plays. He once played Berenger, the lead role in Eugene Ionesco's *Rhinoceros*, which touched on the tug between conformity and individuality.

One early morning, close to 1 A.M., there was a crunch in the gravel driveway and his mother went to the door. Out front was a black truck with the word "Ghost" on it. The driver asked for Henry Holland. The widow said he had died a year ago. It was a motorcycle delivery. Hank Holland had ordered a fast, jet-black Ducati from a legendary New York motorcycle dealer. It was, said his uncle, "something which gave all of us some concern considering Hank's harum-scarum attitude."[3]

Hank also began to quote Ayn Rand. Her *Atlas Shrugged* was being passed back and forth inside his Yale circles and her theories on super-individualism, the deadening effects of collectivism, seemed a natural gateway to his immersion in something else—eugenics. His belief in eugenics, like many things he threw himself into, was not faint-hearted.

One day Hank Holland asked his sister if there was "anything" she thought he couldn't do. She thought about it and settled on music. Their grandmother, a pianist, had once played Carnegie Hall; Ann herself played the piano until she was nineteen. (Their father had prohibited the playing of anything more contemporary than Gershwin at the house.) Ann told her brother that she didn't think he was particularly musical. Holland immediately called Julius Baker, one of the greatest flutists in modern history, and who played for many of the leading orchestras, including the

New York Philharmonic: "Maestro, you don't know me but it is an honor for me to call you. I want to buy a flute from you and I want you to be my teacher." Baker sold him a Gemeinhardt and arranged for Holland to study with one of his students. He muscled his way through Mozart, very intensely, and played for his sister. It was precise, but mechanical, she thought—just like her brother.

"He was ferociously intense and intellectual. He was strange. Very self-aggrandizing," says his sister.[4] "He loved to be the center of attention. He was good at it. Was very compelling. He was a driven guy. I mean he really wanted to be an Ayn Rand super-hero." He wanted to excel at everything, and he believed that there were selected men who could almost always master the things they chose. In the Ivy League circles, preppie students occasionally came to Yale, asking to play a game of tennis against Hank Holland. The night before each match, he would get a laundry basket stuffed with tennis balls and practice his serve for hours and hours. He was, his sister believed, at war with his father's shadow—just like other Yalies such as George W. Bush. "In his striving to transcend my father's accomplishments he sabotaged himself."[5]

While dancing at debutante and gala parties, Holland would suddenly flop to the floor in a paroxysm, jump up, and then—in a mad blur—twist and dive back to the ground.

⁂

Sometimes he and Ivins would visit his sister in Greenwich Village. She was attending New York University, was in love with the musician Paul Winter, and was moving in directions different from the ones her brother and Molly Ivins seemed tied to. She listened to speeches by Dr. Martin Luther King, Jr., took part in sit-ins, and eventually went to work teaching at Brandeis High. Ivins would come to visit, seeing things in the Village far removed from what passed for culture at the Shamrock and the River Oaks Country Club. It was less than a decade since she attended the same summer camp as Luci Baines Johnson.

In the spring of 1964, Hank and Molly talked about being together overseas—she was going to study in Paris in her junior year, he was going to study in Munich, maybe explore Nietzsche at a deeper level. "He and Molly really saw themselves as, and for different reasons, products of a very superior gene pool and deserving of each other. It was like 'we deserve to be together because we are of a superior strain and only we can recognize that in one another,'" says Holland's sister. "Accomplishment was very important to them. Accomplishment was really important to my father and they fulfilled any parent's expectation of accomplishment and beyond."[6]

Ann Holland later felt that Molly Ivins, the fully realized public figure, had remarkable similarities to both Henry Holland and his son Hank. The two Holland men knew how to draw a crowd, tell a story in a mad, funny rush. She believed Ivins had an "ability to leave a room with most everyone feeling that they had the inside track to her friendship and her personal life. My father had that gift. So many people thought 'Henry, Hank, understands my consciousness. He is my advocate.'"[7]

When Ivins and Hank Holland were together, they played off each other and seemed to use up the room's oxygen. They egged each other on, ratcheting up the energy, *insisting* on things, ideas, places to go, descriptions of people. Some people who knew them as a couple said there really wasn't a comparison. They were made for each other. They would probably be married. Sometimes, they would be in one of the sitting rooms at the Holland mansion—smirking at each other, speaking in some sort of secret alphabet—and Holland's mother, perfectly coiffured, would emerge and begin playing her harp. Maybe they'd go for a swim at the beach at Tod's Point, or they would talk about plans to visit the Davis estate near Lake Sammamish, close to the epicenter of the Weyerhaeuser lumber empire. Davis's parents had just returned from Italy; they had brought home a real Italian gondola, and flying to Washington would give Ivins and Holland a great chance to try it out.

Holland, in his way, might have been the super-idealized end game for Ivins's ties to the world her mother knew at Smith and the world her father willed himself to join. If her parents wanted her to have some lasting proximity to power, some man from the upper reaches, she had certainly found the edgiest embodiment. "Hank really wanted to manipulate the world. He wanted to be a power-monger. I know that he and Molly sort of envisioned themselves in a dynastic way. They believed that they breathed rarefied air. Very much an Ayn Rand scenario—and perhaps they would rule the world from an unseen location," said his sister.[8] He was, she said, somewhere beyond aloof. It was as if he had no time to waste with ordinary people, he wanted to be around the movers. He was painfully judgmental and quick to draw caricatures, to home in on perceived weaknesses, to lump places and people into narrowly defined camps. He was like the unleashed, fulminating version of what Jim Ivins had espoused—someone who believed that the world was black and white rather than shades of gray, with little room for ambiguity or even melancholy, and that bittersweet hesitations were for fools.

Holland's father and Ivins's father were protocol-driven diplomats in their way—but Hank was averse to the bullshit of long-term ambassadorial massaging. It was hard to imagine that he could one day patiently ladle the prep school–cum–Ivy League balm that his father, Jim Ivins, George H.W. Bush, Gardiner Symonds, and James Baker III brought to their mega-deals in Washington and on Wall Street. He was like a private-school banshee, feasting on the things that he knew might vault him far above and beyond his expected station in life—and he didn't really want to be the anonymous broker in the white silk suit, doing the CIA's private work over endless banana daiquiris and hotel lobby meetings in pre-Castro Cuba. If he had lived, he might have been comfortable with the zeitgeist of some of the modern CIA emissaries, the ones who dispensed with tedious formalities, Geneva Conventions, and went for the jugular, bad-to-the-bone style. He could learn any language; he was a fierce capitalist without any religious millstones. "He was not a compassionate person. He was calculating. Hank grew up with a really cold indifference to social issues or societal issues of the heart. So power and money were Hank's world. He really did feel that religion was the opiate of the people—at the same time he was a very cold capitalist," says his sister. "In a sense, Hank might not have been all that different from Dick Cheney."[9]

Ivins told people she loved him.[10] They would probably be married, thought her friends. "Exactly, exactly . . . in those times, it was kind of that way. You were making your matches, you were matching up. It would probably play out that way. It kind of looked like she was getting matched up with Hank."[11]

People in her family saw it too, including her brother Andy: "Hank Holland, he was the one. She had professed that she was in love with him and that they planned to marry. And I had never seen that before."[12]

She would also tell another lover, just a few years later, that she and Holland were once engaged to be married.[13]

Friends who literally grew up with her and stayed with her through the different phases of her life sometimes viewed Ivins through the prism of her relationship with Holland. Given her future political inclinations, her constitution, it is difficult to imagine that Hank Holland was, at one time, the most important person in her life. Their relationship was so far removed from those forgotten ditches along Buffalo Bayou where the mosquito larvae made the fetid water shake, far from the shotgun shacks on the edge of River Oaks leaning like they had just given up, far from the putrid smell and grinding roar of the oil refineries that paid for her college education. Given her final evolution, it would be difficult for friends to think she once was willing to entertain thoughts that went beyond Ayn Rand, scientific atheism, and rugged individualism:

"Hank deconstructed things so that he could reconstruct them on a higher level. This was the kind of thinking that he and Mary shared at the time. I think he and Molly talked about a master race."[14]

⋯

Ivins visited Yale several times to attend galas where the women wore gowns to the "very, very elegant formal dances."[15] The men gave the women corsages and the women gave the men boutonnieres. Once she presented Holland with a flower that squirted water and he wore it to that evening's fête. They slipped into the society cycles in New Haven, in Boston, in Greenwich, going to football games and to more galas and formals. They made weekend trips to Greenwich Village to see Ann Holland and marvel at how she was living like a pauper, sharing a room, hanging out close to where Bob Dylan was trying to survive. And there was always the prospect of heading west to the lakeside estate in Weyerhaeuser country. Molly thought hard about going with Hank in the summer of 1964.

Before then, on campus, she had become interested in the student newspaper, *The Sophian*, where Gloria Steinem had begun her career by writing book reviews. On her résumé she would note that she was the news editor in 1964 and in 1966. She later joked that she was writing "several impassioned editorials on the need to eliminate Brussels sprouts from school menus."[16] Meanwhile, her father was arranging an internship at the sleepy *Houston Chronicle*. He had to pull some strings, but not very hard. It would keep her home and he could take her out on his Lightning yacht. She could work on the "women's pages" at the paper. It would be a nice filler for her, a way to stay busy over the summer and to earn her own money. (Compared to the parents of many people she knew at St. John's and Smith, he was always tight-fisted toward her, to the point of sending her pointed notes about how much money he had spent on her and how much she owed, sometimes with very specific repayment plans.)

She hadn't yet told her parents that she wanted to live in France with Hank Holland and write stories. One rainy day on campus, she'd put on her trench coat, had a smoke dangling from her mouth, and was standing with Anne Seifert watching the parade of people going by. Seifert knew there were students on campus who had no clue what they would do, other than search for some certitudes in marriage. With the rain coming down, still puffing on her cigarette, Ivins said: "I'm going into journalism. I'm going to write. That's what I'm going to do."[17]

⋘⋙

Holland decided to spend the summer of 1964 in Washington with Dan Davis, his friend from Yale and part of the extended Weyerhaeuser empire. They struck a deal: Holland would drive Davis's car from Greenwich to Seattle, and he would also tow his black Ducati, the one that had been delivered in the dead of night by a truck named Ghost. He hadn't really sat still at all. Lately, he'd been writing short stories, inventive little tales:

> He is in [a] car with a date. He looks at her, sort of virginal and plump in her strapless dress. They are moving slowly, in a line of cars headed

> to the front door of the country club in Greenwich, where they expect to [be] helped out of the car by valets. Inside, Hank began musing about dancing with his dumb date. And then he would slip into his dervish dance, she would step back in amazement, and a circle of other dancers would form around him. And he leaps up into the air . . . and, poof, at the top of his jump, he simply disappears. And he's never seen again . . . until, years later, stories start coming out from a remote valley in the Andes of a young genius who had developed a flying machine, not unlike some of da Vinci's schematics for flying devices that one man can step into, this one set in motion with a bio-fuel, yak urine. The genius, raised by descendants of the Incans, is never really found—he remains mysterious, influential, powerful and unseen.[18]

Holland arrived in Washington on July 2. The next day he registered for a summer course at the University of Washington. On July 6, he took his motorcycle out for a spin. A sixteen-year-old girl who lived near the estate asked for a ride. He told her to ask her parents for permission. They gave it, the girl jumped on back, and they roared down the driveway to the country road. Almost immediately, a dog charged into the lane and Holland swerved hard. The girl flew off the bike and Holland slammed headfirst into a steel guardrail. His head was crushed and he died instantly. The girl was alive but dazed. Dan Davis sprinted to the road and held Holland in his arms. He screamed: "Leave us alone, can't you see we're fine!"

Things moved quickly. The family was notified, and Ann Holland suggested that Hank's body be cremated—going through another burial after her father's recent death would be too much. Holland was cremated in Seattle and Dan Davis flew with Holland's ashes back to Greenwich for a memorial service at an Episcopal church on July 10. There was a throng at the service—including the dean of Morse College at Yale and one of Holland's professors. Ivins arrived and "she was wrapped so tightly . . . she looked like a widow in mourning. Molly almost seemed like a statue. She seemed very straight, very self-contained, very emotionless. She had a lid on, a tight lid on."[19]

The next day, Ann and her uncle took the ashes to the beach at Tod's Point and she opened the can and scattered the remains. She thought they looked like gravel. There were bells ringing in the background; it was Sunday and church services were unfolding nearby. As she watched the matter float away, she could see a family standing in the water—a man and woman holding the hands of their children. She thought they looked like paper dolls and wondered if her family could ever be like that. Ann thought, then and for years, that her brother's short story about disappearing and still being alive might be true. She would look for his face in a crowd. One thing became extremely clear to her and other close friends: Molly Ivins was never the same person after Holland flew over the handlebars of his Ducati on a back road in Washington.

⥈

Ann Siefert says:

> It was not the same. The party was over. We were trying to function again and it just wasn't working. In my mind, she lost that part of her dream. I do know that as career-minded as she was . . . we both felt in the back of our minds that these are the guys we will end up with. We can do all of our coquetting, and playing around and all that stuff, but eventually this is the plan. Molly will be with Hank and I will be with Dan and that's how it was going to happen. . . . I think that in her mind, that he was the one. And in her mind—maybe there wasn't anybody else. He would have been a really, really hard act to follow. The two of them together were dynamite.
>
> Molly and Hank kind of fed on it. They were back and forth like a game of badminton. They could just keep doing this sort of thing. It was a really happy time and then it was like everything came crashing down. We were just young. The world was all in front of us. He was somebody that you couldn't imagine could die. He really had it all. Smart, good looking. Good family. In this case, we were all kind of very privileged and in a very, very special situation for people our age—and it just came crashing down. So we weren't protected. There was no protection with all that wealth.[20]

Their plans to get married added another dimension to the tragedy, especially considering that Ivins realized there were many women at Smith who were there primarily to marry someone: "It was part of the deal at Smith. You knew you were supposed to. It wasn't a very liberated time. Many of the women there were jockeying to find the best suitor that would maintain that social connection and lifestyle that we were all sort of expected to have. That was the expectation, that if you were there and meeting the right people, and having the right connections, and getting the good money, your life would be pretty sweet."[21]

Ivins's friends said that after Holland's death she was especially disgusted with the expectations, and maybe that's why she mocked her upbringing and Texas even more—and smoked more cigarettes, drank more, and insisted on telling people she was going to do something, that she was going to work, have a job. But, for a while, Holland had been a way to cling to some of the bourgeois conceits and own them, really, at some superior level. He was rich, wanted to be rich, but he loathed his mother, religion, and all the tired protocols of his father. And after Holland's death, Ivins wrote poems about him—ones in which she blamed herself for not being there for him—as well as several letters to Holland's sister: "Zut alors, Anneth, Hank said that you were worthy of my friendship and because of Hank's commendation, I will consider it. . . . I scream in agony to think of the long muscles of Hank's back."[22]

Ann was stung by some of the letters, the intimacies revealed about her brother. Ann hated to get the letters, she was shocked, she felt them to be arrogant—but she also perceived that Ivins was doing what she had to in order to cope, and that the content and tone of those letters were part of that.

The foursome of Ivins, Holland, Davis, and Seifert essentially disintegrated. Seifert wondered if Ivins would ever marry. She assumed that Ivins's sense of what money could buy had been irrevocably altered. Other friends said that Holland had to die so that Ivins could begin her steady march toward progressive politics, toward activism, toward delivering blows against the empire. Hank Holland and Ivins had taken the rarefied air in a dizzying corner of a prep school–Ivy League–CIA–Wall Street world—with impeccably dressed parents playing the harp, importing a giant wooden gondola from Italy, navigating giant yachts across the Atlantic—and reduced it all to some combustible essence. Holland wanted to be superman; he wanted to speak in every language, to disappear because he could. It was as though his father's world, her father's world, was all muscled-up and filled with rationalized selfishness—and filtered through the prism of wealthy children lugging jackboot expectations. It was, in its way, a brand of moneyed madness born of societal incest and perhaps inspired a bit by a desire for revenge—Ivins and Holland had never really fit in before, and they had convinced themselves they were operating on another plane. (She had once written that joking note to her parents, from France, that she was the "Superior One.") Ivins and Holland pushed each other, reinforced each other, goaded each other with a jibber-jabber pastiche of the new things they'd heard in school and read in the self-actualizing books of the time.

Their camaraderie was also very, very funny, but a brittle, cold kind of funny (Holland's sister said he lacked any form of compassion)—like sharing a hushed, clever joke at someone's expense. It was as if Ivins and Holland had charted a new caste system in which they were far beyond the River Oaks and Greenwich Brahmins in so many ways. All of it blew away with the ashes at Tod's Point in Connecticut. For the rest of her life, when it came to many of her friendships with men, Ivins would prefer the company of mercurial types—radical activists in a war against "the pigs," Pulitzer Prize–winners who had seen dark fires or had a proximity to power, balls-to-the-wall politicos who carried guns and turned shallow men into presidential candidates, Ivy League professors who pinned their anger to their chests.

Holland could perhaps have been any of those people if he wanted, and he might have done it more brilliantly, in pluperfect colors. Arguably, she would spend her life meeting men whom she knew never measured up to him but possessed bits and pieces of his energy. Either way, marriage would hardly emerge as an assumption or a long, lingering possibility. Some men might have believed it, hoped for it, but it really was not going to happen after Holland rode that doomed motorcycle delivered by the Ghost. As one friend said: "She may just not have met somebody else that quite fit the bill."[23]

⋘⋙

The summer Holland died, Ivins returned to her home on Chevy Chase Drive and also experienced her first, limited exposure to the inner workings of the *Houston Chronicle*, a paper that managed to be both moribund and obsequiously deferential to the powers-that-be. The *Chronicle* was seen by many as a jingoistic house organ for the oligarchy of America's sixth-largest city. It had been owned by the former secretary of commerce, Jesse Jones, and after he died the paper moved into the control of his heavily bankrolled and very private Houston Endowment. The latter was an influential body that endorsed the notion that, once the patricians had accumulated enough money, they could segue into civic ventures coated with the patina of noblesse oblige. The tax-free Endowment, founded in 1937, gave away millions and had a major reach, with "an important interest in 32 corporations, a majority interest in 25, including half a dozen banks, three hotels, several downtown office buildings, real estate and the Mayfair House hotel on Park Avenue in New York."[24] Aside from the newspaper, it owned a prominent radio station and a chunk of one of the leading TV stations. The trustees (five in all) all worked for Jones, were related to Jones, or had significant roles running major banks and holding companies in the city. The publisher, through 1965, was Jones's nephew John T. Jones, Jr.

When Ivins visited the paper that summer during the first of what would be three internships there, the Endowment was busy buying and shutting one of the *Chronicle*'s major rivals, the gritty *Houston Press*. The *Press* had long featured the work of Sig Byrd, a gumshoe reporter who out-Breslined Jimmy Breslin in terms of celebrating working-class heroes and ordinary saints in the alleys, bars, and boiler rooms of the city. And she was joining the *Chronicle* at a time when Lyndon Johnson would become the only Democrat endorsed in a presidential race by the paper until Barack Obama in 2008. The circles of power in Houston had remained exactly the same since she had gone to school in the East, and the Endowment's philosophy was that the editorial process should never block the mega-deals that were being cooked at the still-segregated River Oaks Country Club, the Old Capitol Club in the Rice Hotel, the Petroleum Club, the Houston Club, and the Houston Yacht Club.[25]

The other paper in town, the *Houston Post*, was owned by the former governor of Texas, William P. Hobby, and his wife Oveta Culp Hobby. She ran the day-to-day operations after having served as the nation's first secretary of health, education, and welfare. Many observers suggested that the slightly larger *Post* had been the mildly better paper in terms of its news content. The *Chronicle*, a sturdy friend of the men who ran the city, had imported editor William Steven, who had recently been fired from the *Minneapolis Star-Tribune*. Steven flogged the circulation with livelier stories, watchdog columns, and improved delivery tactics.[26]

During her summers at the *Chronicle*, Ivins was assigned to a variety of low-level tasks: answering phones, filling paste pots, cutting out articles for the library morgue, and running errands for the grizzled veterans, including caustic, local-legend-in-the-making Zarko Franks, who would remain close to her for years. Franks was a man who could have walked off the pages of A. J. Leibling's *Telephone Booth Indian*. He was loud, intense, proud of his work, and liked to stroll down the block from the *Chronicle* building on Texas Avenue, in mid-afternoon, to hang out at the Rice Hotel's Old Capitol Club, sinking into the red leather couches that had been stuffed with hair from horse manes. Or, he'd head down the highway to the naughty possibilities in wide-open Galveston, run by the once notorious Maceo family, and have drinks at a joint called the Rickshaw under the welcoming eye of smooth proprietor Diamond Athanasiou. Franks was a player, mingling with the reporters in fedoras at the courthouse and immediately drawn to the tall, twenty-year-old redhead who liked to smoke. He would call her "Molly Bee" and "Viking Goddess" and tell her she had "lake blue eyes." He liked to send her working versions of stories he had banged out on his typewriter, asking if she had ever seen anything that good. Every paper in Texas had at least one or two journeymen like him—ballsy, working on a novel, and willing to play the crusty-but-benign role for awed newbies.

When Ivins was going downtown in the mid-60s, before Houston had built most of its six miles of underground tunnels, the streets were still full of grifters with pencil-line moustaches and nicknames, dreamers outside the Greyhound bus terminal whose luck was flatter than a gambler's wallet, and shoeshine men who played the blues as good as Lightnin' Hopkins. Zarko fit in, knew many of them; he was a Runyonesque rooster who sent roses to women and dreamed of getting his book *Goodbye, Golden Girl* published.[27] If not that book, then it would be the one he wanted to write with a forensic pathologist, with the working title *I Live with the Dead*.

He constantly made fun of the process, of the earnestness that editors clamored for in his stories and that he hammered out a few minutes before deadline. Years later, he sent Ivins a story he had written with a note attached: "Ask your city editor, the sardonic bastard . . . if he's got anybody on that sterile rag capable of doing something like this. I mean, with a phony heartbeat to it, so it sings and cries like pro copy should."[28] Franks was influential on several levels—including his ability to bat out copy on a dime, something Ivins would do for the next few decades. His seemingly perpetual, comedic contempt for editors he viewed as less than his equal was something else she absorbed.

Another reporter who made an impression on her was Stan Redding, who had filed the *Chronicle* stories when John F. Kennedy visited Houston just before his fateful journey to Dallas. Redding was more than predisposed to view the world with black humor and healthy skepticism: He interviewed Frank Abagnale four times and wrote the breathless *Catch Me If You Can*, the story of the teenaged con man that was eventually made into a Stephen Spielberg movie starring Leonardo DiCaprio and Tom Hanks. There was also Billy Porterfield, a Jack Daniels–drinking and whip-crackingly funny reporter Ivins would encounter for years in Texas. He had covered Elvis Presley's first visits to Houston and, like Franks and Redding, had literary aspirations well beyond the realm of the smoke-filled city room of the *Chronicle*. He would eventually produce a telling memoir, published by HarperCollins, of the paths he and his family took as they danced around the expectations and limitations of Texas.

In Houston, Ivins took her father's sailboat out at the yacht club, visited her mentor Bob Moore, and tried to put Hank Holland's death out of her mind. She liked the idea of going to work at the downtown newspaper; she liked having a desk in the building on Texas Avenue, in the middle of the power complex where her father had cut his own deals. She'd never been around reporters before, including the itinerant ones who would work for a few months in one city and then move on to Laredo, El Paso, San Antonio, or Corpus Christi—hired guns who were brought in to maybe bird-dog a long-running murder trial and who lived in rent-by-the-week motels on the edges of downtown.

She liked the newspaper code talk, the lingo about picas, double trucks, slugs, and reefers. She liked the gallows humor. For a twenty-year-old who had essentially done stand-up comedy routines at Smith about holy rollers in Texas, who told people she played hoops with plastic-curler-girls from Bed, Texas, this was something closer to the marrow. The newsroom was only a three-minute drive from her home on Chevy Chase, and it seemed to have come directly out of one of her favorite books, Nathanael West's *Miss Lonelyhearts*, the bitter saga about a man assigned to the "agony beat" at the big city daily, exposed to too many things, hardened to concrete—and who then "killed his great understanding heart by laughing."[29]

⇽⇾

That summer, Ivins decided to follow through with her plans to study abroad—it was supposed to have been a trip she and Hank Holland would take together. She had turned twenty that August, the day after the movie *Mary Poppins* was released. She met her father in New York for a dinner at an expensive restaurant, and at some point in the evening he jumped to his feet and yelled out: "Yahoo, my little girl is going to Europe!" The next day she flew to France to spend her junior year at the Institut des Sciences Poletiques in Paris, a place that some called the "French Harvard." Among the students, educators, and staffers affiliated with the school over the years were United Nations Secretary-General Boutros Boutros-Ghali, Canadian Prime Minister Pierre Trudeau, Monaco's Prince Rainier, French president François Mitterrand, Columbia University president Grayson Kirk, Harvard president Derek Bok, Marcel Proust, and Christian Dior.

While she was abroad, students were buzzing about the bigger issues. Dr. King was awarded the Nobel Peace Prize, the Warren Commission said Lee Harvey Oswald acted alone in Dallas, Malcolm X was assassinated, China detonated its first atomic bomb—and Parisians were mulling over the fact that Jean Paul Sartre had declined his own Nobel Prize for literature. In California, the Free Speech movement was intensifying. A month after LBJ was elected president, the largest mass arrest of students in American history, involving some 800 people, took place at the University of

California, Berkeley. In Paris, that same year, students were taking to the streets to protest government educational reforms. Tensions were building between the United States and France, and in the middle of it all Ivins worked hard on a lengthy analysis paper about Charles DeGaulle.

It was good to be in France, away from anything that might immediately remind her of Hank Holland. She smoked constantly and stayed up late with other students, drinking and debating and telling hard-to-imagine stories about Texas. She cultivated a love of cooking, fine food, and wines that would be a mainstay for decades. With Johnson winning the presidency, there were more questions about her home state: What were Texas and LBJ really like? Were there still Indians? And what about "Giant" and the oil gunslingers—was it all real, imagined, exaggerated? The students loved her, this towering, well-read redhead from Texas, of all places—who cursed like a sailor, could out-drink anybody at the table, peppered her stories with literary references and snippets of country songs by Kitty Wells and Patsy Cline, and insisted that everyone go out dancing. Just a few years removed from her first trip to France, she was now seeing Paris at a more intimate level, sans chaperones, and walking the Left Bank instead of viewing it from the tour bus window.

At the Institut, she had to prepare a final paper and began to dwell more on her project on DeGaulle—and about how she thought he had been objectified, how he managed to be a visionary superman who was never taken seriously enough, who had righteous reasons to tweak the United States. Titled "In Defense of DeGaulle," her never-published seventeen-page draft on DeGaulle was something she was exceedingly proud of, to the point of sharing it with her family. In it she wrote that he is "one of the last of the Great Men" and that his books "are not only strategically brilliant, but beautifully written as well." And, she said, people misunderstood and underestimated DeGaulle: "the butt of countless jokes, some of them quite cruel. An inordinately proud and peculiar-looking man he was an easy target. . . . He was ignored, upbraided, snubbed, ridiculed and insulted."[30]

She called him a visionary leader for the times, quoted Louis Auchincloss's 1964 novel *The Rector of Justin*, and checklisted McGeorge Bundy and Robert McNamara. She talked about the Maginot Line and Churchill's "heaviest cross." And then, as if she couldn't help herself, as if she was suddenly channeling Margaret Robbie Milne Ivins's take on Lucille Ball in Houston, Texas, she uncorked: "He looks as much like an elephant as it is possible for a man to look. He is a walking caricature. The 6-foot-6 DeGaulle is sometimes known to his irreverent countrymen as Charlie the Big Asparagus. . . . DeGaulle has a sort of ponderous, pachydermal dignity that impresses even scoffers."[31]

In France, for the first time, she was beginning to tinker with writing about people in power—and doing it by zooming down from the hovering sweep, the historical panorama, and making a crash landing on the high-and-mighty. It seemed too overtly intellectual, and full of shit, to do so in a droning, preachy, academic way. It wasn't really complex: She wanted to write the way she talked. Like Holland, she'd suffer no fools; like her father she'd work like a dog; like her mother she'd roll with the absurdity.

She also read, constantly, and it informed her search for a style, a voice: John Steinbeck's *Travels with Charley*. Rachel Carson's *Silent Spring*. James Baldwin's *The Fire Next Time*. Theodore White's *The Making of a President*. She told people she loved Thor Heyerdahl and his book about rafting the Pacific, *Kon Tiki*. And she wrote more and more, filling up her notebooks with indecipherable handwriting, exclamation points, and doodles of dandies and clerics and fools. She also grew more comfortable holding forth in public, dominating the discourse. In France, strangers would look at the looming American, and she knew they were staring and she would start jabbering in French. Then she would start talking with a Texas twang. Then she would use some Upper East Coast Smith inflections. And then she would start laughing. She told friends she still felt physically awkward, but rarely intellectually intimidated. The goal, too, hadn't changed—it was the same goal she had written down on a piece of paper and put in her wallet back in high school. "She always wanted to be famous," said one close friend.[32]

CHAPTER FOUR

Naturally Backwards into Journalism

There is nothing to be learned from history anymore.
We're in science fiction now.

—ALLEN GINSBERG

The longer he was in office, the more editors in New York began to wonder what hellish wellspring had produced Lyndon Baines Johnson. Kennedy was, for many of them, so much easier to understand and relate to. So was Nixon, for that matter. But Johnson was another prickly beast entirely, and his devilish manipulation of the media in spot-specific ways—making reporters wait for him while he clearly was taking a leak—was confounding the issue of how exactly to cover and interpret him. It wasn't just his style, of course, and the sense that half of it was calculated not just to disarm reporters but to mess with their heads and maybe even humiliate them: Some editors were also aware of the shadowy suspicions that Johnson and other Texans like John Connally and the members of the Hunt family must have had some hand in the deadly affairs in Dallas. For New

York- and Washington-centric editors it was like another world down there; it was even beyond the easier-to-read evils in the other, less-powerful Southern states. Johnson's ascent, his presidency, raised endless questions about how exactly he got to power in the first place, what he would do in the Oval Office, what his intentions were as the United States fell deeper into the muck of Vietnam. It was a propitious time to be a Smith-educated, Paris-trained, budding journalist from Texas—someone who clearly had ambitions beyond the backwater, who was able to apply to Texas the same kind of Ivy League focus that others usually applied to matters in Washington, New York, or Europe. Johnson's presidency, and the resulting influx of reporters coming to the state to try to "interpret it," to see what it suggested about huge turns in American political tendencies and future presidential races, helped steer Ivins more firmly toward a life in journalism. Editors wanted, needed, to know what the hell it was like below the Red River and north of the Rio Grande, and maybe they would one day want a reporter who both knew the place and could explain it in Northeast-educated English.

Their bewilderment, and her predisposition to articulate the ridiculousness of Texas, would eventually put her in a position to do what A.J. Liebling had done for (or to) Louisiana in 1961 when his dispatches to *The New Yorker* were turned into "The Earl of Louisiana," a chronicle of corruption and regional absurdities that reinforced the belief of editors "back east and up north" that Reconstruction and reunification had never really taken place. She had continued to read *The Texas Observer*—in part because having it in her hands was a subversive slap to almost everything her father had stood for. She knew that *Observer* editor Willie Morris, the former editor of the student newspaper at the University of Texas at Austin, had followed a career arc to New York. He was hired at *Harper's* and was on a path to being the editor-in-chief—and, of course, he was working on a memoir about alienation and affection as he grew up in the South, a book that arguably inspired a sub-genre that included works by other Southern journalists who went to New York such as *New York Times* writers Howell Raines and Rick Bragg. Morris was one early role model for Ivins, proof that you could make a living as a political journalist–cum–cultural anthropologist, and could come out of Texas and be taken seriously in New York. He could be from the South but hover above it and dissect it and translate it. There would be other role models too, people who helped more specifically to shape her writing voice, but as an early, working paradigm, Willie Morris was certainly a figure she was very much aware of.

She settled in for her first serious internship at the *Houston Chronicle* in the summer of 1965, assigned to a small warren reserved for interns and almost hidden behind a row of large, clunky black typewriters, and it was as though she'd been dropped by parachute into the funniest, and most cynical, bunker imaginable. She worked on short "filler" items, answered the phones, dealt with reader complaints, took in wedding announcements—and, on one occasion, mixed up the names in the stories and said a college graduate had a B.O. instead of a B.A.

She began hanging out with the smart-ass reporters going to City Hall and the courthouses. She was turning twenty-one, bringing home $62 a week, still inviting people to go sailing and drinking on her father's Lightning boat at the Houston Yacht Club. She joined the rolling amoeba of journalists going to drink at clubs around Market Square, behind the *Chronicle*. She met other lifelong friends. Dave McNeely, a twenty-five-year-old cub reporter who had graduated from the University of Texas at Austin, dropped in on the supposedly stern Tuesday intern meetings and became an extremely loyal, close personal friend and productive political source over the years. McNeely would also become one of the leading political reporters in Texas, writing a long-running column for the *Austin American-Statesman* and co-writing a book about Bob Bullock, the mad genius who had a stranglehold on Texas politics and essentially paved the way for George W. Bush's run for the presidency. (McNeely, arguably the David Broder of Texas, eventually taught a course at his alma mater with Paul Begala and then Karl Rove.)

At the *Chronicle*, Ivins was increasingly influenced and inspired by the attention she was getting from the Mad Hatter of the newsroom, the eclectic and combustible Zarko Franks. She was also fitting into a circle of sarcastic young interns and new reporters, many of whom were openly quacking about whether the *Chronicle* was too stodgy, too wedded to the various businesses and boards that the Houston Endowment kingmakers presided over. It was an early manifestation of what would become her lifelong suspicion of newspaper ownership—the high sheriffs, as she called them. She was exposed to the business at a time when the editorial pages often perfectly reflected the groupthink of the citizen-kings. It was also a time when the paper was designed and laid out by hand, when boys delivered it on bikes, when muscled pressmen would fold up a newspaper sheet into a "pressman's hat" to keep the ink mist from spraying on their heads—and when most women were relegated to the back sections of the paper, the softer news, the "women's section."

But she was also exposed to a particular newspaper at a time when it was becoming increasingly difficult to ignore the disparities, and the inequities, that persisted as Houston grew. The "Eighth Wonder of the World," the Astrodome, had opened and baseball was magically being played indoors—but its best seats were reserved for the wealthy white citizens. It was a stunning new addition to the city. But the growth of Houston, each glittering triumph, only made it harder than ever to ignore the harsh juxtaposition with the Fourth Ward, the former freedman's town that had been neglected and finally butchered by highway and office construction throughout the '60s. When Ivins drove to work at the *Chronicle*, she skirted the south side of Buffalo Bayou and she could see the Fourth Ward, the boundaries of it easy to identify and the bleak look of it so singular. The whole place, a gulag festering directly between her River Oaks neighborhood and the oil-fueled downtown office complex, was even more tattered. Its clapboard shacks were an aching reminder of the new prosperity.

The titans had built a new airport, a stadium with air conditioning, and they were busy laying out all those tunnels downtown so that you would walk from your bank to your private club without breaking a sweat on Texas Avenue. And the city's intransigence toward the Fourth Ward—as well as the sister zones where the blacks and Latinos were exiled, the Second, Third, and Fifth wards—was only made more clear with each new highway expansion or building crane looming over downtown. There were even homes in the Settegast neighborhood, a place dotted with "affordable" homes that might lure blacks away from any encroachment into white neighborhoods, where there was still no running water and raw sewage simply flowed into ditches and streets. There was nothing subtle, in the least, about the disparities. It was in the architecture, and in the language. Reporters coming back from interviews with the police said some of them were still talking about the "niggers." The police force was widely viewed by critics as one of the most racist in America. And at the courthouses, it was easy to see that the separate water fountains for blacks and whites hadn't yet been removed—one person at the courthouse told a reporter that they had been kept there "for historic reasons." It was 1965 in the meanest, richest city below the Mason-Dixon line and Ivins was looking at the very occasional, but still enlightening, moments of how journalism could shine a light on a dark corner. A week after a reporter mentioned the drinking fountains in a small item in the *Chronicle*, they were no longer separate.

That summer, the city was also on edge over the fact that a local attorney named Barbara Jordan had co-founded People for Upgraded Schools in Houston and had recently steered a demonstration by 2,000 people protesting the fact that 85–90 percent of the school system remained aggressively segregated. White flight was under way as families began to anticipate desegregated neighborhoods and schools. And Ivins was learning, as were the other interns who had gone to extraordinarily exclusive schools like St. John's and Kinkaid where there were no minorities beyond the janitors and landscapers, that Houston was not just multi-hued but twitchy, restive, and getting hotter all the time.

⟻⟼

Carlton Carl, another *Chronicle* intern, was someone Ivins had bumped into in private-school circles. He had gone to Kinkaid, George W. Bush's school, and when he and Ivins worked at their various high school publications he would run into her at a local printing shop. They talked, early on, about the absence of minority students at the institutions they'd attended. She made an impression on Carl when they reconnected at the *Chronicle* in the summer of 1965: "She was all full of energy, always seemed sure of herself even when she wasn't. To her, journalism was something more than putting words in a newspaper, it could have influence and should have influence. I don't know whether it was absolutely clear in her mind that that was what she was going to do, but I think it was a part of her from early on. Partly, I think she loved reading, she loved writing. I think it originates with reading a lot."[1]

Some of the *Chronicle* staffers Ivins befriended would later profess their aspirations to do something beyond the limitations they perceived at the paper and, more generally, in Texas. One sent her a note on Texas governor Preston Smith's stationery in which he talked about the "intellectual wastelands of Texas." (Ivins once immortalized Smith for the nation when she wrote about the befuddled governor wondering why there were angry black people outside his window shouting "Frijoles! Frijoles!"—the Spanish word for beans. The protesters were actually shouting "Free Lee Otis"—referring to a black activist who had been busted for one marijuana joint and was facing thirty years in jail.)

Zarko Franks constantly shared his literary goals with Ivins. When he wasn't on deadline, Franks would often be harrumphing around the area where the interns and cub reporters were quartered. It remained obvious to others that he still had an abiding interest in Ivins. "He clearly saw some spark there that he liked. He liked people who wrote with a little flair."[2] He read her copy, critiqued it, wisecracked about how she might be more like him some day. She wasn't the only one who hadn't really met men like Franks before—someone who liked knocking back beers with young people at the ice houses close to downtown. He was closer to her father's generation, and she simply hadn't seen or heard adults who were so skeptical about who was below deck and greasing the big machinery in Houston. She liked the vulgar, obscene bonhomie and camaraderie that the reporters had—the hanging out, the way the real stories were the ones that never made the paper because no one would believe them or the editors wouldn't allow them.

At the bar after work, after some drinks, the fact that she was so damned funny blurred the fact that she was often the only woman in the room. Few people had seen or heard a woman as loud and funny as Ivins, and at least one said she was channeling both Katharine Hepburn's political columnist Tess Harding in *Woman of the Year* and Rosalind Russell's cocky reporter Hildy Johnson in *His Girl Friday*. "Molly was a large and powerful presence even then," said McNeely.[3]

⋯

She returned to Smith for her final year in the fall of 1965. She wrapped up the final requirements for her major in modern history with an emphasis on Europe and the Middle East, and a minor in French. And she told her parents that she wanted to go to journalism school. "I decided I should figure out how to make a living in case it turned out I wasn't a great writer. The only talent I had ever shown was writing, and the only deep interest outside of literature was current affairs, so I just fell kind of naturally backwards into journalism."[4] She was aiming for Columbia, in New York, which some said offered the finest graduate program in the nation and she thought offered the best chance for her to eventually live in France and be a foreign correspondent. Her father was somewhere between skeptical and deliberately unenthused. He liked the idea that she would be in New York, at an Ivy League school. But he had never expressed any great affection for the muckraking side of journalism, in either newspapers or magazines. His world was predicated on cloistered business deals and an off-the-record, confidential, lubricating protocol.

In her final year at Smith, her love for alcohol deepened and she developed a willingness to experiment with other things. A college friend sent her a crackling, conspiratorial note asking if her mother had ever found her "stash." Ivins still continued her awkward letter-writing to Ann Holland, trying to ease her way back from Hank's death. She was still weaving Texas tales, solidifying friendships. There was an especially vibrant kinship with the mercurial Nancy Dowd, from Framingham, Massachusetts, that would continue for years. Dowd was irreverent, loved to write, had studied French, and, like Ivins, spent part of her school year in Paris. She would earn a master's at UCLA and go on to write what some say is one of the most authentic sports movies ever, *Slap Shot*, and then be caught up in extremely contentious debate about her contributions to the Academy Award–winning screenplay for *Coming Home* with Jane Fonda.

Dowd's friendship with Ivins suggests she was pushing Ivins to break from her River Oaks upbringing and whatever Smith-related path her parents had in mind for her. They communicated for many years, and Dowd would ship copies of her screenplays for Ivins to read. In a striking parallel to her college friend, Dowd would later write an essay suggesting that she herself had escaped her upbringing. Dowd and Ivins bonded at college and for years after, linked, in part, by their denunciation of whatever exactly it was their parents had in mind for them.

Their close relationship was obviously grounded in rejection of the stultifying limitations on what women were supposed to be and do in the world, an issue that Friedan, Steinem, and others were analyzing at the time.

Ivins told her parents that she planned to come back home and do one last internship at the *Houston Chronicle* in the summer of 1966, but she had already made up her mind about that hometown paper. She decided she needed to plump her résumé in a different way. "In those days it was much harder for women to get hired and for women to get good assignments . . . and it was pretty clear, at least on that provincial paper, as the *Chronicle* then was, that they were sort of automatically relegated to food, club and fashion. The women's page was actually called the 'snake pit,' and that was where you would end up unless you had an extra credential. That was why I went to graduate school."[5]

The changing campus politics, Friedan's emergence, and, in 1962, a groundbreaking *Esquire* article by Steinem about women, contraception, and careers solidified things for her. As one of her friends from then said: "It was during a time when the objective was to get married before you finished school. And there was tremendous pressure, to get married and to find the right social register person that kind of matched your credentials or at least would allow you to stay within the lifestyle you'd been enjoying. To Molly it was not important. . . . It was not having babies and it was not being married, that wasn't the first thing on the agenda."[6]

The notion that she had to play the female socialite primogenitor seemed less and less interesting the more she was exposed to the irreverent possibilities in journalism. That traditional route certainly seemed a hell of a lot less fun, and a waste of a good education. Years later she reflected on her time at Smith: "I had been on school papers both in high school and college and knew what I wanted to do fairly early on. . . . I really did get an education there [at Smith], and over the years I have come to value what they did for me more and more. . . . I guess I had just absorbed . . . self-confidence."[7]

⟻⟼

In the summer of 1966 she was back at the *Chronicle*. She wrote a series of articles with Carlton Carl that were compressed into one long piece about poverty in Houston. It wound up on the front page, a major coup considering the topic and the fact that it was spearheaded by interns. On Saturdays, she invited the newer interns for the usual moments aboard her father's yacht, people sometimes laughing so hard they fell overboard, and she spent weekends on the slivers of beach on Galveston Island, walking out onto the piers where the mob still ran their illicit casinos.

In the Third Ward, students at Texas Southern University (the school "set up" for "the colored" years earlier) were meeting and on the verge of coalescing into one of the most intense confrontations ever with the police. The pioneering psychedelic band known as The 13th Floor Elevators was playing in Houston clubs, escorting rock music into some faraway, other place. She gave parties at her house on Chevy Chase Drive, and for some of her friends it became a home away from home. She had a swimming pool, something magical and not yet ubiquitous in the well-off areas. Food and jokes abounded, and there was plenty of beer and booze. And she made sure that people were not intimidated by "General Jim." He demanded, when the interns went sailing, that people know the difference between a halyard and a lanyard. Molly taught them how to rig the boat and take it down.

She was still clinging to a certain Yacht Club aura. Terry O'Rourke, another intern in the summer of 1966, used to peer at her over those black typewriters on the city desk: "She spoke with an East Coast, educated elite diction, inflected by a junior-year abroad French accent. She sounded like

Jacqueline Kennedy. And like Jackie, she not only spoke fluent French, she also read novels and political theory in French. Molly was tall and slim and beautiful. In her unpretentious, classic, expensive clothing, Molly exuded a soft, confident aura. Molly taught me to sail her father's 32-foot racing sloop at the Houston Yacht Club. She was the daughter of corporate power and wealth."[8]

O'Rourke was, after Hank Holland, someone she could relate to at a deeper level. Like Holland, he rode an Italian motorbike. "We were the children of the privileged," said O'Rourke.[9] He had grown up in Houston, been a page in the Senate and House in Washington, enrolled at Rice University in Houston, and was planning on a law degree from the University of Texas at Austin. If there was anyone in her life after Hank Holland who could channel some of his spirit, it might have been O'Rourke. He wrote long, passionate letters to her, ones that she kept with her for decades. "I think that for most people what may be challenging to understand was how pretty she was at that stage in her life. She was actually a very lovely woman. It's very difficult for those who knew her later in her life to understand that she was a fashion-conscious, attractive young woman," he said. He also sensed that she already had her own distinct political viewpoint that was driven by her own background—a background that allowed her to see the power structure from a personal standpoint.

"In the summer of 1966, she was already an East Coast liberal. She was liberal, yeah, she'd found her inner liberal . . . and yet she was still fascinated with the power structure, and she worked for the *Houston Chronicle*. When Molly and I worked for the *Houston Chronicle*, it was an overt, racist institution. It was owned by the Houston Endowment. The editor was Everett Collier and he worked as an inside member of the conservative Democratic establishment unapologetically."[10] O'Rourke says that Collier once told him he was, in fact, a spy for Lyndon Johnson and would go to Washington to listen in on the White House press corps to find out what they were saying about the president.[11]

One day in the newsroom, Ivins was perusing some textbooks that had been recommended to incoming students at Columbia, where she would start her nine-month program in the fall. She read out loud from one of them: "Gone are the days when the newspaper reporter had his tie undone, his cigarette hanging out of his mouth, with a bottle of whiskey in the top drawer of his desk, with a deck of cards sitting out." Right in front of them, of course, was Zarko Franks, who was exactly like the words in her textbook. They laughed their heads off—not just then, but most days at work.

O'Rourke thought that the girl who seemed more like Jackie O than most people—with the fluency in French, the East Coast education, the "well-modulated" voice—wouldn't stay long enough in Houston to be the heir to Sig Byrd or Zarko Franks and their ink-stained meditations on the inner city. She wasn't going to Telephone Road, talking to the oilfield workers from Lake Charles and Lafayette who were looking to spend their money in the city; she wasn't going to Segundo Barrio and Antonio Gonzalo Bustamante's bar, the Laredo; she wasn't going to the vestiges of Catfish Reef, where you could buy both catfish and reefer; she wasn't going to Vinegar Hill or Produce Row, where the callused working-class heroes of Houston built the bedrock of the city.

But she *was* developing an interest in understanding the big process and policy of power. It was a function, most likely, of trying to figure out how her father, her family, fit into the oligarchy. A process of self-examination. She was learning where her family ranked. Studying power, ruminating on who had it and why, would became a constant focus for her. She was not going to specialize in telling stories from the bottom up—long narratives based on intimate details about race, poverty, and injustice. Instead, she would more often touch on those themes by exploring the system, the historical context, and the very specific policies and policymakers.

She emerged in an era in Houston when it was rare for whites, let alone WASPs, to venture into the Fourth, Fifth, and Third wards for the length of time necessary to overcome neighborhood suspicions and do lingering narratives—and when it was rarer still for the local newspaper to even assign stories in those neighborhoods. She was watching how editors tied to the most powerful politicians and businessmen in Houston would routinely avoid addressing the systemic problems. Meanwhile, of course, the muckraking, investigative, and condemning work she was reading in *The Texas Observer* continued to serve as a harsh contrast to what she was seeing in most big daily papers.

There were a few people in the city who were trying to make sense of the minority experience, trying to shed light on both the despair and the richness. As one example, the important musicologists Chris Strachwitz and Mac McCormick were busy out on the streets and in the alleys, capturing the profound music of Lightnin' Hopkins, Juke Boy Bonner, and other Houston-area geniuses who were extending and inventing essential American roots music in Houston's African-American neighborhoods. In a sense, they were doing the grassroots reporting that most journalists in the city were not. Ivins, as a function of her upbringing, and her insistent rejection of her father's world, was developing a métier shaped by a broader, more panoramic view of history—and filtered through a critical and chiding view of the powerbrokers.

Those journalistic summers in Houston were the early foundation for her boldly skeptical voice. It was as if she was ultimately determined to reprise the beery rap sessions, the laugh riots with the rat pack of reporters topping each other with insider accounts of some moke or pinhead who ran things in town—all those skittering-toward-cynical talk-fests with the awestruck interns and the jaded reporters, all those after-work deconstructions of what was *really* going on and who was *really* in charge. She learned that you could work at a newspaper and laugh your ass off—maybe because so many people in power were far less intelligent than the people they served and the reporters who covered them. She would later admit that she learned a shitload at the paper, the kinds of things that weren't in any of the texts at Columbia University, where she would eventually go to study journalism. "At that time, I was not a grateful child, but I learned [at the *Chronicle*] that a really good city editor could teach you as much as I had learned at Columbia."[12]

Terry O'Rourke rode his Vespa to Chevy Chase one day and asked Ivins if she wanted to go for a ride. She was turning twenty-two. He was turning twenty and he felt immortal.

She grew serious: "I can't get on it. I don't like the fact that you're riding it."

She said she had a boyfriend who died in a motorbike wipeout and she "wouldn't, couldn't" get on the back.[13]

She spent time at Château Dijon—the southwest Houston "singles'" apartment complex where George W. Bush would live during his acutely beery, boozy, nomadic years chasing go-go girls and airline stewardesses—working on a three-part series ("Faces from Other Places: Newcomers Bring Business, Brains to Booming City") about how "newcomers" found Houston so attractive. The series seemed custom-ordered by the chamber of commerce, with its outline of how Humble Oil was providing jobs and had turned into a "major importer of skills and brains." A week before her birthday, she did a piece on the Houston Cocktail Bartending School ("These Students Spend Their Time Mixing Drinks"). It was funny, in a way, to be able to skip out of the office and talk straight-faced to people about how much they loved their swinging lifestyle—people her age who couldn't wait to be like her old man. But she told friends she was ready to get the hell out of Houston; it was funny but not fulfilling. In her room on Chevy Chase, she packed the books she wanted with her on the Upper West Side of Manhattan at Columbia.

O'Rourke unabashedly felt she was a genius destined for something larger. "She was one of the smartest people I'd ever met. I can say that easily."[14] She was formulating, he thought, an understanding of how things were *supposed* to work in Texas and how they *actually* worked. It was an outgrowth of seeing Texas through her father's eyes, then working at the *Chronicle* with reporters who were already somewhere beyond cynicism—maybe because they worked for the very men who ran the city they were supposed to be covering objectively. It was a vicious loop, a circle, and she was coming to clear beliefs about government, the hallways of power. Deals were cooked, compromises made, and there were always angles and endless, sometimes illegal "corner shoots"—the Texas oil term for drilling just close enough to a big oil find that you hope to suck away some black gold of your own.

For the sons and daughters of the Tenneco-style aristocracy in Houston, the ones smart enough to see how the game was being played by their elders, there were clearly two sides to that trip on the petroleum rocket ship. Ivins told friends, later, that she knew too much, heard too many things about price-fixing in her father's living room and in the smoky newsroom downtown, to think that everything was unsullied and equitable in the gilded corners she had grown up in. The injustice and the comedy in Texas were everywhere. Most reporters she knew just moved along the periphery of the silly, sometimes authentically scary mess. But she was beginning to see it as an orchard of lush, low-hanging fruit. There were things in Texas worth examining up close and personal.

⋘⋙

At the end of her last summertime stint at the *Houston Chronicle*, she worked on various drafts of a funny goodbye speech for the "graduation ceremonies" for the members of the intern "Kiddie School," as she called it:

> Now we all realize that, contrary to reports in some national magazines, the *Houston Chronicle* is NOT a reactionary newspaper. Nevertheless, we are haunted by doubt: where WAS [reporter] Elmer Bertelsen when [civil rights leader James] Meredith was shot? Another aspect of life on Houston's Family Newspaper that puzzled us this summer was the copy boys. But someone finally explained to us that the *Chronicle* has a policy of hiring the handicapped, which accounts for a great deal.
>
> On August 1, the Big Story of the summer broke when Charles Whitman set a new world's record for shooting people from the University of Texas tower. . . . On August 15th, the quote of the year came in from Ku Klux Klanners who said, "We don't believe in violence, and we don't intend to have any violence if we have to kill every Negro in America."
>
> Such quotes make us all realize what a truly inspiring profession we are about to join. . . .
>
> But of course the really big event of the summer, the capstone, as it were, occurred on August 22, last Monday, when the *Chronicle* finally acquired a new publisher. However, as the "atlantic" will doubtlessly note, the *Chronicle* did not run a story on it.[15]

She didn't need any extra prodding to leave Houston and forget about working there again. But if she did, it was spelled out in the "atlantic." *The*

Atlantic magazine, in its August 1966 issue, had devoted a devastating piece devoted to the *Chronicle*. Called "Houston's Shackled Press," and written by Ben Bagdikian, the story eviscerated the paper, accusing it of constantly being on bended-knee to the royal families of Houston, of burying an important story (by Saul Friedman, who had been a Nieman Fellow at Harvard) about slumlords and abysmal living conditions for minorities, and of failing to note the firing of editor William Steven for being "too liberal, too pro-Negro and too militant a reporter of the town." The paper also had a new publisher, the millionaire oilman and investor John Mecom, who had countless business interests in Houston.[16]

In the fall of 1966, Ivins was on the Upper West Side of Manhattan. Some people called the area "White Harlem," because it was set on Morningside Heights, almost floating above one of the most influential black communities in America. It was a short stroll from Columbia to 125th Street, to the famous Apollo Theater, to all that Harlem meant—but, like the Fourth Ward in Houston, it was not a place that she normally detoured to, explored. She spent her time at the student haunts, bars, dives, diners, and burger joints filtering out from Broadway and 116th Street and the main gates to Columbia—the pizza place that Vincent and Tony Curcarato had opened on Amsterdam, the Marlin Bar, Chock Full O'Nuts, the College Inn, and the famous West End where Columbia students Jack Kerouac and Allen Ginsberg had hung out. She could walk, on a nice day, north to Grant's Tomb or south to the tiny "Latina y China" restaurants that dished up Cuban, Puerto Rican, and Chinese food on heaping plates.

She had won the Perle Mesta Franco-American Friendship Foundation Scholarship to the school, named in honor of the wealthy oil-and-steel heiress who held legendary fêtes for film stars, power brokers, and politicos at her magnificent Washington, D.C. apartment. Columbia's dean, Edward Barrett, had his roots in the South and in gilded Northeast schools—he was born in Alabama, educated at Princeton, and had worked for *Newsweek*, for the government, and in public relations before becoming the fourth dean in the school's history. A key faculty member was

Richard T. Baker, a worldly man who had taught in China, had become the school's "historian," and was well known for his elegant, patient manner with incoming students. There was the intense Penn Kimball, also Princeton educated, and someone who had worked at *Time* and *New Republic*; Kimball was interested, as were some other new faculty members, in seeing Columbia become more attuned to politics, government policy, and international and national reporting. Toward that end, Donald Shanor, a veteran foreign correspondent for the *Chicago Daily News* and *United Press International*, had joined the faculty. The school had also embarked on a tradition, one it would continue for years, whereby it dipped into the large pool of New York–based journalists to serve as part-time faculty—including several members of the *New York Times*.

Ivins's two semesters at Columbia were marked by the indelible impression left on her by Melvin Mencher, a relatively new teacher who was emerging as the flinty mentor for hundreds of students. Mencher, like him or not, by design or not, was a frequent focus of attention among those who said he was a tough-love instructor needed by students in an intense, compact graduate journalism program like the one at Columbia. Detractors said he overplayed the taskmaster–city editor role a bit too much and was out of sync with the intellectual, ambassadorial wings of the Ivy League school. He did seem, for years, to be the in-house populist, at war with his elders, almost as if he was still the pugnacious reporter who had gone from working-class roots to the University of Colorado and then to jobs at the *Albuquerque Tribune*, *Albuquerque Journal*, and *United Press International*. His work at the *Journal*, on infant mortality in the Navajo nation, led to a Nieman Fellowship at Harvard. He returned to the McClatchy chain as an investigative reporter and then began his teaching career in the late '50s at the University of Kansas. He served as advisor to the student newspaper, which occasionally ran stories that angered the school administration, including one piece about discrimination in housing for students. When the paper won an award from the National Conference of Christians and Jews, he traveled to Columbia in 1963 to accept the award and it led to a job offer.[17]

Mencher's philosophy, that a guiding purpose of journalism was to scrutinize power and it practitioners, cleaved perfectly with Ivins's welling notions of what she wanted to do with her career. And his sometimes barbed confrontations with his bosses at Columbia might have helped nurture the same kind of feisty relationship she would have with her future employers. Mencher, she told people, seemed to have a low tolerance for the pretentious, pontificating urges that she thought some people in New York journalism and publishing circles exhibited. He was in New York, but hadn't succumbed to some parochial view of life beyond the Hudson River.

Meanwhile, the on-campus climate was increasingly conducive to the bubbling skepticism that Ivins brought to Manhattan. The student movement at Columbia was intensifying, geared up for its full exposition in 1968 when the school would become an epicenter for campus revolution. At Columbia, it was driven by both anti-war sentiment and a belief that the university had been behaving like an intolerant slumlord to its Harlem neighbors. She had to have seen the links between what she had left in Houston and what was unfolding at Columbia. The *Houston Chronicle* had given her many things to think about: the reportorial acquiescence that often existed in daily newspapers, the pecking order that still plagued women in journalism, the way business and politics were completely intertwined in major American cities. Columbia gave her other things to mull: the collective rallying against authority, the bridge between local issues and the bigger historical context, the thread between those local issues and national trends. Above all, Columbia offered her a level of critical thinking that served as an adjunct to the baseline journalism skills she had absorbed in Houston: "It turned out that I had picked up more important thoughts at Columbia than just technical skills—how to write a story, how to cover this, that, and the other," she once said.[18]

Out toward the famed sundial on campus, under the wary eyes of the university administration, protestors were assembling in late 1966 and then in early 1967 to demonstrate against the seemingly grandfathered-in CIA recruiters who were back on campus.

⇹

The former president of CBS News, Fred Friendly, had just joined the school as the Edward R. Murrow Professor of Journalism. Friendly's insistence on the constant examination of the role of the media, especially in matters of national and global importance, served as another template for Ivins. He wanted to look at the macro-conceits of press and power, how the two danced with each other, what one meant to the other in terms of the U.S. Constitution and a functioning democracy. (A similar examination by Ivins would lead to a powerful relationship with her true First Amendment mentor—John Henry Faulk, the blacklisted broadcast personality—that began in the years after she graduated Columbia.) Friendly had just started at the school, and his philosophy—shared by some other faculty members—that the school should think hard about the broader issues, take a panoramic view, would also foreshadow Ivins's later interests.

She was picking up *The Village Voice*, reading Jimmy Breslin and Norman Mailer and Truman Capote, reading stories in *The New Yorker* that went beyond anything she had seen in Houston. Beyond the inverted pyramid leads, with all the important Who, What, When, Where, Why information stacked in the first two paragraphs. Beyond the High Altar of Objectivity, where all reporters were trained and sworn to not take sides or points of view in their copy. At Columbia she began keeping a notebook filled with quotations she liked. She wrote page after page of one-liners and jokes, random thoughts and snippets of conversation—many of them seemingly nonsensical.

As she settled into school, her father remained faithful to his pecuniary post-college threats. Struggling for money, she had to make do with eating Campbell's split-pea soup with ham and pitching in her pennies when her classmates went on beer runs. She lived near a Woolworth's on 79th and Broadway and walked in one day and secured part-time work as a saleslady, in order to make ends meet. Her father, meanwhile, was weighing a move now that she was out of college and Andy was beginning to shuttle to a variety of schools and programs. To many family members, Andy was always faithful in his communication with The Mole. He watched her progress, wrote her from his various travel destinations around the world, and shared stories about their parents and their new plans to relocate outside Texas.

At Columbia, Ivins was surrounded by people who would make names for themselves: author and filmmaker Paul Wilkes; *Orange County Register* editor Tonnie Katz; network news executive Paul Friedman; *Newsday* editor Howard Schneider; magazine and *New York Times* reporter Carey Winfrey; financial writer and columnist Allan Sloan; public television producer Linda Winslow; *Atlanta Journal-Constitution* columnist Carole Ashkinaze; *New York Times* reporter Joe Berger; OPEC head of communications Edward Omotoso. Ivins was pleased to be around so many ambitious students. She wrote letters to O'Rourke about how excited she was to be at Columbia. He replied that "you sound so fired up over Columbia, it is alarming"—and he also noted that he was "still a freely moving commodity in the unfree market of marriage." He signed a letter to her, dated November 28, 1966, "I await you with passion, Terry."[19]

Her father was writing to her as well, espousing the theories of Robert Ardrey, a dramatist who had turned his hand to cultural sociology and anthropology and joined the vanguard of "big thought" books that conveniently emerged at a time when essayists and commentators were earnestly trying to make sense of the smoke, fire, sex, drugs, and revolution of the '60s. Ardrey, Desmond Morris, and other writers were inclined to explain it all through the prism of man's primal roots and inclinations, and her father liked that. Jim Ivins, still arguing with his daughter via mail, sent her a note: "I'm enclosing a little bit gleaned from *The New York Times*, which I know will gladden your heart. It's what Ardrey has been propounding in his books; now authenticated in a highly responsible (?) paper by recognized scientists. When I question the *Times*' integrity, I have reference to their editorial on Agnew. That was really a low blow. Incidentally, had lunch with Gardiner Symonds yesterday. Quinta is at the Metropolitan Museum in early American art."[20]

In one stroke, he threw several things in her face—her affection for the *New York Times*, his admiration for Ardrey, and the fact that a girl she'd grown up with and gone to camp with (the daughter of the founder of Tenneco) had gone in the artistic direction that General Jim might have envisioned for his daughter. Of the unsettling aspects of his note, the one that might have resonated on some intractably deep level was the mention of

Ardrey, as if her father was seeking a pseudo-academic-intellectual affirmation of something way inside his soul, something he had come to believe on his Coast Guard vessel during WWII. Ardrey himself would write these controversial words:

> In the small black race—which I much suspect, from its numbers, to be the youngest of races—we have such evidence of superiority of anatomical endowment and neurological coordination that it must be regarded as a distinct subdivision of Homo sapiens. If racial distinction on the playing field is to be accepted, then can there exist theoretical grounds for banishing distinction in the classroom? In the United States the evidence for inferior learning capacity is as inarguable as superior performance on the baseball diamond; yet the question of intelligence remains distinctly unsettled.[21]

Her mother, too, was unrelenting in her admonitions as Ivins prepared to move from Columbia into her first full-time job in journalism. Her mother knew that Ivins had changed at Smith, during her time at the *Chronicle*, during her stay in New York. But she still harbored hopes that, if her daughter was going to go into journalism, she would be like longtime *Houston Post* reporter and editor Marguerite Johnston, perhaps the best-known female journalist for years in Houston. Her letters to Ivins had to rankle: "Dearest Mole, this is the last of Marguerite Johnston's columns. I send it to you because she has done what I'd like you to do. She has coupled it [the column] with raising a family and watching Houston grow. To be sure, it has often been a mite sticky but along with four children and her dogs, she has recorded the growth of Houston. . . . She wrote a book about [Episcopal] Christ Cathedral from way back. Often it was too personal but fairly humorous to boot—with a very *kindly* humor." She also, in the same letter, chastises her daughter for complaining about St. John's. "I think St. John's was very good for you and I don't see what your point is in trying to dictate policy."[22]

⇜⇝

At Columbia, as at Smith, Ivins was making a lasting impression among some professors, including the erudite, student-friendly John Hohenberg. She also embarked on lifelong friendships with students preoccupied with whether they would be drafted and shipped to Vietnam. For self-preservation and anti-war reasons, some of her closest friends from both Houston and New York were scrambling to make arrangements that would keep them out of the military—getting educational deferments, lining up teaching gigs that would lead to exemptions. She saw two things coalescing in the student movement on campus—the anti-war sentiment and the heated suggestion that the arrogant isolationism at the upper reaches of the ivory-tower university had continued to flourish. There was, in her view, an oligarchy in Houston. And some version of it existed at Columbia. Her politics, by now, were well beyond those of Hank Holland's hyper-individualism. And she saw some collective cause-and-effect, maybe some satisfying possibilities that were emerging when people protested: In particular, the Journalism School dean, Edward Barrett, would eventually resign in the wake of the turmoil at Columbia, and he would suggest that the overseers of the university were out of step with what was happening around them.

Meanwhile, there were other lessons, exceedingly practical ones that would influence her thoughts about both the day-to-day journalism process as well as what it might mean to have a "permanent" career. Hohenberg would run students through harrowing "speed drills"—demanding that they crank out stories in just a few minutes. And he urged everyone to keep $100 set aside. It was basically a Fuck You account—so that if an editor ever demanded that you do a story you hated, you would have at least $100 to help you walk away from the job.

Ivins was constantly dragging on a Marlboro, swirling a cup of Chock Full O'Nuts coffee, and seemingly often rolling her eyes when some hot-air speaker was invited to talk to a class. She would mutter an insult in French and stare in a different direction when someone turned to see who had been talking. At the bars and diners, she was a good debater, someone who pushed back against Mencher when she felt she was right. For a school assignment, she wrote an article trying to explain Texas and particularly Texas liberals. She said they were too damned paranoid, too damned drunk all the time, too prone to depression. All, perhaps, for no good reason except some sort of self-invited fear, some sense that they were operating in isolation and only a handful of trusted Texas souls could ever really understand them. She surmised that Texas liberals had essentially drawn a circle of cracked glass against unseen conspiracies—and then drank some more, went into some bunker, and then drank some more. It was a paper that she later decided was pretentious. Friends who saw it would say that it was, in fact, brilliant—that Ivins had accurately described a certain circle of dedicated, hard-drinking, and occasionally paranoid Texas liberals who were chased by demons both real and imagined. In just a few years after leaving Columbia, she'd be in the heart of what she had presciently described—shoulder to shoulder with the pioneers of Texas liberal politics, reinforcing each other in both very good and very debilitating ways.

At Columbia she met Jack Cox, who shared a desk with her in the "newsroom" on the second floor of the school. Cox had studied at the University of Wyoming, been editor of the school paper, and would maintain a close friendship with Ivins in the months and immediate years after they both left Columbia. Her correspondence with him and other students indicates that she was more than just comfortable with the expansive level of anti-authoritarian thinking at Columbia. Columbia, she told friends, was a composite that pleased her: an intellectual environment that was a refined, catholic extension of St. John's and Smith—and a community that didn't just endorse skepticism but, inside and increasingly outside the classroom, preached a righteous distrust. Columbia was a perfect distillation for her, a place where her literary–and–public affairs inclinations and her wide-open Texas smack-talk style were welcome during the late-night smoke-and-beer sessions. She made lifelong friends at the school, and some of them would even wind their way to her home: She took delicious, smiling delight in the fact that classmate Edward Omotoso visited the house in River Oaks on Chevy Chase Drive—and she not only let the Nigerian student use the swimming pool, she let him borrow her father's swimsuit.[23] She laughed about a Nigerian man, a "nigger," frolicking in her father's pool.

CHAPTER FIVE

Young Radicals

Any newspaper, from the first line to the last, is nothing but a web of horrors.

—BAUDELAIRE, "MY HEART LAID BARE"

A kind of dual existence—her "Texas friends" vs. her "New York friends," her Texas roots vs. her Northeast inclinations—was taking shape. This sense of bifurcation would increase over the years, sometimes with her Texas friends wondering if she was spending too much time with an uppity New York crowd—and the New York crowd wondering if Ivins was being ill served by her dishabille pals in Texas. (It was, perhaps, no accident that after her death there were two major memorials for Ivins—one held by her friends in Texas, the other by her friends in New York.) She would be tugged in both directions, sometimes willingly, sometimes not. While she was in New York, Zarko Franks sent her another of his madcap letters from Houston: "One of these days, Rebecca West will be a memory and the name of Molly Ivins will be emblazoned in the hearts of those who love pure writing. . . . Keep in touch. You're one of the rare ones. There are so few, Love Z, Zarko." She was also hearing from Terry

O'Rourke, someone she was still fond of: "I love you because you have a challenging mind and a beautiful body," O'Rourke wrote her.[1]

She graduated from Columbia on June 6, 1967. It was a Tuesday afternoon and after the 3 P.M. commencement exercises, students assembled in the striking World Room at the journalism school—a room dominated by a stained-glass window depicting the Statue of Liberty that had been rescued from the building that housed the late *New York World*. Two months earlier, Columbia had been on edge when Students for a Democratic Society protestors gathered against Marine Corps recruiters—and counter-protestors lined up. It was "jocks" versus "pukes," as they called each other.

At the journalism school, some students and faculty were frozen by indecision and alleged journalistic objectivity; others were too fixated on their careers, their student draft deferments, to do anything other than remain neutral: "The classes of 1967 and 1968 seemed intent on moving ahead with their careers and staying out of activist politics. . . . [T]he graduate classes may have absorbed unconsciously, even too well, the school's newer ideal of the job-oriented neutral—or neutered—journalist."[2]

Ivins had decided that Albert Camus, George Orwell, and I. F. Stone were her literary and journalism heroes. She was also reading the new journalists, the writers who had an edge. Richard Goldstein, who would become one of the better-known rock journalists of his era and an editor of *The Village Voice*, had graduated from Columbia the year before. He'd clearly gotten more quickly to where Molly Ivins the columnist would finally emerge almost fifteen years later. After Columbia, he would write about "the struggle for subjectivity" and how to dance between objectivity and the nagging doubts, fears, and history swirling in his head: how to inject your own voice, your own subjective sets of experiences—and basically run counter to particular rules espoused at Columbia or at the *Houston Chronicle*. The dictum that was usually preached over and over again was to never make the story about you. But Goldstein was immersing himself in as many entry points inside the crackling counterculture as possible—and bending the hell out of conventions that some were dutifully outlining at Columbia. Most mainstream educators and editors wanted journalists to speak truth to power, but they wanted it done in the usual time-honored fashion—dig, report some more, write a linear story devoid of any subjectivity. Goldstein and others were on another path—

covering the news, speaking in their own voice, and weighing the cost of using it in stories about the Real Politick edges of the '60s and '70s. Hunter Thompson hadn't yet risen up like the homunculus born to feast on Richard Nixon and his ilk, but his brand of subjective journalism was coming. Ivins would later chuckle and call her short-form version of it "storytelling," in honor of her Texas mentor John Henry Faulk, the blacklisted humorist who specialized in Southern-style homilies and parables. Whatever it was called, there was a new set of possibilities, something way the hell beyond the hometown woman columnists in Houston that her mother was praying she would be like.

She had prepared a résumé and mailed it to several newspapers from her West 78th Street apartment in Manhattan. Under career plans it read: "Am interested in foreign correspondence. Want job as reporter on a metropolitan daily with the object of getting abroad either at once or as soon as possible. Am particularly interested in North Africa and the Middle East. Can cover politics, features and general assignment in the States." She listed herself as five-foot-ten and 140 pounds, fluent in French and some Spanish, an experienced photographer, unmarried and having had experience on "everything from obituaries to murder trials: did mostly features stories and one series." She wondered how the mostly male newspaper editors would react when they read that she once had a part-time job in a five-and-dime store hawking girdles to women on their lunch hours. "Have also worked as a lingerie saleslady, a telephone operator, a sailing instructor, a lifeguard, a cleaning woman, a camp counselor and a waitress." She listed deposed *Houston Chronicle* editor William Steven and John Hohenberg, her teacher and the assistant dean at Columbia, as references.

She had time to reflect on what Columbia had given her. The place was deadly serious at times, but she had met people she would call enlightened wiseasses—friends who were constantly amazed, to the point of laughter, at how blind some authoritarians and institutions could be:

> I suppose the teacher I was closest to was Mel Mencher, a pint-sized, bearded iconoclastic man who had been one helluva good investigative

> reporter. . . . Then he became a sinner and fell into academia. . . . [H]e concluded that the only useful thing he could do for journalism students was to pull their minds open. He got very graphic about it. He wanted to explode their heads, force them to question all their assumptions about life, people, and the world. Make them THINK, make them realize that what is will not always be. . . . I think Mel Mencher did a good job.[3]

Among some career advisors at Columbia there was a belief that young reporters should head out for what was often simply called the "heartland," join "solid newspapers," and work their way up the ladder. And, perhaps, wind their way back to New York and grander, loftier ambitions.

Minneapolis Tribune assistant managing editor Wallace Allen called Ivins in early June, offered her a job, and they settled on a start date of July 3. She would report at 9 A.M. to the personnel department, undergo an orientation, and be handed her "schedule for the next eight days." She was moving to the Twin Cities in the middle of a lingering, dreary summer rain—and settling into a newspaper whose culture was informed by people who seemed to work at a slightly artier, intellectual level than those at her newspaper in Houston, but who were still, in their way, wedded to regional dictates.

As she settled in Minneapolis, she wrote to both her Texas and New York friends, including O'Rourke and Cox. She talked about the mores of Minneapolis, scrubbed and very white, and how it was almost the anti-Houston and even the anti-New York in terms of diversity. But, she arrived at a time when parts of the city were restive and protests were breaking out—what the newspaper would come to discreetly call "disturbances." There were rumblings on Plymouth Avenue and in other areas, where a loosely affiliated network of community organizers, old-guard Socialist Party members, university students, clergy, and musicians were beginning to bring to Minneapolis some moments that would rattle the staid, white establishment at the paper.

Ivins quickly bonded with some sarcastic, grumbling, anti-authority staffers—while she was assigned to work on stories that didn't seem far removed from the fare she had worked on in Houston. The rodeo at the

Minnesota State Fair ("Backstage, at the rodeo at the Minnesota State Fair, stink. It stinks with the good, strong smells of animal, sweat and leather"). The camp that ten Mennonite teenagers were attending. The local roofing business going great guns ("Are your soffits in sad straits? Having trouble with the old pitch, gravel, over-hang, trim, tar, build up, downspouts, dead level, eaves, emulsions, fiberglass, sill casing, asphalt, siding, shingle or steep?"). The latest United Fund campaign ("United Charity Campaigns to Begin 50th Year in City").

She told friends in Texas and New York, and college buddies Dowd and Seifert, about how the intense cold spells could freeze your spit, how her cats seemed to be having more sex than she was, how she had bought a cranky car that sometimes had to be shoved by hand. She moved into an apartment on Pillsbury Avenue and laughed about the street name. She became good friends with photographer Skip Heine, Harvard-educated reporter Fin Lewis, and arts critic Mike Steele—and joined the regulars at The Little Wagon, the watering hole where the foot-soldier reporters would gather to bullshit and toss back cocktails, hoping that any upper-echelon editors were out of earshot. In the newsroom, she was smoking, guzzling mugs of coffee, taking her shoes off—and people were wondering if she was really working on a story. She was guffawing, the cigarette bobbing on her lips, her head thrown back as she chortled so loud you could hear her across several desks. Meanwhile, she was continually assigned stories that only underscored the disconnect between the paper's inclinations and her interests and personality: "Singer Accentuates the Positive," her story about Ronald Reagan's eldest daughter Maureen, was a typical example. She wrote: "Miss Reagan, a tall slender blonde, is pleasantly enthusiastic about her activities, which are politics and singing. 'I just feel that too many people in this country are negative about America. . . . I love this country, and I want to tell people so.'"[4]

Away from the paper, she told friends that she was seeking a permanent relationship, that there were one or two men she was interested in. Ivins wrote to one friend that she was torn in her affections between Columbia classmate Cox and Terry O'Rourke, the former *Chronicle* intern who was on his way to becoming an assistant Texas attorney general. Cox now happened to be in Minneapolis at the same time as Ivins. He had gone there after they graduated from Columbia to take a job as a university teaching assistant. "She was pretty poor. She lived in a studio apartment. . . . [I]t was in an older part of town, certainly not suburban," says Cox. Their relationship remained platonic; Cox was going to get married to someone else. "We just became real good friends. We spent a lot of evenings drinking cheap jug wine together."[5] Cox and his wife would remain close to Ivins for many years. He would spend a long career at the *Denver Post* as a reporter and editor, and apparently name one of his daughters Molly in partial tribute to Ivins.

At the paper, she toiled under the withering tutelage of Frank Premack, the cantankerous city editor turned news editor, whom she later concluded was "driving half the staff to alcoholism."[6] Premack was a legend-in-the-making, a newsroom denizen out of the old mold, issuing tough feedback, barking out profanities, and marshaling reporters as if he was building a plateau to war. Ivins felt that Premack was yet another male authority figure who had been promoted beyond his true calling, that he should have remained in his position as a political reporter. He was, to her, a classic hard-ass and someone she could howl with laughter about because he seemed so intentionally "on" all the time.

In March 1968, she wrote a letter to O'Rourke and shared her hesitations and reservations about her career. Her *Tribune* portfolio was almost schizophrenic in content. She would work on stories about the Minneapolis Junior Folk Dancers, rodeo clowns, a visit by Julie Nixon and David Eisenhower. And in between, she would write about David Dellinger and local students who once had "Ivy League haircuts" but had now become members of the SDS. She was talking to close friends about the giant stabs of history: LBJ was teetering and in France, which she watched with a passion, Daniel Cohn-Bendit was leading a stunning student-led revolt. Writers she followed with enormous interest, including Jack Newfield at *The Village Voice*, were seemingly in the middle of the bigger issues and stories. She was frustrated. The stated plan on her résumé—to be a foreign correspondent—was simply not happening. She was doing stories about ice storms, leaky roofs, septic tanks, a canary singing contest, Casey the gorilla at the local zoo, contract bridge tournaments, and the State Fair. She had started at $140 a week and after two years was making $183 a week. She told friends she was more than mired, that the experience was deadening, soul-eroding, and that she was succumbing to imaginary illnesses and the occasional eccentricity.

She was thinking about leaving Minnesota. "I've come down with my annual hypochondriac's case of cancer, which adds poignancy to incipient Spring. I am also getting non-sequitory—a sure sign I ought to quit." In a letter to O'Rourke she said: "Let's write about ideas, what you think. It's hard to find people to talk to about ideas and barring a few beautiful people on the *Trib*, I am hungry for conversation."

On March 28, 1969, she wrote another letter to him, espousing some of the ideas she wanted to explore:

> Well, about life, which is a catchy way to start a graf, I think you've got the wrong verb. It's not do. It's be. Which is a revelation which came to me one night on a beach in Galveston (I dare say not many people get revelations in Galveston). I was out there squatting in the water about sunset, see, watching the water run over a sand dollar, see, there was only that moment and only me. Or as Hayakawa said, "open your eyes and take in what is there"—only that—embrace it—insight comes first from experience and from the reflection upon experience and only secondarily from literature, poetry, drama and the arts, which are more meaningful against a background of psychology, cultural anthropology, sociology and general semantics. . . . It's just there and you live it and you're not called upon to decide anything about it. Except that whole thing leaves me uneasy because it's faintly akin to the whole Eastern mystic bag, which I do not dig because my whole training is Western rational and you can't beat good early training, as Amy Vanderbilt will tell you.[7]

⊰⊱

As the paper tried to make sense of student unrest and the complaints from the black community and women, Ivins simply volunteered to take on the stories. And she dutifully proposed that the paper devote a variety of series to help capture the times: "Young Radicals," "Alienated Students," and "Young Conservatives." She also became the default reporter for news that touched on labor issues, tenants' rights issues, and community organizing.

When Yippie leader Jerry Rubin came to town, she was sent to cover the event. And through her affinity for underground political movements, she met the next key figure in her private life following Hank Holland. Any lasting relationship she might have hoped for with Cox or O'Rourke was not going to happen. She wrote to a friend: "The love of my life these days is a hairy rad[ical] named Jack Cann, who dropped out of Stanford before getting his PhD and has been earning about $300 a year since then. I fear the thing is doomed. Here I am, quintessential bourgeoisie—even if I reformed, who ever heard of a fat radical? Trauma, trauma. I'll live."[8]

John "Jack" Cann attended Carleton College before doing three years of graduate work at Stanford and becoming a key figure in the small activist community in the Twin Cities. He helped to found the Minneapolis Tenants Union, and Ivins wrote articles touching on the group's work—including a piece about a rock musician who was evicted from his apartment, but not before Cann's Tenants Union tried to intercede. They met at the University of Minnesota when he was giving a talk, chatted briefly, and then Ivins saw him again at a potluck dinner for anti-war activists in December 1968. She told him she was thinking of doing a series on young activists, she interviewed him, and they went out drinking.

She was sometimes dressed in a long red maxi-coat and walking with a sort of regal bearing—like she was sizing things up. He thought she was interesting, loud, funny. A few days later she called and asked if he wanted to do something after work. By January 1969, they were dating regularly. They moved in together and friends wondered where the hell it was all going, what her parents would say if they knew. She worried that her upbringing would predispose him to objectify her and her family. Perhaps as a salve, she told him personal stories about her family—how Andy and her father got into a fistfight by the swimming pool, one of those family moments that was actually more high comedy than high rage.

They fell into a pattern. She would go to work at noon, work until midnight, and then they'd go hang out with other newspaper people, friends. Several months after they began dating, Cann was set to go on trial after being arrested, along with a local black activist, for taking part in a fracas that had erupted between police and protestors at a George Wallace rally. Ivins was moving beyond her work at the paper, and had begun going door to door with Cann, helping him solicit people as part of his work with the Tenants Union. "She wasn't just an observer but also a fairly active participant," he said.

During a break in his trial, Ivins came up to him and told him that she had heard a policeman saying "we're finally going to nail that nigger." Cann quickly asked her to testify, she agreed, and her story made a deep impression in the courtroom. Cann was acquitted, but a week later she received five parking tickets and the week after that the Minneapolis Tactical Squad adopted a small, black, female pig as a mascot. In an undated article a detective said the pig was named Molly and that "it's named after one of the famous pig haters . . . a person they [the squad] have no respect for, which I think is appropriate."[9] At least one officer said there was no truth to the rumor that it had been named after a local reporter.[10]

By the summer of 1969, Cann and Ivins were arguing. She began writing to friends—and in diaries—about the relationship. By July, he had moved out. She'd dutifully troop to the dull-looking *Tribune* building on Plymouth Avenue, walk the linoleum floors to her desk, and fire up a cigarette. When people thought she was working on a story, she was sometimes filling up her "official" No. 800 reporter's notebook with thoughts about her life, career, self-image, and former lover. She wrote some words in French ("creuser"—which can mean to hollow out, to dig a hole) and code words she shared with Hank Holland (like "PTR"—which apparently stands for "Play The Role," perhaps a reference to the "role" some women were expected to play in a male-dominated society). And she wrote words ("not") that she then crossed out:

> Oh fuck. I don't want to write on this—I wanted to give him warm gloves for Christmas. . . . [A]t the back of my mind is the hope that somehow this "harrowing" experience will creuser my soul and either make me capable of writing great books or make me a better person. I also have a reoccurrence of hope that someone will see or know of my tears, I feel so sorry for me—pity me. . . . Jack returning, asking what are those wet spots. . . . I was crying . . . but mostly I am as real tonight as I'll ever get. . . .

I threaten him & now more than ever, Jack doesn't need that kind of reproach. His defenses are higher because he is more vulnerable. All he can take now is love and support. Though he can't take either in an owning sense, which again leaves me no latitude to define myself as a real person to him. PTR as Hank would say. Yet perhaps Jack knows me in a more real sense for never having listened to my intellect—my definitions, perpetually false, and self-flattering of myself. . . .

I think I told him the truth the night he left—I love him & made a bad choice—one of the most difficult human relationships I have ever known in any sense. . . . Even if I were to smash through sometimes and say, look Jack, here I am—real live, thinking, feeling a hell of a lot more than you know—we wordlessly fall into the same habits I forebode (good). Ah, thus women's lib—the hope, so faint, that the real reason I play the role is not because he demanded it or even that I am incapable of more, but that somehow it's THEM, out there, the system, even the establishment (GHM) which prevents breakthrough communication (& which has really unforgivably made those words into clichés) which demand that perhaps we, certainly I, play roles. . . . I half want to say he must recognize my profession, this is what I do, I want to be proud of it, because of him I will never have the, for me, earnest fervor of your basic J school grad—but I think part of it at least is personal on his part. Not only that he finds the *Trib* plain shitty, or even maleficent (should be an uglier word) but he puts it down in part to put me down. . . .

So we're trapped for at least [these] two very strong reasons. He doesn't want to get involved . . . and he's hung up in shit . . . doesn't want to let me compete with him, much less win on any terms (even the Establishment's). . . . I dare not tell him any of this for fear (or is certain knowledge) that A. his petty male ego can't take it and he will go away for good (more on this later) or B., I'll fuck up the telling of it, soften it, prettify it, play the role, wind up back in the shit hole role I was trying to get out of (aside: the night he left, I tried B. and it proved true, yes, I inadvertently spoke Truth—a rare thing for me). . . .

God knows I have occasionally engaged—since he left—the feeling of being FREE. I don't like going through this shit. I don't like the strained silences, I don't like him crapping all over me and everything

I have. . . . Jesus I would give an arm and a leg, a million dollars, anything I might ever have if somehow I could make Jack laugh more . . . if I could make him enjoy being alive more. . . . I want to make him more giving, more accommodating, more compromising (yes, a noble word—since JFK), well, I want to serve! Pin a rose on me—I want to serve Jack—hand me a prize and some grits.

But another morsel of female wisdom comes to mind. IF you can't love a person as he is without wanting to change him, forget it—well in fact, I do love Jack as he is and it makes me horribly unhappy and that's why I want to change him—he doesn't love me as I am, if at all. Occasionally (very occasionally) Jack's wisdom astounds me. He doesn't know fuck—me in particular, or people in general, or about how to get along with anyone. Maybe because getting along is not one of his values. He was right to leave . . . he was right one night, early, when he yelled about me not being radical, a dumbshit, etc. I then said, when I didn't understand why he yelled, that it was something we would go over and over because it mattered so much to him.

Two points—One: he tried to change me. I am flattered, I am not being sarcastic, that he cared to try. Two: . . . all the children in my wildly aggressively wired, strange Texas Irish lousy tempered family have turned out to be pacifists . . . we are personal pacifists, we grew up with fighting between parents, who are still fighting, and now none of us can stand the sound of fighting.

Jack, having you, or anyone I care about, yell at me makes me sick. I mean that it makes me feel physically ill. Queasy, like I might vomit. I can't stand it. That's why I never fought with you by yelling back. I think sometimes you might have thought I was scoring points by keeping my cool, remaining rational, whatever, it's not true. I prefer any kind of sham truce to a fight. That's why I don't yell. Not wise? Yes, but that's the way I am. I suppose any psychiatrist would say it's better to bring it out into the open but I can't fight it out.

One other thing my loving family left me with which bears on this—my mother used to tell me, bitterly, viciously, "You are an ugly girl, Mary, you are a very ugly little girl." I believed her and still do. In a sense I consider myself unlovable. I do have a self-image that has value only on an intellectual, professional plane. I would say of myself: I did well in school. Everyone said I was bright. I won a few honors. I am a competent journalist.

I think I almost expected Jack not to love me. I am ~~not~~ ugly fat & dull. But he attacked on another flank. By refusing to accept or even entertain my ideas, he attacked me on those grounds on which I have built whatever self-confidence I have (so give the game to him, he hit where it hurt). And what a shaky confidence it is—I would call myself pathetic. I am certainly one of the most pitiful cases of perpetually seeking after praise to bolster my self-confidence—mostly the game I know. But I don't like myself well enough to work up much pity, so pathetic is the wrong word. I think I am probably right in thinking that one of the few things that binds Jack to me now is pity. Poor Moll, he thinks, got to go back and see her, so she won't slit her throat. (I won't. . . . Never!)

But I loathe the thought of binding him to me like that. Pride, baby, pride forbids it—so I reveal myself as an emotional basket case and give the poor guy horrendous guilt complexes about running out on me. . . . The son of a bitch is out of work, he is down, at odds with his would-be comrades in arms. I wish I were right so I could give him an allowance anonymously. Talk about pride, he's got it. He probably won't even come to dinner anymore 'cause he's hungry.

I would like to take care of him, not that I'm competent to take care of anyone. Someday, when he's not down, I would like to tell him three other things: One is that one of the reasons we broke up is because I have shitty working hours, maybe not all that important but he spent too many nights here alone waiting for me. Another thing is that the real reason I wouldn't change and become radical is a combination of sexual antagonism and personal identity. If left to myself, I might easily become the kind of rad Jack admires (Tautology: one of the reasons I admire Jack is because he is that kind of rad) but he kept telling me what to do and how to be.

I fought my domineering father too long to give in to another man. Plus, good healthy sex antagonism—one has to do something to retain one's self identity in the face of a personality to whom one wants to give, submerge one's self.

And the last thought is that I love Jack: I don't know what it would take to make it work out right, but, Oh God, it's a shame we can't do it. Jack, remember the day we drove up to Fargo—I think it took six or eight hours but it seemed like 15 minutes.

⊰⊱

In Minneapolis, as her relationship with Cann took its twists and turns, Ivins turned to even more work that consistently ran counter to the usual news items in the *Minneapolis Tribune*. She covered the Socialist Labor Party of Minneapolis convention as well as state proposals to punish student demonstrators. (When the latter story appeared, it was cut out of the paper and marked up by an editor, who dryly pointed out some errors in style.) Her "Young Radicals" series included an editor's note:

> Who are these young radicals? What are they like as persons? Why do they talk, dress and act as they do? What do they hope to accomplish?
>
> Some persons view this small group of young people as publicity seekers, irresponsible troublemakers; others see them as profoundly moral, imbued with ideals and gifted with the vision to create a better society.
>
> Whatever emotions they may inspire, the young radicals are with us and they are making themselves heard. They are playing a part in the shaping of our world.
>
> To answer some questions about young radicals, *Minneapolis Tribune* staff writer Molly Ivins has talked with five from Minneapolis, probed into their backgrounds and explored their motives.[11]

The series was promoted in the paper, along with Ivins's photograph. She did other work, too: a review of an Aretha Franklin concert, a piece about the first anniversary of the American Indian Movement, a story about the "West Bank Peace Force" complaining about police harassment during a protest. ("About 20 young people in unconventional clothing gathered in the rain Saturday afternoon at the 3rd Ave. entrance to the Courthouse and sang sadly to policemen who hurried in and out.")

She began to get letters—personal ones and letters to the editor—complaining about her work and, in one case, threatening her. One writer, upset over her calling David Dellinger a pacifist, said, "I wish I could conceal my contempt for the things you always seem to write about, but I can't." Another letter came on stationery from the Curtis Hotel and Motor Lodge in Minneapolis: "How can you condone the doings of Maria, a colored savage filthy, uneducated crummy Nigger. She and four other Nigger savages beat up a white girl after first robbing her. You call letting this Nigger go free, justice. All Niggers belong in detention camps, like the Japs and Germans of World War II. Only they are a far bigger Menace. Hope you choke, when reading this letter bitch. . . . We will get you bitch."

In November 1969, she received a letter from Carlton Carl, the man she knew as an intern at the *Houston Chronicle*: "It looks as though the paper values your skills more than it despairs of your radical activities. . . . [A]lthough I generally catch an undertone of bitchiness towards the *Trib*, Establishment, World, in your letters, I still envy the hell out of your being able to do what you want and raise hell, and organize."[12]

⁂

Meanwhile, her parents still seemed to be holding out some hope that she would move into some version of their lives. They were mailing her from various places they had sailed to, filling her in, in breezy tones, about the various well-placed Houston friends they had encountered—and how successful the young people she had grown up with appeared to be. Her mother seemed to acknowledge that there was some distance between her and her parents: In one letter, her mother wrote "Love to you, Maggot Mother" at the bottom. Ivins's relationship with her father, in particular, took on a more pointed tone as the sociopolitical urgencies of the '60s reached new flashpoints. In his letters, he tried to debate and sometimes bait her. He chided her for her politics, and he urged her to take more responsibility for her finances and her health. Money, especially, still seemed to be a very testy, lingering matter. She needed some to travel to Texas, to New York, to see friends around the country. She needed some for a car. Her letters show that, on occasion, she had to negotiate her bills with her father even as he remained entrenched in the upper echelons at Tenneco.

She spent more time at The Little Wagon, still drinking, still lighting up Marlboros. The shared distrust of the editorial power structure at the paper could still be felt there. Some of her colleagues suggested they coalesce into "The Group," which might meet more or less semi-officially to air grievances about the weak-willed direction of the paper. The mutineers began having meetings on Sunday mornings at 11 A.M. at the home of a newspaper photographer.

She wrote a letter to Terry O'Rourke and kept a copy in her files and archives:

> Life here is slightly more schizo as I move into the radical bag. I fear my solid middle class foundations are crumbling rapidly. Can't remember if I told you this, but as part of my efforts to create a new life style (I think what I am trying to do is see if it's possible to hold a straight job and do well by it while simultaneously working to get rid of the System which employs me), I'm moving. Leaving my relatively posh middle class pad with its early-hotel appointments going into kind of a neat dump in an Indian slum which has a million bookcases. Not that the move itself will prove or change anything: it's just a symbol to me.

Her work was being recognized: She won awards in the Twin Cities Newspaper Guild competition for her "Young Radicals" series and for a news feature she did on another confrontation on Plymouth Avenue. She won an award for a story about a soldier killed in Vietnam. She won the sweepstakes award in the first annual Minnesota Associated Press newswriting contest. She kept every notice of every award and put them in folders—along with any positive memos or letters to the editor she received—and saved them for the rest of her life.

In September 1969, she and a handful of staffers sent a note to publisher John Cowles, Jr., and high-ranking editors, accusing the newspaper of sexual discrimination. A staffer, they claimed, had been denied maternity leave. "We protest this refusal. It is unjust and discriminatory. . . . We do not feel that any woman should have to justify having a child. . . . It is our understanding that the company wishes to enforce a blanket policy against maternity leaves for any woman employee. We are opposed to that policy and will work through our unions to make a maternity leave an automatic right."[13]

While researching her "Young Conservatives" series—meant to counterbalance her "Young Radicals" series—Ivins arranged a visit to a furtive meeting of Nazi sympathizers. "I had finagled for weeks and swore myself to eternal secrecy, etc., in order to get into a meeting. Finally arranged it and was late, of course. I dashed across town, flew up three flights of stairs to the attic of an old house in St. Paul, plopped down in front of seven Nazis and gasped, 'Oi vey!'"[14]

Privately, she joked with friends about Senator Ted Kennedy's career nadir—driving off a bridge with a woman who drowned. They invented a mock Kennedy press conference where he was asked whether he would resign, and Kennedy replied, "I'll just have to drive off that bridge when I come to it." And she wrote what she called a "double dactyl for the occasion":

Groggily, soggily
Edward M. Kennedy
Drunk drove his blonde to a watery grave
Master of wenchery
Plenipotentiary
What an impolitic way to behave.[15]

In case there was any doubt about her intentions, or her impatience with the *Tribune*'s perceived limitations, she spelled it all out to colleagues: She began referring to the newspaper as "*The Daily Chuckle.*" She advised some friends that she had published her work in *The Militant*, the voice of the Socialist Workers Party—but also that she was doing freelance work for *Life* magazine, researching stories that never got printed. And she began telling friends that she was thinking of joining the Peace Corps or even traveling to Russia—maybe becoming more closely aligned with issues she could not fully address in her stories. And, meanwhile, her family seemed increasingly unaware of how she had changed. The last week of April 1970, there was a letter from her father: "Dear Mole: Trust you did your bit for Earth Day. I mowed the lawn."[16] (Close to the same time, her sister Sara sent a note that concluded, "Love to you and practice talking less profane. . . ."[17])

The day her father's letter arrived, editors agreed to let her cover Yippie leader Jerry Rubin's visit to Minneapolis. She wrote: "More than 3500 people roared to their feet and cheered last night after Jerry Rubin screamed, 'We're gonna make Honeywell stop makin' bombs and go back to makin' honey!'" She described it as "the big yippie-rad-pacifist pep rally" at Macalester College. At the rally, a twenty-two-year-old Yale student named Charles Pillsbury, an heir to his family's Minneapolis flour empire, talked about being anti-corporate even while carrying one of the most recognizable brand names in America. Ivins, only three years older and with a father at Tenneco, made sure to dutifully quote him in her story. She, of course, lived on a street named Pillsbury.

Two weeks later, there was a bloody confrontation between police and activists occupying buildings scheduled for demolition to make way for a branch of the Red Barn hamburger chain. It was just three days after antiwar protesters were gunned down by National Guardsmen at Kent State. Her story about the charged atmosphere—protestors talking about domestic imperialism, cops using billy clubs—would be one of her last at the *Tribune*.

The weather was changing, winter was finally fading. She had recently attended the memorial service for veteran socialist leader V. R. Dunne, where Farrell Dobbs, the national secretary of the Socialist Workers Party, had spoken. She was writing more pissed-off memos to colleagues at the paper ("thanks for another piece of shit on your editorial page"). Nothing, really, as far as she was concerned, was going to change at the *Tribune*. She was also convinced that her relationship with Jack Cann was irreparable. She was writing to her friends and talking about the difficulties and worries of living with men, and also about not being politically radical enough. Her soul-searching extended to the core notions of what journalism was all about; she increasingly mulled the worth of objectivity. Living with an activist, being confronted by his accusations, had clearly affected her thinking not just about personal relationships but also about her image as a journalist trained to be neutral and objective in the extreme. She knew she wanted to leave Minnesota, and she knew that some people still viewed her through the prism of her upbringing. She had been offered a pointed analysis of her life:

> [Y]ou have some of the biggest, fattest establishment labels going—some little WASP prep school, some lawyer father, some Smith College, some junior year abroad, some Columbia Journalism School master's degree, some Minneapolis paper. You have tried . . . to convince people that you were not a part of those worlds, that you were different, the ghetto kid who was hanging around those honkies just for a big yuk-yuk and also to hone your fine mind on all the books in the library, but you were never one of them, no no.[18]

She decided to write one more internal Fuck You memo, this one asking editors what constituted a "conflict of interest" at the paper—asking if it was a conflict to have "a Boycott Grapes sticker on a car, a McCarthy for President sticker on a car, a Peace & Freedom Party sticker? Is it a conflict of interest to work for a political candidate in any way? What about writing freelance articles for politically oriented publications? Say 'New Republic?'"[19] The issue was personal, of course. She was telling friends she had been in love with Jack Cann, perhaps the city's most consistent activist—and she was covering the protests and issues he knew better than most people in the city. She had been at his trial, helping his legal defense. She had canvassed the neighborhoods with him.

⤛⤜

That spring in Texas, Terry O'Rourke ran into Ronnie Dugger, longtime founder-editor-publisher of *The Texas Observer*. Dugger told O'Rourke that he was fielding applications for editors. O'Rourke mentioned Ivins. She had continued to read the *Observer* and she told friends that the publication consistently painted a portrait of a heinous state.[20] She was a long-distance admirer of Dugger, who fought for years to keep the publication afloat, and she had once told Jack Cann that Dugger was one of her heroes. She quickly applied and sent a résumé and some clips to Texas (including a story she had done about once attending the same summer camp as LBJ's daughter). Her application included some of the stories she had done at the *Tribune* on the student upheavals in Minneapolis. Dugger thought they were very well reported and had a "boldness and fairness" but "no showing at all of a sense of humor in them."

He and the *Observer* staff, always in dire financial shape, decided to bring her to Austin for an interview. She arrived at Dugger's house with a six-pack of beer. Dugger, associate editor Kaye Northcott, and business manager Cliff Olofson were impressed. She was funny and she seemed really alive, chortling about Texas, about growing up in Houston.[21] Northcott thought that she was damned tall. Northcott had roots in the Midwest but was raised in Houston, so she knew about the River Oaks neighborhood and about private schools like St. John's. She was impressed that Ivins didn't seem to carry any airs, but she also sensed that Ivins wasn't overly broadcasting her pedigree. "I knew her family lived in River Oaks," says Northcott. "She'd rather that people didn't know that."[22]

Dugger eventually narrowed his choice down to five or six candidates, with Ivins and Billy Porterfield (her old colleague at the *Houston Chronicle*) as the finalists. Dugger liked Porterfield's literary inclinations but wondered if Porterfield was averse to politics in some way. Dugger began to look more closely at Ivins and eventually offered Northcott and Ivins positions as co-editors. They decided to pay themselves the same amount of money that state legislators got—about $8,000 a year.

Ivins made a collect call from Texas and told Wallace Allen, her editor in Minnesota, that she was resigning. When she got back to Minnesota, a friend handed her a hand-drawn award: The "Chutzpah Of The Month Award—presented, with deepest feelings of admiration to Mary T. Ivins for calling Wally collect to resign."[23]

She composed a formal resignation letter in Minnesota on June 25, 1970:

> Dear Wally: It is with deep regret that I submit my resignation from *The Minneapolis Tribune*, effective July 25. I am leaving to take the position of managing editor of *The Texas Observer*. I would like to take this chance to thank you and all the other *Tribune* staff members from whom I have learned so much during the past three years.[24]

⊰⊱

After she resigned, she began writing what can only be described as The Mother of All Fuck Off Stories—a piece that would appear in the local alternative paper in Minneapolis. It was a raised middle finger of colossal proportions, directed at the man who had hired her and to whom she had sent the polite letter of resignation. Some of her friends revered the piece but said that she had recklessly quoted *Tribune* staffers and put them in danger of getting fired. The story ran across eight pages in the August 1970 issue of the *Twin Citian*, and it both shredded her editors and neatly outlined her philosophy that objectivity was virtually useless. The defining piece, one of the best tools for understanding her entire career, was written against the backdrop of several personal matters: being best friends with men trying desperately to avoid the draft, living with a man who was one of the city's most intense activists, thinking about leaving the country as part of the Peace Corps, thinking of traveling to Russia, writing for *The Militant*, chiding friends who were working for conservative politicians, telling people she was insecure about her physical appearance and her sexuality. It was the culmination, perhaps, of other things, too: Hank Holland's death, her father's vice grip and buried racism, her mother's socialite naggings.

"I worked for the *Minneapolis Tribune* for three years. No, the paper is not hell—just a stone wall drag. . . . *The Trib* doesn't permit its reporters time, money, freedom or space and so we continue to crank out schlock. The horror stories are endless—every reporter has dozens."

As for objectivity: "I don't believe in the stuff myself—I've seen the truth murdered too many times in the name of objectivity—but I'm open to the argument that what we really need is a better definition of objectivity."

And: "to look around the newsroom is to see living tragedy in terms of wasted talent" and "the Channels of Communication are silted up with the corpses of stories that never got covered and ideas that were never pursued. Some reporters quit and others quit trying." Some reporters "point to letters attacking us as communists and letters attacking us as Birchers and claim they must be doing something right. On any given controversy, they print what A said and then what B said and think they've produced an adequate piece of journalism."[25]

Tribune staffers would talk about the article for months. Editors issued an internal response. In *Tribune* Staff Memo No. 77, Wally Allen laid out his feelings: "If objectivity means dull writing, failure to show what an event really means, destruction of color and humanity, then I'm against it. If it means a retreat into the past, a new emphasis on trivia, timidity in reporting on social issues, I'm against it." The objective story, he went on,

> tells what happened by giving the reader the facts, accurately, fully, fairly, dispassionately, to the best of our ability as, let's admit, prejudiced, fallible human beings. It tells what happened in terms of facts, and facts are beautiful. They are not dull and bland. They do not lack color. They do not bore the reader. They do not lie. They need to be piled up, one on another, until the reader understands and sees and hears and smells what is being written about. My objection is to the reporter's assuming the role of the advocate, playing with the facts, insinuating his feelings into the story, using loaded words, pointing his story toward proving what he himself sees as the truth. My objection is to the reporter's assumption that he alone sees the truth, that because he is "involved" he knows. Spot news isn't enough, of course. It's merely the beginning, because the facts aren't always what they seem. We have to go far beneath the superficial daily event to find out why it happened and what it means. . . . We can do this digging objectively—through background pieces, through analysis and, yes, even through first-person stories. . . . Personal opinion can't do the job. For those who want it, there is the editorial page. But don't let it into the news columns.[26]

It would be twelve years before Ivins would do exactly what her managing editor advocated—get her own column on the editorial page. First she'd go to Texas and sharpen her sense of how power works in one of the most inscrutable places on Earth. It would be a sweet place to move to, in 1970, and to do two things at the same time—practice advocacy journalism and develop a voice. "Reporters, along with being chronic bitchers, are great prima donnas. In fairness to editors, it should be noted that reporters are impossible. They need a lot of encouragement; but all they were getting was a lot of shit," she said about her last days working at the *Tribune*.[27]

She was listening to music, to the people who had miraculously emerged from Texas informed by the blues that gurgled up from South Dallas, the Fourth Ward in Houston, the East Side of San Antonio, and those haunted woods in deep East Texas. Janis Joplin from Port Arthur was channeling it. So was Johnny Winter, the albino bluesman from Beaumont. Every time they sang, it was the second-generation spirit of T-Bone Walker, Mance Lipscomb, and Lightnin' Hopkins floating out from the pine trees, the dismal swamps along the coast, the bittersweet side streets that skirted the downtown skyscrapers. Ivins liked Winter. He knew about how Big Money and the oily underbelly of the Lone Star State were constantly rubbing against each other in an overheated, pregnant way. He had Texas pretty well-pegged, and she'd later quote his lines in her work: "Going back to Dallas, take my razor and my gun . . . there's so much shit in Texas, I'm bound to step in some."

She moved to Texas in late July, driving down from Minneapolis in her Mercury, with two cats and a rubber plant. A few weeks after she had moved to Austin, she received a letter from a friend with the World Press Institute, who said that he had taken careful notes from a talk Wally Allen had given at a luncheon:

> I took copious notes of some of the comments made about you by Wally Allen. . . . "She came to us and we took her on and trained her; taught her as much as we could. She's a bright girl and a fairly good writer. We could have brought her along and made a good reporter out of her, I think, but now she's lost in this advocacy press.
>
> "She had pipelines to the underground, so we decided to take advantage of this and do a series of profiles on some of their leaders. Well, the things she wrote could never have been printed in raw form. She was on their side—this was advocacy journalism—and we had to rewrite it and edit the hell out of it. We used the series as a training piece for her and I think she did learn something from it. What our readers couldn't know was that that piece could never have gone in as she wrote it.

> "She told me that this job at the *Texas Observer* was the only one she'd consider taking. If it hadn't been for that, she'd have stayed on here, so I don't really think she was fair in criticizing us as she did."[28]

He wasn't the only unhappy one.

When her mother read the anti-*Tribune* piece, she dashed off a note to her daughter: "I too was devastated to read your hatchet job on the *Trib*—you're like me, always sound stranger than you intend."[29]

⤛⤜

The division of duties at *The Texas Observer* quickly took shape and Northcott and Ivins—both in their twenties, both on the same political wavelength—easily accepted their titles. Some people in Austin said quietly that Dugger had settled on the co-editor format because he was worried whether one woman could do the job. Northcott was a good reporter and writer; Ivins was a funnier writer and could clearly drink with many different people, which might not have been Northcott's strong suit—especially in the hallways of the pink-granite capitol, with its miles of wood and swinging-dick legislators yodeling about all the women they had picked up the night before in Austin.

Her first piece in the *Observer* appeared at almost the same time as her cluster-fuck attack on the *Tribune* in the *Twin Citian*. In a direct nod to *North Toward Home,* Willie Morris's epistle on his process of self-discovery and riding the lines connecting the South and the North, she decided to call her piece "South Toward Home":

> "Going back to Texas? Ivins, you're out of your goddamn mind." And they told me again all the things that make Minnesota a better place to live. The schools are better, the health care is better, the mental institutions more humane, the prisons more enlightened, and the courts more just. And also, Minnesota has bars.
>
> And Minnesota's newspapers are superior and its politicians are progressive and its climate no lousier and its laws more sane. And its racism is thin-blooded and polite. I can't help it. I love the state of Texas. It's a harmless perversion.

She gleefully talked about visiting her brother at UT-Austin two years earlier, getting drunk at his fraternity, and having to endure a fraternity brother groping her breast. She condemned the culture of violence in the state and the crazed juxtaposition with the surface politeness, and suggested that things were just more interesting in Texas because the evil deeds and people were easily on parade. "Down here the baddies wear black hats and we can loathe them with a cheerful conscience. . . . Hatred is hardly a thing to take pride in, but I believe there is a difference between the anger of bitterness and despair and the anger of righteousness. The latter, when not wholly lacking in humor, is a just and cleansing thing."[30]

And she said that the liberal wing of things was prone to infighting, afflicted by group depression, bad drinking, and the sanctimonious game of I'm-more-radical-than-thou. With her forum—and her willingness to write about Texas politicians in a funnier, more caustic and unfiltered way than anyone else had ever done—she would actually become a grounding focal point for the liberal movement in the city and the state.

In August 1970, a few days after her introductory essay, there was a letter waiting for her from Willie Morris, sent from the Park Avenue offices of *Harper's Magazine*:

> Dear Molly: Your piece on coming back to Texas is delightful. And I agree with it, Yours Sincerely, Willie.[31]

She had taken a different tack, obviously, in her exploration of being back in Texas. Her approach was frontloaded with wisecracks, self-effacing humor, and it was not nearly as elaborately poignant or as much of a literary meditation on race and society as Morris's had been. For years, Ivins would share with her friends the notion that she, too, wanted to do a lengthier treatment on "East Texas"—on race and society in the South. Something akin to what Morris had done, what Walker Percy had done, maybe even John Howard Griffin, the Texan who had written the startling *Black Like Me*. (Years later, her former editor at Random House, the publishing house that put together collections of her columns and essays, would refer to her as a "sprinter" as opposed to a long-distance runner.)

⟡

In 1970, the twisted political deals at the Texas State House were endless and impossible to fathom. There were byzantine dealings among the independent populists, Southern Democrats, new-breed Republicans. Deciphering it took endless daily immersion, flattery, and reportorial seduction. It took a lot of hanging around, trying to stay awake and trying to unravel the obtuse language, the planned obfuscation that masked billion-dollar political maneuverings, appropriations, and policy decisions. It took a lot of lingering in the hallways—and sometimes, more importantly, it entailed hanging out late at night at the bars and private clubs where the most intense political players drank and drank some more. The legislature was to convene in January 1971, but Ivins had a lot of learning to do before then.

Early on, it was clear that that lush-life turf was going to be covered by Ivins, not the teetotaler, nonsmoking Northcott. Ivins was the one who had the carton of Marlboros and the ability to drink almost anyone under the table. She would be Ms. Outside and Northcott would be Ms. Inside—in the sense that Ivins would spend her days and nights trolling for news, slipping into the women's restroom at the capitol to add something to her notebook, whereas Northcott would hold down the fort at the *Observer* offices, do her stories in a less-overtly-social way, and make sure the publication actually got to the printers on time. Ivins, meanwhile, had plenty of smokes and she would bend her six-foot frame a little so people felt like they were really in her orbit. People laughed at the Mutt and Jeff routine. Northcott was a hummingbird and Ivins was a whooping crane. She hovered over Northcott, her voice gushing and swirling and laughing. They clicked and worked very well as a team.

There were no fact-checkers; they had to rely on each other, and in the end they also had to weigh ways to keep the publication vital and alive. The *Observer* existed by virtue of the goodwill of its supporters and the lone ad that the deep-pocketed, liberal, Jewish insurance executive Bernard Rapoport took out every issue. (Rapoport would become a favored figure for a long line of liberal, Democratic politicians—including Bill and Hillary Clinton—as they sought his financial backing over the years.) For years people wondered what was more amazing about him—that he was

Jewish and living in the heavily Baptist town of Waco, or that he was considered to be a semi-socialist in one of the most reactionary warrens in Texas, a city where people still kept KKK robes in the closet and where time hadn't exactly washed away the fact that in 1916, a black man named Jesse Washington fell victim to one of the most brutal lynchings in American history.

Ivins's exposure to these deeply entrenched bits of complicated Texas history, things she hadn't learned in Houston, intensified in Austin. LBJ was occasionally in the city, visiting from his nearby ranch, and his presence served as a reminder of the national influence Texas had exerted—and even how Texas and Texans were sometimes objectified by the rest of the nation. It was as if she was relearning the history of the state she had grown up in, the one that her father had brought the family to. Her relationship with her father was still complicated; still, of course, defined by money. (He would finally loan her $300 for a Toyota, but complain about her buying a foreign car and then constantly demand, on his President of Tenneco stationery, that she pay him back immediately.)

She was almost always broke. Friends in Minneapolis had known that she was chronically short of money. Some wondered if it had permanently embittered her toward her father, and why he wouldn't regularly help her out. And, as she was re-immersing herself in Texas, her father told her he had decided to move from Houston to Maryland. He wanted to be closer to the Tenneco Incorporated offices and to sail in something other than the oil-polluted waters at the Houston Yacht Club. Leaving Houston was going to be hard on her mother, but her father was very eager to go. For him, there might have been other urgencies: There were rumblings in the Third Ward, at all-black Texas Southern University, and racial confrontations were welling up in the city. Now, her father was going to be sailing on Chesapeake Bay. The house on Chevy Chase Drive in River Oaks was sold.

Austin in 1970 was a mellow oasis for stoners and groovers seeking easier temptations than the ones in Dallas, Houston, and San Antonio. Doug Sahm was the city's legendary musical master and the fast-talking genius-heir to the cross-cultural genre-bending work that Bob Wills had started in Texas—and Sahm had always used Austin as his headquarters until hippie chic washed over the town and he fled back to his native San Antonio, lamenting the presence of too many yuppies and not enough good enchiladas. He symbolized the eclectic possibilities of the state and of mixed blues, jazz, rock, and German and Mexican polkas, and he wrote the Austin anthem, which was perfectly, aptly, called "Groover's Paradise." You could score Thai sticks or Oaxacan pot outside the famous concert venue called the Armadillo World Headquarters, you could see beatific Freddie King for the price of a beer, you could swim topless at Barton Springs or naked at Hippie Hollow and the cops eventually looked the other way. There were collectives, a few communes, the evolution toward a couple of cults—and a steady stream of musicians, like the Vaughan brothers and Willie Nelson, coming south on Interstate 35 or west on Interstate 10. The University of Texas at Austin and the State Capitol dominated the city, but that unhinged legislature met for only a few months every other year. When it did, it was as if Rush Limbaugh was sneaking into Lollapalooza and scoring the first trick bag of oxycontin—at every legislative session it was almost guaranteed that some state senator or representative would be caught with his pants down at a rent-by-the-hour South Congress motel. Or get thrown in the drunk tank. Or wake up at the side of the road, literally asleep at the wheel. Billy Lee Brammer, the mercurial, drug-bedeviled Austin writer and former *Observer* associate editor, chronicled some of it in his masterful book *The Gay Place*—which some said had nailed down Austin, LBJ, and the Texas Big Top political circus.

It was a place, in the 1970s, where the university, growing into the largest one in the nation, existed as its own fiefdom, still moving beyond whatever hellish objectification it endured after Charles Whitman's shooting spree atop the school tower. It was where horny, megalomaniacal state lawmakers tumbled in from Pecos, San Angelo, the Panhandle, and the Piney Woods, looking for something beyond everything back home—more power, more money, more women. It was a Texas sock-hop on steroids, with chess moves, counter-chess-moves, and a flurry of last-minute deals that were done by handshake over a Pearl beer at the old Scholz's beer house—or in the back of a Lincoln Continental parked outside.

There were stories and more stories: the mistress of LBJ who used to wait for him in a tub at the Driskill, the politicians who had to put tape on the inside pockets of their suit jackets (they were packing heavy guns that were constantly pushing against the fabric). The nation took note. Folksinger Phil Ochs was writing tunes about the swindler Billie Sol Estes and everyone assumed, rightly so, that this episode of massive West Texas–style corruption—a complex con game involving fake farm subsidies—was just one of many to be revealed. And as if on cue, not long after Ivins settled in to work at the *Observer*, the Sharpstown Scandal blew up and snaked its way to Governor Preston Smith's door. A Houston banker and insurance man, Frank Sharp, had loaned money to state officials to buy shares of his insurance company at artificially inflated prices—so that they could be unloaded later and everyone would walk away with skimmed profits, except, of course, the dupes who were saddled with the hyped stock.

The fog lifted on the scam in 1970 and 1971, and Ivins dug in. The *Observer*, unquestionably on a longer leash than any of the major dailies, feasted on the affair. Some of Ivins's friends assumed that her father knew all the principals involved; Houston was a tight place at a certain, rarefied-air level. The scandal made national headlines and prompted editors in New York and Washington to study her *Observer* stories. Ivins was roaming the halls of the State Capitol, trying to figure out the well-fed men. For many of them, she was an unusually striking figure: Tall redheads who huffed Marlboros, drank Southern Comfort, and knew how to play the magnolia-scented socialite were in short supply in Austin. It was a perfect convergence. She was the only woman left standing in the power zones, and she was the only woman able to hold her own in the back rooms, in chambers, in the lubricated mosh pit that the politicos tumbled into after work "officially" ended. It was as if everything—River Oaks, St. John's, Smith, Columbia, the *Chronicle*, the *Tribune*—had been a boot-camp preparation for going undercover and embedding herself in the biggest, free, political freak show north of Mexico.

It was a journalism revelation and it crystallized the notion that she could be part of the story, really inside of it, and then step outside and write about it. She could work the room like a politician and then go to a typewriter, fire up a smoke, drink several more beers, and begin the process of hovering over her own reality—looking down on it, in all meanings of that phrase, and writing about it as if she was filing letters from a distant land. As if she was sending out missives from deep inside a very queer coal mine in the South. Messages back to civilization.

The gambit that she had embarked on back in college, of toying with Texas, of laughing at her father's Nouveau Texas Riche ilk and mocking her mother's Old Texas mores, was shifting to a pure-play political journalism template. And, almost exquisitely, she could deliver on the things that newspaper war dogs like Zarko Franks dreamed about when he used to send her notes ("To the Viking Goddess of The North—hey ma, look at me, I'm writin'") about wanting to be a real writer. She could actually try to *write* the news—to inject the fucked-up news with the righteous black humor that it deserved. For years she would tell people that *The Texas Observer*, really, was the best thing that had ever happened to her.

Dugger watched her closely, moving to almost editor emeritus advisory status. He was pleased that he had two feminists working together, maybe the only all-women editorial team in the nation. He was unprepared for the humor in Ivins's work—how constant it would be. When he'd hired her, all that he had seen were what he called her "excellent public interest" stories from the *Tribune*. "As she got funnier and funnier I enjoyed it like everybody else. She was like Will Rogers but in an entirely new way, in that she was as vulgar as a stevedore's daughter . . . she was new. She was a great sensation." And he tried to remain somewhat hands-off in the editorial process: "I would criticize the work of the two [Northcott and Ivins] in the following way: I would sometimes raise the issues of fairness or libel in writing and then give them the issue and then leave them to it, not giving them orders but helping them—if I could—put out a slightly better paper."[32]

Without question, the freedom Dugger extended to Ivins would stand in marked contrast to what she got from subsequent employers.

⊰⊱

A welling hallmark of Austin was its self-congratulatory sense that it was better than anywhere else—or at least anywhere else in Texas. Never mind that it was one of the least racially diverse big cities in the state—Dallas,

Houston, San Antonio had far larger minority communities and were often, by necessity, more integrated. Austin had, if one had to guess, far more pot, far stronger pot—and far more musicians per capita. It had beautiful rivers and hideouts in the nearby Hill Country. It had the university feeding the '60s and '70s sensibilities—and it had very little of the symptomatic urban angst that welled up in other places. And it was paradise, in its way, for liberal politicians, activists, and lobbyists—many of them fleeing from Houston or Dallas, or from small towns where it wasn't ever a good thing to be affiliated with the American Civil Liberties Union, to quote from *The Texas Observer*, to say that you hated Lyndon Baines Johnson, to argue that you felt that Kennedy was killed in Dallas because, well, Dallas was filled with arch-conservative-reactionary hate and racism. Austin was considered more laid-back, far more so, by people who possessed what euphemistically could be called progressive politics. And there was a clear sense that like-minded political souls were reinforcing each other and simply wanting to hang out together just like the real hippies—running around outdoors, camping, smoking dope under the starlight, drinking more beer, and disappearing into the looming cluster of live oak trees at the edge of a wildflower meadow just outside the Austin city limits. Texas gave many people good reason to be paranoid. And Austin gave some Texans a sense of being able to mingle with "fellow travelers"—of having a wink-and-nod solidarity with their political soul mates.

When the *Observer* relocated its offices from near the university to the second floor of an old mansion at 600 W. Seventh Street downtown—courtesy of liberal lawyers Dave Richards and Sam Houston Clinton, who owned the building and used it for a law office—Ivins was that much closer to building a core group of friends who would protect her, stonewall on her behalf, perform interventions on her, take her home at night, feed her, and even clothe her until the day she died. Richards and his wife were among those people—and they had high-tailed it out of Dallas, coming to Austin in 1969. He went into labor law and civil rights arenas, invited the Texas Civil Liberties Union to share space in the same building as the *Observer*, and introduced his wife, Ann, to Ivins. Ann Richards had been involved in local Democratic politics in Dallas and she had begun exploring options in Austin. She was a parent, eleven years older than Ivins. Her father was from Bug Tussle, Texas; and her mother, from Hogjaw, Texas. Both of them were from somewhere on the tumbleweed end of the caste system, worlds apart from what Ivins knew growing up. Richards went to Waco High, not St. John's. She attended Christian conservative Baylor University, not Smith College. Her parents were dirt-poor, as she said, not sailing yachts with the men from Tenneco.

Still, Richards and Ivins hit it off fairly quickly. They were feminists in a state where that term was still being defined, where there were not many reinforcing role models, networks, or social structures. They liked to drink and drink some more. At 5:30 P.M., when work was deemed done at the *Observer*, Ivins and Richards would sit on the wisteria-covered veranda at the old mansion-office, watch the crimson sun go down over the Hill Country, somewhere in the general direction of where LBJ was in his self-imposed exile, and repeatedly dip into an ice chest filled with Lone Star and Pearl beers.

Richards and her husband liked to camp and owned some land along the North San Gabriel River, near Liberty Hill outside of Austin. Before the Central Texas rivers were overrun with margarita-crazed, sun-fried visitors in inner tubes, there were hidden, peaceful places where the ancestors of the early German settlers still spoke a little of the old language. They ran small farms or ranches and didn't seem to mind if over the barbed-wire they could hear some strangers playing Marty Robbins songs on a guitar, hear some muffled laughter and a splash in the water, or maybe see sparks floating up from a very late-night campfire. Richards began inviting Ivins to the campouts—and it drew Ivins into a circle of Austin-based activists, musicians, writers, and other kindred souls. The nexus, as always, seemed to be politics. And she learned to not be surprised when Democratic loyalists, insiders, even kingmakers, would show up at the smoky campouts. If there were still some starched creases left over from Smith, some faint hints of plastic Houston breeding still on her sleeve, they were being removed in Austin, a place where everybody she liked seemed to be in on the joke. Nobody really cared, in certain circles, how you dressed. Or where you went to school or grew up. Being in Austin, the fact that you had gotten there, was enough.

"A spaceship from a magic place" is how ever-smiling Doug Sahm, the hippie angel who channeled every form of Texas music, was describing Austin to people around the nation.[33]

CHAPTER SIX

Us Against Them

I alternated between fear and seething anger.

—JOHN HENRY FAULK

"Hi, Sweet Pea," she'd say with a chuckle when she saw someone she knew out on the streets filtering off Congress Avenue. She'd arrive at the new *Observer* offices, hardly ever when she was supposed to, in "The Tank"—the Mercury with a problem: it would not go in reverse. Dressed in a work shirt and blue jeans—she and Northcott had both vowed to dress that way as part of a proletarian gesture—she'd sit at a typewriter and lay out a brown notebook filled with her almost illegible, cursive handwriting. She disliked working the old black phones, maybe as an outgrowth of having had to do too much of it at the *Chronicle*. A cloud of smoke over her head, she would smile at her carbon copy, pleased with what she'd just written, sometimes making breathy noises and snorting to herself.

As she and the *Observer* prepared for the opening rounds of the 1971 state legislature, she pushed open the imposing doors that led to the impressive, wood-paneled second-floor chambers. There were two good ol' boys guffawing. She perked up when she overheard one say to the other: "You should have seen what I found myself last night . . . and she don't talk neither." She'd endured three years of emphasized objectivity at the *Tribune*, and she'd had some exposure to "serious" political reporting as practiced by the veteran New York-and-Washington journalists she studied with at Columbia. Now, at *The Texas Observer*, she had free rein not just to address issues that barely dented the pages of the mainstream papers—the out-sized issues of poverty, racism, systemic corruption—but to do it with a chiding, confiding derision that two-stepped back and forth between a mocking condemnation and a can-you-believe-it kind of wonderment. From her first pieces there was that sense of an extension of the beery sessions in Houston, in Minnesota, in Austin with her friends—an invitation to the reader to come behind the curtain and study the cartoon characters, malapropisms, and bourbon-and-cash-laced rationalizations for a million political mind-fucks.

She was headed to The Lege—as she called it—every day, sometimes walking up Congress Avenue past the small, old-time downtown jewelry stores where the lobbyists liked to buy wristwatches for the pols and brooches for the wives of those same pols. She'd make the stroll up the slow incline leading to the towering front doors of the capitol, shaking her head at the Confederate memorial, the old cannons, and the pensioners feeding the squirrels that darted under the towering live oak trees. It was a grand building, built from huge blocks of granite unearthed in nearby Marble Falls, and it was, essentially, a private club filled with silver-haired Satans and their eager, well-connected aides. The older, wary, foot soldiers in the press corps slowly let her in. She also had Northcott and Dugger as early guides. Northcott had been the embattled editor of the student newspaper at UT-Austin, writing courageous anti-war editorials that university officials loathed—with one bureaucrat claiming that Northcott's work had led to the university's loss of massive donations. She distrusted many people in authority, and told people that she had a hard time being around others who didn't share her politics, beliefs. She grew to like Ivins more and more, and she couldn't help but laugh when she overheard Ivins on the phone and drawing people out, cajoling them into some tidbit she needed for a story. And when the two would sometimes step outside for fresh air, they would laugh until they almost couldn't breathe.

Even as their friendship deepened, Northcott didn't dwell on Ivins's upbringing in Houston, her Smith College education. Nor did Ivins. She still didn't tell people she was from Houston. "She did not like to say she was from Houston," says Northcott. After listening to Ivins talk to lobbyists in white suits they had bought at Joseph's Men's Shop on Congress—and watching her work the younger, preening aides to the state officials, and watching her clutch another beer and lean down and seem to *really* listen to the politicians at Scholz's Garten—Northcott concluded that Ivins had a rock-hard constitution.

Northcott would leave Scholz's by 9 P.M., when everyone had had too much to drink and started repeating themselves. Ivins stayed. Northcott thought she had the physical will to stay up late, smoke, and drink—and to stare deeply into the eyes of people she considered existentially damaged salesmen of crooked dreams. And an even stronger stomach for trying to extrapolate some higher meaning from the bullshit infighting, parliamentary gamesmanship, subtle blackmailing, and contracts with the devil that dominated the political process in Austin.

"By the time she had gotten to Austin, she seemed fully bloomed. She had such a natural voice and she had only been in journalism a couple of years. She seemed to me to know so much more than I did," says Northcott.[1] In particular, she seemed to know innately how to conceptualize stories in a less-straight, nonlinear, non-inverted-pyramid style. Northcott learned a lot from Ivins, thinking about ways to wrap her hands around the bigger stories, the ones that could drown in endless ruminations on obscure sub-committee hearings on water, electricity, and minerals—and that would often result in deadly boring, paint-by-the-numbers approaches. As always, there was the nod to subjectivity: Ivins had been reading the work of the muckraking Jack Newfield, the *Village Voice* journalist who once talked about the freedom inherent in working for a publication that made "no pretense of objectivity."[2] Newfield argued that journalists should never mistake objectivity for the truth. He wanted to "combine activism with writing" and "create a constituency for reform. And don't stop until you have achieved some progress or positive results."[3] Newfield never ran from his associations with politicians; rather, he sought out the elected officials he deemed to be the most progressive and then championed them. He knew members of the Black Panthers, traveled with Bobby Kennedy, and was famous for throwing his typewriter out of his hotel room window and toward some cops beating demonstrators at the bloody Democratic convention in 1968. Friends of Ivins would talk about how they had made pilgrimages to see Newfield in New York. Ivins followed his work for years, cut out his articles, and underlined them.

She was doing the same thing with other writers, including Andrew Kopkind, Murray Kempton, and David Broder, and the journalist she felt a Texas kinship to, Willie Morris. Kopkind made his bones with constant, personal insights into the lives of the committed foot soldiers of the hard left. Ivins knew his history, how he walked away from day-to-day journalism at big daily newspapers and wrote for progressive publications with a barely concealed advocacy and righteous indignation. Ivins knew his career arc.

It was in Minnesota that she first wondered whether she could be both a leftist and a journalist. In Texas, she continued that dialog with friends, wondering if it was better to use the bigger mainstream media to subtly advance a political philosophy—or work for a smaller, independent organ like the *Observer* with its 12,000 subscribers, where she could just say what she wanted to say.

At the *Observer*, she simply took advantage of the overt possibilities to experiment with her voice, to see what resonated with the dedicated, supportive, receptive audience. She had no editor other than Northcott, who in turn was politically attuned to Ivins, impressed both by her stamina and by her giddy depictions of the ridiculous theater unfolding in the capitol. Ivins, Northcott decided, had an early ability to clinically deconstruct the elaborate, million-dollar budget matters being crafted in the state house—and to see them through the prism of the cowboy-hat gladhanders who viewed the place as their personal playground.[4]

Politicians, too—those in power and those who wanted to get there—quickly picked up on not just her overview abilities but her potentially useful muscle. *The Texas Observer* had only a few thousand readers, but it was required reading inside certain political circles. Willie Morris had said in his memoir that "by the sheer force of its ardor and its talent, it was read by everyone in Texas whose opinions had authority."[5] The mainstream papers were dutifully covering The Lege, but they were doing their usual he-said–she-said pieces and precious little analysis—let alone Jack Newfield-level commentary. By the time the legislative session wrapped up in late spring of 1971, she had already developed a growing reputation as someone who went beyond the pronouncements that came with the final thud of the gavel—she had some sense of the slimy process, the way bills wormed their way into existence, and what the macrocosmic guiding influences had been. And her stories were funnier, more free, than what was popping up in the dutiful dailies—she had a sense of place, of political theater, and she wasn't afraid to import it. "We wanted Molly to be unleashed, that was why we chose her. Her stories were interesting right off the bat. She had an eye for details. She would go into dialect in her stories. She could pick up the old-time German Central Texas accents, she could write in dialect," says Northcott.[6]

⟹⟸

She had the base, the hardcore liberal faithful, as her audience, and people shared her stories with one another. And it wasn't just Ann Richards but other political players who were studying her byline—especially the scary funny, manic depressive, and raging alcoholic Bob Bullock. Like an LBJ on angel dust, Bullock carried guns, slept four hours a night, got into fistfights outside of bars, and dove out motel bathroom windows. He was an arm-twisting, ball-breaking, ultimate insider who was on his way to his defining Faustian moment—helping George W. Bush forge alliances between Democrats and Republicans, so Bush could easily move toward the presidency. During his various stints as secretary of state, state comptroller, and then lieutenant governor, he developed a very close relationship with Ivins, first forged over beers at Scholz's Garten or bourbon-and-coke at the Quorum Club—and then cemented with straight whiskey at the wet bar in his state office, with cocktails at a variety of downtown clubs, and god knows what else on those Hill Country campouts where he wound up paddling canoes with Ivins.

There were reporters who assumed they were lovers at some point, but could never provide the proof. If Hank Holland had been born in Hillsboro, Texas, like Bullock, there was a strong chance he would have been just like him. It certainly wouldn't take too many psychiatrists to connect the dots from Holland's mad spontaneities and megalomania to the dizzying, snarling Bob Bullock. He was clearly entranced by Ivins. He once sent Ivins three roses with a handwritten note: "One rose for each decade of your life." He called her, repeatedly, for rounds of hard drinking.

The eventual depth of their friendship, the relationship between the Smith College daughter of the president of Tenneco and the unfiltered Jerry Lee Lewis of Texas politics, surprised many people who knew them. He had clawed his way up from a rural Texas town, attended college in deep West Texas, and then joined the Air Force before he began his dive bomb into the political scene in Austin. They were, on the surface, opposite—and it was frequently difficult to pin his political persuasions down, apart from the fact that he was a registered Democrat. But he became her mentor, teaching her more about how the game was really played than anyone else in Texas. It was a relationship—a form of mutual access to opposite worlds—that startled other reporters, some of whom either resented the tie between Ivins and Bullock or were condemning of it. He knew the rules inside the state house. He had written and broken some of them. Though she towered over him, he liked the fact that she was equally foul-mouthed and as hard a drinker. It wasn't really a stretch to say he had known a lot of women—he was a regular in divorce court—but no one like Ivins.

Bullock drove over 100 miles per hour, went to parties in the heart of the city where his pals trained machine guns at targets, and carried a pistol that he once pulled out, cocked, and aimed at the head of a scared-shitless waiter at the Quorum Club. He jumped out of at least one motel bathroom window trying to flee from a husband looking for his wife. He fell into a thirty-foot-deep ditch, lost his sharkskin loafers, and walked in his socks back to the state comptroller's office, praying the cops wouldn't stop him. He was hospitalized for depression and put on suicide watch. He dated women who worked for him. He married a woman twenty years younger. He excitedly told reporters he "wanted to fuck" Rena Pederson, who ran the editorial page of the *Dallas Morning News*. He called state house reporters and accused them of firing up joints in the pressroom. He went to treatment centers, what he called "drunk school," after he had begun boozing from morning to night, all while trying to do the state's business—and remaining the most feared figure in Austin political circles.

He once passed out in the back of a stranger's car. The driver stepped into the vehicle without seeing Bullock, started it up, and blissfully hit Interstate 35. Bullock, realizing something was awry, decided to pop up and introduce himself: "Hi there, I'm Bob Bullock, your secretary of state."

It wasn't the last time he almost frightened someone to death. He busted the backs of anyone who stood in his way at the State Capitol, and did intense reconnaissance on both his enemies and allies. But Ivins ultimately came to believe that Bullock deserved credit for doing the dirty work of corralling all the twitchy and greedy state lawmakers, as if they were rabid cats, and forcing them to pass bills, to make law, to reconsider past wrongs. Like him or not, he made the trains move on time, and he seemed to sometimes possess the same kind of populist streak that had maybe once stirred in LBJ's soul and had its true fruition in Ralph Yarborough, the senator from Texas whom she idolized. Bullock tried to hire minorities, gave a nod to women's issues, tried to collect taxes from people and businesses that had cheated the law, and sometimes seemed obsessed with legislative efficiency even more than with partisan politics.

In the end, she had never seen such a free radical operating in politics, in business. To her, he was a mad, damned funny genius—the political link to Hank Holland: "Not since Lyndon B. Johnson has there been another pol who could so dominate everyone around him by sheer force of personality . . . probably the smartest person I've ever known, which is partly what makes both the good and the bad of him so outsized."[7] She liked Bullock because he was so in the moment, and post-cynical about it all, that he could essentially hover above the State Capitol. He didn't have easily predictable allegiances because he was so inherently suspicious—and he had an almost psychotic understanding of Texas as a place so huge, unregulated, untamed, and coated with oil money that, even in the best-case scenario, it could be managed but never really completely reformed. He was a master tactician, an utter pragmatist, whose life—in uncertain

Texas—was utterly defined by knowing who would be loyal to him. He thought Molly Ivins could perhaps be loyal to him, especially if he drew her deeper into his confidences, his circles, and made her drink with him over the years at The Quorum, The Filling Station, and The Cloak Room. And she was loyal, crediting him with many things, sometimes refraining from calling him out for not doing more with his often unlimited abilities and power. For her purposes, Bullock was truly worth knowing. She worked her way through her connections to try to know him even more. Carlton Carl, her friend from the internship days at the *Houston Chronicle*, had moved from writing press releases and speeches for the Texas governor to working for Bullock.

In time, she grew accustomed to the fact that the phone would ring and Bullock would be on the other end. It was 4 P.M.—drinking time. The reporters who had occasionally experienced the same kind of call knew that it went this way: "You goddamned better get your fuckin' ass over here if you want me to talk to you." He wanted to drink and he wanted to talk, and she grew closer to him even at a time when more and more snakes were coiled inside his head. Bullock was a hurricane-force inevitability, someone you had to deal with, and Ivins almost saw him as a challenge. And vice versa.

One weekend evening when they were side-by-side at a joint called The Office and he refused to let her out of their booth, she hip-checked the state comptroller hard and knocked him to the ground. As she stepped over him and walked out the door, a stunned Bullock yelped with a sort of red-blooded giddy-yup in his voice:

"Son of a bitch. Did you see that? I love Molly Ivins!"[8]

Years later, on his deathbed, he would slip in and out of coherence—occasionally bolting upright, grinning, and suddenly shouting that Molly Ivins was one "hairy-legged liberal."

⇷⇸

It was almost required around the campfires, along the North San Gabriel River, that you come up with some story, some anecdote, and Ivins listened as Ann Richards played with the language, the dialects, the devastatingly funny caricatures. Richards was effortless and her unthreatening delivery only underscored the drop-dead effectiveness of her punch lines. Bullock had given Ivins the political manual to Texas and Ann Richards would certainly share hers eventually—but in the early 1970s Ivins was more often picking up style tips from "Miss Ann," as she sometimes liked to call her new friend.

"All of a sudden we were part of Dave and Ann Richards's circle. And she always spent a lot of time with him and with Ann, at the campouts," says Northcott. Ivins studied Richards. "Ann didn't write but she spoke so well and you could definitely learn how to make your point from Ann. She was sort of the instigator, she was sort of our troop leader, and this was incredibly wonderful. Ann was very practical."[9]

Early on, Northcott also knew that she and Ivins shared a generational quirk—they were both very glad to listen to older people, to be around older people, especially if they espoused some link to the feisty populism embodied by people they either studied or mingled with—Maury Maverick, Jr. (the rabblerousing attorney from San Antonio whose family, famous for not branding their cattle, inspired the popular use of the word "maverick"), liberal Senator Ralph Yarborough, populist Senator Fred Harris in Oklahoma, and Texas humorist John Henry Faulk. They also weren't constitutionally opposed to Ann Richards just because she was a homemaker-cum-politico and a few years older. Her campouts were almost like annual, informal political conventions in the woods—with some heavy drinking, a bit of pot smoking, and many tales spun around the fire. Ivins continued to take center stage, and one time she and Bullock found themselves in a canoe, rocking down the river, and it suddenly tipped and sent them both into the water. As the years went on, the campouts would be enshrined in a sort of Austin subculture mythology, remembered by the people there not just as a gathering of liberal, like-minded souls but as part of a semi-historic, conscious collective of "everybody who was on our wavelength," as Northcott puts it. "The Richards campouts were just so wonderful . . . by the time people would be done telling their stories, it was just precious. There was more of an us-against-them feeling. I had many, many good friends in the past, but I had never had 'my people.' Everybody took turns telling stories."

Northcott says Richards was, really, a "nobody" at the time—a likeable politico with normal hair who would write out cute invitations to the campouts, including hand-drawn maps decorated with bunny pictures, and urge people to bring kids if they wanted, to sing songs, to go swimming. There would be similar campouts, traditions, that welled up and lingered for years—State Representative and, later, Land Commissioner Bob Armstrong held gatherings that Ivins and Northcott attended, and these, too, gained a certain cachet in the pantheon of insider Austin history. Dave and Ann Richards knew so many people, and it led to other river runs around the state with Ivins, botanists, geologists, and poets. And, finally, through Congressman Bob Eckhardt, she met more people in the extended liberal network in Texas.

In Austin there were protests, student activists, underground cartoonists, and easy-to-find pot shipped across the Rio Grande—dealers from campuses like Columbia were flying to Austin to buy Acapulco Gold in bulk and bring it back to New York. Some Texas musicians, fried from the helter-skelter in California, were coming home to Austin and following Doug Sahm's advice and lead. And, for liberals who cared mostly about politics, *The Texas Observer* was the only publication that mattered. *The Rag*, a groundbreaking underground newspaper that featured the work of artists Gilbert Shelton ("The Fabulous Furry Freak Brothers") and Jim Franklin, was more attuned to the overt counterculture in Austin and Texas. It touched on the Black Panthers, city politics, the objectification of women in *Playboy*, alternative lifestyles, and altered realities—and interviewed the troubled genius Townes Van Zandt, investigated police brutality in Austin, and railed against the University of Texas and its reactionary leaders. At one point, the university tried to halt the distribution of *The Rag* on campus. Dave Richards successfully defended the magazine in court. As a medium, *The Rag* might have been too much of a countercultural segue for Ivins. She liked being at the *Observer*. It was what she had surreptitiously read while a student at St. John's; it had a literary tug, as evidenced by Willie Morris; it was something that got referenced and quoted by the bigger mainstream publications that she had begun telling people she ultimately wanted to work for in New York and Washington.

The Texas Observer wasn't underground, but it was independent and respected by the prairie socialists, progressives, and liberals who had fought the fight in Texas. And during her six years at the *Observer*, Ivins continuously tinkered with the comic possibilities. She told friends that she assumed some of the politicians were so dulled by their work under the big state dome that maybe they didn't really get the joke. She was always amazed that she could essentially suggest a particular politician was as refreshing in his thinking as a dead armadillo, and then, when she'd see that same politician, he would shake her hand, hug her, squeeze her in ways that she didn't want—and thank her for getting him mentioned in "yah little magazine."

Northcott loved Ivins's lampooning. They were becoming better friends. They would take the final galleys of the magazine to the Futura Press offices on Tuesdays and then they would do their laundry on Wednesdays—Northcott was anxious to get the smell of Ivins's cigarette smoke out of her clothes. Sometimes, they'd go to the library downtown to check out murder mysteries. Northcott knew one of the founders of the legendary music club Armadillo World Headquarters, which came to embody the hippie-blues-rock-country-music ethos of Austin, and she brought Ivins to the music club that was a far cry from the days when Ivins sat in a Greenwich mansion and tried not to snicker as she listened to her lover's mother earnestly play the harp. Some Austin things, things that once drew a buttoned-down Willie Nelson to a countercultural Austin, were being ingrained in her.

Throughout the early 1970s, Ivins began to walk in The Lege as if it was her second home. She worked the room, told jokes, and endured more of the unwanted shoulder rubs and ass grabs. "She didn't think of it as being behind enemy lines. It was just covering good stories. She never felt uncomfortable at the legislature. That was a great advantage for her. I still didn't want to talk to people I didn't agree with. I hadn't matured as much as she had in some ways. I thought it was great, I just wished I could do it. It took me a while, because I watched Molly," says Northcott.[10] When another writer, John Ferguson, joined the *Observer* staff, he and Ivins would sometimes press the deadlines. Northcott would be waiting—Ivins came to call it "an eloquent silence." Ivins blurted one time: "If we just left now, we could get to Galveston and watch the sunrise and commit suicide and not have to finish these stories."

She was invited to speak at a Unitarian Church, her first speaking gig in Austin. She had done some speaking when she was at the *Tribune* and she had gone door-to-door doing community organizing, maybe being more loquacious than Jack Cann. Still, she had reservations about getting up and giving a real speech about public affairs. "In some ways she was insecure, she said she was nervous before speeches, and maybe she was," says Northcott. But she was studying Ann Richards, holding her own at the campouts and making her voice heard in Bullock's circles. She was developing a voice on the page and one process would inform the other. She was also learning to speak in different languages, so to speak "She was in a sense her own medium, she cultivated this voice," said Lou Dubose, who would co-author books with her many years later.[11]

Her friends in Austin also began to see something else emerge as the work piled up, as she spent time with Bullock and Richards—both of whom would eventually embark on intense struggles with alcoholism. Ivins was beginning to drink with a ferocity that scared colleagues for years. Some quietly wondered if it ran in the family, if her mother and father had not just driven her to drink but had passed along a genetic predisposition. On the surface in Austin, it was easiest to blame Bullock. He was certainly a steady drinking partner of Ivins. He was "a political mentor and a very good friend, I think that's all it was . . . fellow alcoholics. He would start drinking at 4:30 or 5 and she would get the call and she would go off to meet him. She was about to go get the information. They were drinking buddies. They went to a place near the office. Wherever Bullock happened to be drinking at that time. Alcohol was very much a part of it," remembers Northcott.[12]

Her friend wondered if there was a problem earlier, and exactly when it was that Ivins developed her addiction. Northcott knew that Ivins had shown up with a six-pack of beer for her job interview with *The Texas Ob-*

server. "It was the 70s, if you weren't drinking all the time, you were dop-ing all the time or taking LSD. And it just didn't seem odd. I was sur-rounded by alcoholics, Ann Richards, you know, some of the most wonderful people I knew were alcoholics. When you bring a six-pack of beer to a job interview . . . that's a sign. It was very freewheeling. I was handicapped because I never drank; it would make me sick."

For Ivins there was no initial editorial downside to all that Jim Beam and her proximity to the boozed-up power circles in Texas. She was still pro-lific, still acerbic, and still unafraid to write about the Sharpstown scandal, the legacy of LBJ, and the lack of anti-poverty funding. In a state as in-scrutable as Texas, she perhaps needed to continue her relationship with Bullock. At times, he seemed on the verge of telling her about an outsized political scandal, one that the daily reporters had no clue about. Her note-books are filled with promising suggestions, no doubt conveyed by Bul-lock, that hinted at massive briberies and payoffs in state government. "Bullock gave her a really deep understanding of government. So that as soon as she got there, she was hanging out with Bullock, drinking with Bullock, and she was finding out everything that was going on and un-derstanding everything," says Northcott. "Bullock had a good brain for politics. She liked him. We didn't have anything to worry about. Molly was writing all these things down on cocktail napkins. . . . [T]here was no downside for the *Observer*, except these alcoholics encouraged each other to drink."[13]

She learned from both Bullock and Richards the art of the instant, inti-mate social contract. People in Austin learned that she was good at giving you her undivided attention; her eyes locked on yours even as she raised a glass to her lips. She read constantly and seemed able to summon, at a moment's notice, sundry historical facts about citrus production in the Rio Grande Valley or the deadly hurricane of 1900 in Galveston—and the state representative, the lobbyist, the visitor to Austin, would be pleased. North-cott listened to her on the phone, working her sources, or just slipping into an over-the-top Texas voice and telling an anecdote. She saw her do it in person when they traveled to the Democratic national convention in 1972:

> I had some reservations that she was just an anecdote machine. . . . [I]n 1972, I would be standing there at the Democratic national convention and she made her way around the room. Very much like a politician and an entertainer. But her repertoire was immense. It was part of her personality, to make people laugh. She wanted to be liked and that was one way to do it. It probably defused her size, her brilliance. She did her good-ole-girl shtick, which was one of her innate personalities. She went around meeting people and lobbyists. They didn't care how large she was; they would say, "C'mon here, honey, and sit on my lap." I was still utterly appalled by the legislature, but she could go in there with a laugh and a joke and treat them like human beings. They immediately knew who she was. They read the *Observer* the day it came out. She was quite the magpie, she just picked up on things. If someone from [New York] called, she could be a Smithie. I don't think she knew it. If you need to speak French, you speak French. But there was the person who was in France for a year, got articles in *Foreign Affairs Quarterly*. I have a picture of her wearing pearls and little white gloves. We shared an office for six years and I could never figure out why she used her accent when—sometimes it seemed contrapuntal.

But increasingly, "her primary character became more Texan, more homespun."[14]

⋘⋙

Given Ivins's professional and social circles and the predilection she shared with Northcott ("we revered the generation before us, we would go to see old folks"), it was a clear inevitability that she would meet John Henry Faulk. He was a patriarch in that extended group that some would eventually call "the *Observer* crowd." It was, really, a small town—relatives of his family helped run the printing press where Ivins brought the *Observer* galleys. The Austin-born Faulk was a folklorist and English professor at the

University of Texas at Austin (where he had been influenced by the so-called holy trinity of historian-writers: J. Frank Dobie, Walter Webb, and Roy Bedichek). He was also a friend of the extraordinarily influential musicologist and author Alan Lomax, with whom he had talked about Faulk's master's thesis—a study of powerful sermons delivered by black preachers along the sluggish Brazos River in Texas. During Faulk's classes, he'd tell stories and mimic voices and personalities he had encountered in his travels, but particularly ones from Texas. According to family and friends, Faulk increasingly relied on mimicry—and exaggerated storytelling and broadly drawn caricatures—as a way to overcome his insecurities inside the ivory-tower circles at the university. The more Faulk did it, the more it seemed second nature—and the more people said he had an ability to absorb Texans of all stripes. After Faulk served in the Merchant Marines during WWII, Lomax introduced him to executives at CBS Radio and he embarked on a career hosting various talk, music, and variety shows that often featured his down-home yarns and jokes—along with dollops of wry social commentary and politics. In 1956, his career was effectively smashed when he was blacklisted and accused of being a communist for his work with the American Federation of Television and Radio Artists, for his attendance of United Nations functions where Soviet officials were also present, for a show he once did with Paul Robeson. He was fired from CBS. Crusading television newsman Edward R. Murrow jumped to his defense, and helped hire attorney Louis Nizer to pursue a libel suit. For the next six years Faulk was locked in a death-grip battle with Senator Joseph McCarthy's witch hunters, including attorney Roy Cohn, the heavy-lidded hypocrite who labored for decades to mask his homosexuality. A jury finally ruled in Faulk's favor in 1962 and said he should be awarded $3.5 million—then the largest libel judgment in history (he ultimately received less than $75,000). He wrote a book, *Fear on Trial*, but never regained the seamless career arc that had been taken away from him. He came back to Austin in the late '60s and was revered in those coalescing liberal circles as a hero, the man who beat the blacklist.

He was in his late fifties, about the same age as Ivins's father, and she began to spend more and more time with him. He was flattered that she hadn't lost track of the issue that had brought him down. For Ivins, Faulk was a living window into something bigger, a battle-scarred link to another era when socialism didn't ring with an insidious alarm, when there were righteous movements in the heartland to interpret, celebrate, and enforce the constitutional tenets of equality. It was one thing to be reaching for bottles of bourbon in the back of Bullock's wet bar, and to be lingering with Richards and drolly dissecting the frailties of the men who ran the political system. But it was another thing entirely to visit Faulk and hear him talk about his firsthand encounters with Senator Joseph McCarthy, Edward R. Murrow, Paul Robeson, Roy Cohn, and the seemingly eternal, epic fight over communism, the First Amendment, and civil liberties. She spent more time visiting Faulk and his wife Liz. Says Northcott:

> He was a mentor. She loved to hear him talk and loved to learn from him. Molly had decided that civil liberties was her thing—and she was learning everything she could about the Constitution and the Bill of Rights from John Henry. And we were writing about it and no one else was. And we were next door to the ACLU. He broke the blacklist, you are talking about somebody with a great will. His career was ruined, he never got it back. Early on, she started going over to John Henry's and Liz's house a lot. They liked her. There was a lot to absorb.[15]

There were others feeding her head, people she would come to call "freedom fighters." In Texas, her true heroes were not journalists. They were men like Faulk—and Dave Richards, Sam Houston Clinton, and Maury Maverick, Jr., lawyers who had made career sacrifices, and lost a hell of a lot of money, by representing conscientious objectors, civil rights activists, and poor people who had seen plenty of cops but never enough attorneys. In Austin, she could trace the circles, find those links, back to the darkest pages of racism and injustice that defined Texas. She could also follow the lineage of people who had taken profound, lonely, dangerous roles—and wind it back to something grander and bigger in American history. Northcott knew that Ivins was obsessive in her reading: She consumed books, eventually building a library of 3,500 volumes; she would reach for the phone to talk to people about obscure cemeteries in France or a water rights issue in West Texas. She began reading more about Faulk and the events that led to his downfall, and she began studying similar issues, ones she defined as matters of civil liberties. She was enraptured by

Faulk's style *and* history—even when some people thought he was a kindly fossil, a "has-been who wouldn't stop talking" as someone in Austin called him. Northcott believes that Faulk was a bigger influence on Ivins than either Richards or Bullock.[16]

"Molly loved John Henry," says his widow Liz Faulk, who would eventually go to work as Ivins's personal aide, researcher, and protector for many years. "He was a very compelling person. People gravitated to them [Ivins and Faulk]. There was something about them. I think a lot of politicians have that."[17] As Ivins and Faulk grew closer, his wife could see the similarities—the way Ivins liked to play-act, to mimic Texas and Southern stereotypes just like her husband had done. Her husband was often "commanded" to play-act, to "put on a show" for people, to "act Texan" for them. The same thing was happening with Ivins as more people read her column, now that it had been picked up and was being followed in New York publishing circles. The Smith College graduate who had gone to an Ivy League journalism school, and then studied in France, was increasingly being asked to talk the way she wrote—with a dialect, with some cornpone. For Ivins, Faulk was a role model for how to do it as an act of erudition. He was, in essence, a cultural anthropologist with a specialty in regional linguistics—he was a storyteller, from the Southern tradition, and she absorbed that facility. But his wife saw one key difference: Ivins seemed to stay in character, to stay on stage, much longer and later into the night. Ivins would go on until 3 in the morning "if she was drinking and she had simpatico people around her," says Faulk. She knew her husband could do that play-acting only until he got tired of pleasing all the people clamoring for it, until he realized it probably wasn't very healthy staying up so late, trying to be so many things he wasn't. "John Henry, his big deal was I can only go for so long with a shit grin on my face . . . which is basically what she had," says Faulk.[18]

Students in Austin would constantly seek out Faulk at parties and social gatherings, always wanting to sit at his knee and hear him tell stories. Ivins would also be there, and as she made a name in Austin, people would gravitate toward her as well. They'd both tell stories and the students—and the hangers-on, the strangers, the earnest visitors—would all listen as if they were in a class. And plenty of times, there would be some pot, some beer, some drinks. But Faulk would be careful; Ivins sometimes wasn't.

"He wouldn't become drunk," Faulk says, but "Molly could become so fucking drunk."[19]

⤛⤜

John Henry Faulk had been the closest of anyone in the extended *Observer* crowd, the Texas campout crowd, to real national fame. He had been a star for both good and bad reasons. His wife knew about the lure of recognition and she thought it held some sway over Ivins, something that other close friends echo. Liz Faulk wondered if the drive to be famous had been all that positive, and ultimately whether Ivins was going to be honest with herself: "I think she was desperate for recognition in many ways," says Faulk. "Even when she got the recognition, it wasn't . . . it didn't fulfill her needs, because one's needs can only be fulfilled by oneself. If you don't have the ability for any self-introspection and willingness to be honest . . . I don't know. You know, to share with somebody in some shape or form."[20]

Faulk was glad that Ivins would eventually seek a counselor as her drinking and depression reached new dimensions. "I know the person she went to. She basically said [to Ivins], 'If you don't open up, it is a waste of MY time.' The counselor, psychiatrist, said, 'If you are not going to open up, I'm not going to bother with you. You're a waste of my time.' But it's true. I think it [the ultimatum] was supposed to make her do that, for her to say, 'Oh, well, maybe she's got a point.' But it made an excuse for Molly not to have to go. I think the psychiatrist was hoping it would push Molly, but instead she said . . . screw that."[21]

⤛⤜

During the early 1970s, journalists on both coasts were aggressively sifting through LBJ's legacy, to try to fathom the extended, foreign-seeming sociology that gave birth to him, the Kennedy assassination, Billie Sol Estes, John Connally, George H.W. Bush, and the heavy-hitting Big Oil merchants. The *New York Times* was sending R. W. "Johnny" Apple, Jr., to Texas; the *Washington Post* was sending David Broder. They were not alone. There were stories in countless publications, datelined Dallas, Houston,

Austin, that often began with the resonating sense that they were dispatches from correspondents who had parachuted down, hired interpreters and guides, and sent secure-transmission messages back to headquarters. Through Willie Morris's national reputation—through his own work and because he had published Norman Mailer, William Styron, David Halberstam, John Updike, and Arthur Schlesinger, Jr., in *Harper's*—Texas-bound journalists were predisposed to be aware of *The Texas Observer*. In 1971, as the scandal dial spun to Sharpstown, people began scouring Ivins's coverage in the *Observer* for clues. In the early '70s, 15 percent of the magazine's circulation was out-of-state, with the majority of that segment in New York and Washington. John Kenneth Galbraith and Arthur Schlesinger, Jr. were among the subscribers.

The out-of-state reporters had to assume that anyone as frank in print as Molly Ivins would be a hell of a source when they came to town to take notes for their grander, loftier, staid pieces. "All anyone needs to enjoy the state legislature is a strong stomach and a complete insensitivity to the needs of the people. As long as you don't think about what that peculiar body should be doing and what it actually is doing to the quality of life in Texas, then it's all marvelous fun," Ivins reported in her "Notes from a Rookie" piece in March 1971, providing a rundown on her first encounter with the system.[22] In June, with the legislative session winding down, she wrote this: "I tell my hapless auditors that the great failure of American journalism is that it has talked down to the people. I am a democrat, small d, and the people may be misled and bamboozled, but they're not stupid."[23]

⤛⤜

The voice, like it or not, was firmly there. And Northcott was right—it seemed to have emerged fully formed as she headed to Austin from the tundra in Minnesota. There were hints of it as far back as the silly rants from Camp Mystic, the papers on DeGaulle, the way she pushed back on the dopey assignments at the *Tribune*, the smart-ass goodbye speeches at the *Chronicle*. But her first pieces in the *Observer* in the early '70s were already several stages beyond gestation. She was mixing literary asides, Texas café cornpone, imbedded reporting, and personal pronouns to come up with something that arguably had never been done in Texas with any regularity—let alone by a woman. Broder was one of the out-of-state journalists who read Ivins and sought her out on his forays to Austin and elsewhere in Texas:

> I'm a very straight and dull reporter. And she was very lively and so on. Molly was very tough in her political judgment but she always expressed her disdain in the most wonderfully, amazingly funny way. And that was, I think, what was unique about her.
>
> She had a voice that was completely her own. I think what was always fascinating to me about her was the psychology of somebody who had grown up as part of the business and social establishment in Texas and then turned so completely. Ridiculed them and in a lot of ways just reviled them. I don't think I ever understood exactly why her mind, and her life, had taken that turn. But she was unique. . . . She grew up, as you know, very much a daughter of the business and social establishment in Texas. And she came to have utter contempt for those people. Where and how that developed is a story I never heard from her.[24]

Broder and other reporters shared her stories, shipped them back, and talked her up. She was supremely generous, almost always willing to fork over a phone number or a statistic and point someone in the right direction. She liked hanging out with the visiting reporters, she liked hopping in cabs with them and giving them tours around town—to Scholz's, to Soap Creek Saloon, to little barbecue joints and Mexican restaurants on the East Side. She didn't seem intimidated, or a clawing striver, and she talked just the way her pieces read—with a truckload more "shits," "fucks," and "motherfuckers."

She began to do stringing work for the *Washington Post*, filing notes on Sharpstown. When she visited her parents in Maryland, she would stop by the *Post*. By the end of her first year in Austin, she was also routinely getting calls for more speeches and freelance articles. Friends in Minnesota, people she used to work for, were writing letters complaining that she was hard to reach, that she didn't seem to be around.[25] She was developing friendships with writers outside the state—people like Broder, who worked for the powerful outlets and had been on the front lines of the political upheaval, watching Johnson and Nixon at a time when newspapers were reaching almost an historic apex in terms of their reach and their influence on both the process and the fate of the decision-makers. The *Washington Post* and the *New York Times* were pushing each other, doing better investigative work and more sweeping stories about hidden agendas and documents, about hubris, about the Nixonian level of deceit and corruption. Ivins felt the tug to those issues. It seemed to her that Washington was now, more than ever, the news epicenter—and she stayed in close contact with Broder, who was in the middle of it all. She also met Myra MacPherson, the Michigan State–educated journalist who had worked at papers in Detroit as well as at *Vogue*, the *New York Times*, the *Washington Star*, and the *Washington Post*. MacPherson was a reinforcing role model for Ivins. She had been through the long march in the regional newspaper newsrooms; when she started in the business in Detroit, editors tried to exile her to the "women's pages" and she balked. She was informed that women didn't work on the city desk doing hard news reporting. Coming up through the ranks, she saw the way women were treated—denied equal access at events she was covering, and often excluded from positions of power at news organizations. She and Ivins were predisposed to like each other—they were mutual admirers of I. F. Stone, they hated the thought of "women's pages"—and the two became better friends over the years as they intersected with John Henry Faulk, Ronnie Dugger, and other figures they believed had fought the good fight for constitutional liberties and freedom of the press.

⋄

At one of the river campouts, people were finally settling in, setting up the tents, rolling out the sleeping bags, and starting the fires. The lineup was often unpredictable. Friends invited friends and sometimes there were people at the campouts that Ivins didn't know. And then there were the regulars. There was one, a hard drinker who was in her face, following her all the time from one end of the woods to the other. Really, in a way, stalking her.

As nightfall approached, some of the campers saw Ivins walking toward the place where they had pitched their tent.

"Can't you do something about this guy, this drunk who's following me? I never met him when he was sober," said Ivins.

The other campers assured her that he was harmless.

"Well, you might want to go pick him up," said Ivins, pointing to a spot across the campground.

When the campers looked, they saw a body on the ground. She had slugged the man so hard that he passed out in a cactus patch.

CHAPTER SEVEN

Necessary Humor

God Bless Texas.
—BOB BULLOCK

Andy was in town, at the university, and living at a fraternity house. His parents—who called him "Ace"—were worried, as always, about where he was headed. He had been sent to military school in San Antonio and finally was admitted to UT-Austin. Jim Ivins was telling his daughter to keep an eye on her brother. He, in turn, helped to steer his sister to a slightly-more-than-passing interest in the University of Texas football team and at times she was sharing beers with him at the frat house. She knew enough to learn the "hook 'em horns" sign, the fan's salute to the Texas Longhorns.

Meanwhile, she grew especially close to Sara Speights, who had written for the University of Texas student newspaper at the time Northcott was the editor. Northcott brought Ivins to meet Speights one evening. She heard Northcott saying, "Sara, Sara! Wake up; I want you to meet Molly Ivins." She rolled over and looked at a silhouetted figure. There was "this Gigantic Person who was just huge, who went up and up and up and up and all this hair on the top of it. I was, like, my GOD."[1] She found out her birthday and Ivins's birthday were exactly a month apart, and they began a long tradition of celebrating together. The closer they got, the more Ivins shared her background, including thoughts about her parents and their influence on her as a child. Ivins was pushing thirty and wanting to talk about her upbringing, about what it all meant, to a new group of people in Austin. It was hard for people who met her in the early '70s in Austin to believe her when she said that she had once been an introvert. Speights, like Northcott, also knew there were those old family photographs of Ivins that Ivins had kept—the ones where she is demurely staring back at the camera, her hair just so, a pearl necklace around her neck.

Her father and mother were now living in Easton, Maryland, a short drive to good sailing in the Chesapeake, and easier access for those business trips to New York and Washington. He was thinking of winding down from Tenneco, but he still had to fly to Texas for work and sometimes he would ask about coming to see her. He would write in advance of his arrival, his notes phrased almost as a warning that he was headed south. Her friends were surprised by him, by her reaction to him, considering all that she had shared with them. "She had a very jaundiced view of the oil and gas industry," Northcott says. "She insisted that she had heard them fixing prices in her living room. And between that and the fact that he was sort of a Nazi father—she was always intimidated around him. The General was in town and Molly wanted to find a sailboat for him to sail on. When they got one, there was no question that Jim Ivins would be the captain and Molly turned into just the little helper. She half-loved her dad. Maybe she wouldn't have been such a good journalist if she hadn't—that put some drive in her."[2]

Ivins painted a portrait, for her new friends in Austin, of an upbringing that rocked with the wild mood swings of alcoholism: "I certainly got the sense . . . [that] her parents were alcoholic. And the yelling and the screaming. I mean her father, you know, he would come home and the tension would rise. The General was home, you got to pay attention, be on duty," says Speights. "The few times I met him when he would come to Austin, he was constantly evaluating Molly, there was no relaxation, no enjoyment of each other. He was constantly evaluating 'was she doing good enough of this or that or whatever. Is she any good at that, is she any good at this.' I found him very unpleasant . . . he was a horrible, horrible person."[3]

⤛⤚

She began typing up notes for a possible novel, with one character bearing a striking resemblance, behavior-wise, to Bullock. Others seemed to resemble friends, including Bullock's assistant Carlton Carl. The material came from her drinking and bullshit sessions with Bullock. She sometimes took notes as he outlined theories, real and imagined, on how wholesale corruption, payoffs, and bribery in state government took place. She would then go to a typewriter and bang out page after page of a hard-to-follow plot—how various high-ranking state officials liked to get their cash, where the cash was delivered, who the middlemen were. Bullock, who late in life suggested that he had felt remorse about his unhinged moments, unburdened himself in almost staggering ways to Ivins. Dozens and dozens of notes and memos—summoning up names that are now barely dim memories for most people in Texas—were dutifully added to Ivins's growing archives. There is a possibility she was interviewing the melodramatic Bullock so she could use the material for her novel, or maybe for a searing, longer nonfiction book that would shine light on Texas corruption, maybe some magnum opus that would be the end-all and be-all examination of political chicanery in Texas—and maybe she would be Bullock's Boswell and help absolve him by writing his epic confession. Bullock gauged people by their level of loyalty; if someone was loyal to him, he would always remember it. For Bullock to entrust her with enough scalding, confessional tales of high-level, insider-baseball greed, either he had to have been seduced by a master reporter—or he was spinning his stories as part of a wicked spy–double spy chess match that once held supreme logic for him.

Around the same time that she was debriefing Bullock, her friend Larry L. King, the former *Observer* writer whom she would visit in Washington, published *Confessions of a White Racist*. It served as a reminder to her that there were prospects of a literary life outside of Texas—he was a prolific magazine writer and his pieces about Texas were done from a literal distance. His book earned a National Book Award nomination in 1972 and he would go on to write the Broadway play *The Best Little Whorehouse in Texas*. She told friends that she still harbored dreams of living, working, in the Northeast.

⤛⤜

She had survived her first Texas legislative session, writing in 1971 that she was constantly being touched, manhandled, and basically groped every time she set foot in the halls of power—to the point, she noted, where she felt like a roll of Charmin toilet paper. Yet she enjoyed her work: "The legislature wants Jonathan Swift's invective and Dickens's gift with hypocrisy to be well portrayed. I humbly acknowledge that I am inadequate; but I revel in having such a rich field to mine."[4]

Her early work was not often marked by lengthy, drawn-out investigative forays, the painstaking I. F. Stone–type work of sifting through wagonloads of documents to piece together a condemning paper trail. Her own sense was that the place was, as she said, "a zoo" filled with exotic creatures. After a day at the State Capitol, she would step back into the searing heat and sunlight, take the gently rolling slope down to the *Observer* office, and begin writing letters to friends in Minnesota, New York, California, Washington—she invoked a sense of place, talking about the rain, the architecture, the places she liked to drink, the way the streets were laid out, whether the people she was meeting were cheerful, pouting, dour, or smart. It had its roots in her days back at Camp Mystic, when she was unafraid to lambaste the counselors and fix them in a time and place.

She also applied all of that approach to the *Observer* and was writing about politicians in Texas as if she was the same kind of politically attuned field researcher as John Henry Faulk—and it didn't hurt that the people she was covering lent themselves to easy stereotypes. They lived up, or down, to expectations often enough to make the methodology easy to pursue and easy to rationalize. Her mentor Faulk had gone to New York and told his tales about the hinterland; Willie Morris had gone to New York and written about the South. In time, of course, critics would emerge to suggest that she had begun objectifying Texas to an inordinate degree. That her caricatures played well with East Coast intellectual assumptions of what

Texas was really like—and that those assumptions were especially well-received by publishers, reviewers, and social critics who, in fact, had also fled the heartland and who were clearly not native New Yorkers.

In her back-and-forth correspondence with friends throughout the 1960s and early 1970s, there are references to "the wastelands of Texas" and that state's intellectual and cultural deprivations. But if she really did feel a certain regional inferiority, it was often softened by a genuine affection for the things in Texas she deemed good—paddling down the Guadalupe River or the Rio Grande, spending hours under the towering trees at a German beer garden, enjoying the random encounters with a roadrunner skittering across a hot road under a yawning blue sky. She loved, also, the Texas things that she sometimes saw in her mother—the folksiness, the lack of pretense, the almost naïve willingness to open the door to strangers. There were snapshot-like moments that she talked about to a friend or two—walking with her brother when they were kids, laughing with her sister when they ran on the beach.

With her first legislative session over, she submitted her first piece to the *New York Times*—an op-ed in August 1971 about the LBJ presidential library, how expensive it was, how it seemed an intimidating place to try to ferret out the truth about the man. It was a cautionary piece and cautiously written, as if she felt obliged to take a somber approach given the topic and the venue for her piece. Herbert Mitgang, on the *Times* editorial board, wrote her a note: "Dear Miss Ivins: You're not what's wrong with Texas! Thanks for the wonderful article on the liberry [*sic*]." He put a postscript: "Please think about doing another piece for us soon. For example, is there such a thing as Women's Lib in Texas?"[5] His note, with its intentional misspellings and its suggestion that feminism might not exist in Texas, conveyed the impression that New Yorkers really did have a certain view of the Lone Star State.

She was thrilled to be in the *Times*. She collected the letters from friends—including Carlton Carl—who had gotten in touch to say how impressed they were that she had a byline. Getting published in the *Times* moved her closer to considering a move away from Texas. She was regularly confiding to friends that she wanted to leave the *Observer*, to get beyond the perceived limitations in Austin. But she was also aware that she had almost unlimited freedom at the *Observer*. Leaving it would mean paying a price. The same month her first piece appeared in the *Times*, she composed a letter to Jack Cox on *The Texas Observer* stationery:

> Of course it was a great ego trip to have it in the *Times*, but it's been a year since anyone edited my stuff, and I had that same cold-water-in-the-face feeling: god dammit, why do they always rip out the best stuff?
>
> Hmmm, it occurs to me that I may never be able to work for a straight publication again. Doing what you want spoils you so. As for my head—it's recently come to a rather interesting conclusion of its own, even tho I don't give it much time to ponder life these days. I think I told you that I knew shortly after I got back down here that I wouldn't be able to take it for long. I hope to last through the '73 [legislative] session. Then I thought I'd go to the *Wash Post*. Not that the *Post* has any idea I'm about to deposit myself on its collective doorstep. Anyway, I had this brilliant career all mapped out for myself but was becoming more and more restless about it—I string for the *Post* and spend some time there every time I get to DC, twice or thrice a year now since my parents are in Maryland. It's a super high-pressure, competitive paper—and I hate the way they edit my stuff.[6]

Her next op-ed for the *Times*, in October, as per the wishes of Mitgang, was about the quirks and frustrations inherent in the women's liberation movement in Texas. Called "Lib in Longhorn Country," it cleaved to the broad-brush depictions of an uncivilized, sexist Texas that would become a mainstay of her writing for the next thirty-five years. In it she wrote that "Lone Star State Culture is a marriage of several strains of male chauvinism: There is the machismo of our Latino tradition; the Southern belle concept of our Confederate heritage; the pervasive good ol' boyism; the jock idolatry (football is not a game here: it is a matter of blood and death) and, most important, the legacy of the frontier, as it was when John Wayne lived on it." She ended her piece by saying that "it occurs to me, when I consider my more serious sisters in civilized parts, that there may be some advantage in the fact that a sense of humor about men is not a luxury down here: it is a necessity."[7]

In Texas, a joke sometimes made the rounds among the capitol press corps—that there were really only 1,000 or so people who read the daily newspaper dispatches from the legislature. That politicians, other press people, lobbyists, and the hardcore, often academic, political junkies were the only ones who followed it all with any zealous regularity. In the *Observer*, Ivins's voice stood out, almost instantly—it was unlike anything that had appeared before. She skipped beyond the insider baseball jargon, and suggested repeatedly, insistently, that the place was funny—for both good and bad reasons. She seemed to study it, mock it, and make it understandable all at once.

With her work at the *Observer* becoming a form of required reading for people who wanted to understand Texas government, and with her name showing up in the *New York Times*, she was asked to do more guest speaking. Texas A&M University invited her to speak on a panel about the Pentagon Papers with William Hobby, the editor of the *Houston Post*. She was only five years removed from her last internship in Houston—but her name was increasingly recognized. The transition didn't correspond to anything noticeably different in terms of money or lifestyle: Her Mercury was still in and out of the shop, going swimming with friends at Austin's Barton Springs swimming hole was still a weekend highlight. She started a Spanish-language course at the University of Texas at Austin but then quit it. She hung out at funky Austin clubs and restaurants with Richards, Bullock, artist Fletcher Boone, musician Steve Fromholz.

In March 1972, she felt comfortable enough to write an *Observer* piece about her political mentor Bob Bullock: "Bullock's style is an oasis of forthrightness in the desert of mush-mouthed politicians surrounding him. Chain-smoking, popping BC headache powders and prowling around his office, he talks about anything and everything with pleasantly profane candor.

One gets the feeling that he would tell an outright lie with no hesitation if he thought there was good reason for it, but that he would never try to weasel out of a question."[8] Later that same month, she wrote a story about the trial in which the players in the Sharpstown scandal were convicted: "The jury was quintessentially Abilenean. They looked like the cast of *The Grapes of Wrath* with an extra 40 pounds each. Plain people. Sensible people. Not likely to worry much about the fine points of the law."[9]

Finally, also in March 1972, she was the headline speaker at the Penney-Missouri Awards banquet at the University of Missouri School of Journalism. When the school noted her appearance, it quoted from correspondence she had embarked on with Ed Diamond, a former senior editor at *Newsweek*: "I think women's pages are going to have to address themselves to the image of the ideal woman in this country. But right now the image seems to be a big-bosomed blonde who has the whitest wash on the block and no dishpan hands. Is that what we really want? If we don't want to become like stereotypic males, aggressive and domineering, what kind of human beings do we want to make of ourselves?"[10]

For the *Observer*, she would write essays about the still-mostly-pristine rivers of West Texas and explore the time-warp way in which the good parts of the extended Central Texas area seemed affixed to another era (German immigrants had settled there in the nineteenth century). She wrote, really, about whatever she felt like and then wove it back to Texas. When the brilliant alcoholic poet John Berryman committed suicide, she composed an obituary filtered through their encounters in Minnesota. Given her own problems with alcohol, the obituary has a painful relevance: "I suppose you should read him because John Berryman knew and wrote about pain, love, sorrow, guilt, fear, delusion and misty Irish mornings with the concreteness of the cold tiles on the bathroom floor under your knees when you lean to vomit into the john of a morning. Because there is more to life than Texas and politics and the tire special on at Sears, and were it not for poets, we might forget that."[11]

She took exceedingly careful notes when sources contacted the *Observer* to check into the controversial death of a black man in Pittsburg, Texas. She did the same for a piece about the Joe Louis Addition in Fort Worth, a place where black residents had been exiled with no sewer service, paved roads, or city water lines. Those two stories underscored the strengths she displayed while stepping far away from the easy drolleries offered up by the State Capitol. In Fort Worth, she did a vivid, sad portrait of a place that had once been optimistically labeled a Garden of Eden—until it fell victim to the usual planned pattern of horrendous neglect by the city and state and federal government. She visited the urban hellhole and spent time talking to people and touring the place; then she offered the reader intimate details: "The outhouses tilt drunkenly and seem to stagger preparatory to falling down entirely. Flies and roaches infest them. There is one streetlight in Joe Louis and two tiny churches. One outdoor, cold-water faucet provides all the water for three families. Broken glass, old tires and all manner of junk litters the edges of small plots where the razed houses remain in heaps."[12]

Her attention to aching details emerged in various articles, here and there, but not usually as the all-encompassing directive behind magazine-length narrative exposition. She was, in her way, preparing for life as a columnist—not a narrative nonfiction, long-form writer. The reporting details she would use in her stories—the fact that a Dr. Pepper clock was ticking away in a Texas courthouse, or that the men in Russia who had been sent to fix her hotel TV were behaving as though they were in a "Chinese fire drill"—were dotted into her essays but they were not part of a huge, unfolding, chronologically ordered narrative. She was sprinting, as her editors would later put it, not pausing for book-length journalism or imbedding herself into a piece for several months at a time. As one of her editors said, it was hard to picture her in a writer's garret for months on end. She wrote quickly, almost spontaneously, and she often wrote about things happening that moment, that day, that week.

Her calendars from the early and mid-1970s show an increasingly crowded schedule—freelance deadlines, speeches, and awards ceremonies. She was becoming an expert as well as an ally of the well-known members of the liberal political vanguard in the state—the office holders and activists such as Barbara Jordan, Sissy Farenthold, Billie Carr, Craig Washington. The more conservative power players—including those like

Charlie Wilson who would trip into national prominence for immensely conflicted reasons—were also buttonholing her and inviting her out for drinks.

Well into 1972, she was still stringing for the *Washington Post*. *Newsday* had hired her to write a piece on the political scene in Texas—and an editor there apologized to her for sacrificing "style and form for content." Max Frankel at the *New York Times* wanted more op-ed work. She wrote for a variety of small publications and she also drew up lists of places where she wanted to appear with regularity: *The Nation*, *Harper's*, *The New Republic*, *The Progressive*. She spent hours reading work in a variety of magazines that she either subscribed to or pored over at the Austin Public Library. She filled up folders with hundreds of articles she had clipped out.

She had mentioned former *Observer* editor Robert Sherrill in the first essay she had done for the *Observer*, and she had read his 1968 book about Minnesota's Hubert Humphrey, *Drug Store Liberal*, when she was at the *Tribune*. Sherrill was another early role model, along with Morris and Dugger, for ways to tackle what she was increasingly calling progressive journalism. He could filter the intimate details of what seemed to be happening in Texas and set them against a bigger, more informed historic and intellectual context. In her early years at the *Observer*, she was putting faces to writer's names, such as Sherill's, that she hadn't seen since her teens and getting a conspiratorial thrill by reading the publication at Margaret Sher's house in Houston.

The *Observer*, especially under Dugger's guidance, had strived for a certain assured, knowing tone, even a literary quotient, and it consistently avoided the slap-dash feel of the underground press alternatives in the state. She took that to heart, especially after meeting John Henry Faulk and Maury Maverick, Jr., and the other older liberals who had slogged away in various ways in the Texas trenches and could connect her to the original themes, ideals, of the *Observer*. Ivins read the back issues that Sherrill and Willie Morris had written and edited. The history of progressive journalism hadn't been lingered on during her education at Columbia. But she was clearly working backwards—she continued to follow Newfield's work at *The Village Voice*, she read Sherrill's pieces in *The Nation*, she looked north to Oklahoma City and the work being done by tough independent journalist Forrest "Frosty" Troy, who basically ran a one-man version of *The Texas Observer*. She read more about William Brann, the nineteenth-century journalist from Texas who had published *Iconoclast* and was famous for witty, deadly attacks on both the well-heeled and religious fanatics—until he was shot in the chest by an angry reader. Brann's one-liner—that the only trouble he had with Baptists was that they weren't held under water long enough—was the kind of humor Ivins would increasingly appreciate.

After writing stories in Minnesota about roofing shingles, Maureen Reagan, and bartending school, she was working at a place with a serious connection to a serious journalism tradition—in a state where the mainstream dailies could hardly lay claim to one, long tradition of independent work. Her tenure at *The Texas Observer* also put her in touch with a self-aware, intellectual liberal circle that had not just lionized its regional and local heroes but suggested they belong in the same breath as I. F. Stone, Upton Sinclair, and H. L. Mencken. The net effect, for Ivins, was a sense that she was an heir to an honorable, iconoclastic tradition—but one that she was going to pursue with a voice, a style, that channeled her mother's absurdism, her friend Nancy Dowd's mocking surrealism, the rattlesnake bite of Bob Bullock, the dry pacing of Ann Richards, and the all-purpose lampooning of Samuel Clemens. "It was a different kind of thing. It was a style difference. She made it more accessible. It was the beginning of the Molly column. She just knew what to do with it, from the start," says Northcott.[13]

Ivins might have been the only *Observer* editor who was perfectly fluent in French, studied in France, immersed herself in DeGaulle and French cooking. But there was also Ann Richards, a daughter of rural Texas who was charting a course toward elected office, serving as a reminder of the practical benefits of retaining a modicum of interest and even delight in what some once called Southern mores. Richards could flip the switch, in a nanosecond, and praise the pecan pie she was being served in Dime Box, Texas, all with a cascade of "howdys" and "y'alls." Bullock had done a better job memorizing the book of Lone Star political chicanery, but Richards was far less coarse, in public, and she knew how to work the front room even better than the back room. As Ivins developed her style, she was being guided by the Sonny Liston and Muhammad Ali of Texas politics: Bullock was a stone-faced marauder, and Richards was a charmer.

There were other links, too—even that wealthy patron saint of the *Observer*, Bernard Rapoport in Waco. Ivins drove up to see him, knocked on the door of his home in Waco. Rapoport wanted to know more about her background. He teased her that their fathers were different—his was a communist—and that she surely couldn't be radical enough.

That summer she and Northcott decided to attend the Democratic National Convention in Miami. They pooled their money and talked to politicians who were going. They had become close friends and supporters of Sissy Farenthold, the Texas state representative who was hoping to secure the vice presidential nomination. In Miami, Ivins called David Broder, who had become an increasingly-closer friend and mentor. That year he was accumulating the stories that would win him a Pulitzer in 1973. She had no money, she never had enough money. Northcott still thought Ivins would overspend whatever she had left over from their crappy *Observer* paychecks.

"Can I crash in your room?" she asked Broder.

"Are you serious?" Broder said.

"Yeah, nobody's paying my way here and I'm just looking for places that I can crash," replied Ivins.

"Of course, you're welcome to do it," he told her.

A thought flashed in Broder's mind: "My God, this is a terrific journalist and she shouldn't have to be bumming floor space at night to cover a convention."[14]

Years later, in an interview, Broder said: "I would say we were friends. Whenever I got to Texas, I would look her up. And later, when she came East to work, we'd see each other occasionally. Mainly when we found ourselves covering the same story. As I mentioned, there was that one weird time when she was looking for a place to crash." He added that, "no," he and Ivins never dated.[15]

⇝

In the fall of 1972, she decided to apply for a Nieman Foundation Fellowship at Harvard but was rejected in early 1973—the curator, James Thomson, Jr., scrawled a message at the bottom of his rejection letter saying "Sorry about this . . . now perhaps we can get you here as a Nieman speaker instead of a Fellow?" There was a sense, perhaps, that she was not a reporting heavyweight, at least not in the "classic" sense of the reporters the Nieman Foundation normally awarded the fellowship. She had clearly wanted to win the fellowship; it was something that people she had worked with at Houston and in Minneapolis had done. She had asked Dugger to write her a letter of support:

> She is, most noticeably, a good and serious reporter, a good and witty writer, and a good and unpompous person. That is, these are the things about her that became very clear to me from my examination of her work before she came to the *Observer* and from talking with her antecedent to her move here, and which have been borne out, causing me no surprise, during her work here. Rather than despair, she laughs; rather than curse, she works; rather than take herself too seriously, she writes with lilting informality and penetrating and irreverent wit. She has broken important stories, exposed comic derelictions, enlivened her yeoman journalism with wit instructive to serious social purposes, become an important person in the collective highly vulnerable conscience of the regional press corps, and attracted the respect, interest, and assignments from representatives of the enlightened national media. So much for what is obvious to us here.
>
> Since I started the *Observer* 19 years ago, I have worked with many good people on it. Two of these people and Molly I would say are even, at her age, in their talent and promise as writers: the other two are Willie Morris and Bill Brammer. None of the others come near these three as writers. . . . Best of all, she knows that to deepen her work now, she needs respite to deepen her knowledge of the

> Southwestern underculture and of the economic power structure of the United States. I hope you will let her come and do this at Harvard.

⥈

"She was always self-conscious about the way she looked but not so self-conscious to get her hair fixed—there were just other things to do," says Northcott. "She had all the equipment to look gorgeous, 'but wouldn't you want to go on a motorcycle ride?'"[16] Increasingly, the primary thing Ivins wanted to do was work for the *New York Times*. In September 1973, she produced a 6,000-word piece for the Sunday magazine section about the new, giant airport being built in the Dallas–Fort Worth area. It was a straight magazine piece, with plenty of statistics, quotes, a hint of controversy, and enough "Timesian sweep" to suggest that the airport was a metaphor for America, Texas, and big business. She followed up with a short *Times* op-ed piece in October, musing on "style" in Texas—about how she drank Gallo because she couldn't afford expensive drinks, about how people in Texas talked about buying their haute couture at J.C. Penney.

Meanwhile, her speaking schedule was becoming constant, and from the mid-1970s on she fielded constant inquiries from civil liberties groups, church groups, and universities—to the degree that it became a significant adjunct to her income. Friends who heard her speak said that she was developing an almost seamless style. "She was honing her skills. I think it's innate—she is an innate storyteller," says Northcott.[17] She was giving more speeches outside the state and those public appearances coincided with a lingering fascination about Texas. She was doing the same thing in her speeches that she did in her essays, telling stories as if she was a *National Geographic* explorer just back from a lost civilization. And in the process she continued to confirm, for many people who heard her, what they had expected about Texas—that it was deadly serious but surreal, insular, to the point of black humor.

The *Times* took note of that growing national reputation and editors let her know that she was already on the short list for a reporting position. Her friends knew that she liked appearing in the *Times*, that it pleased her father—a lot more than being in the *Chronicle*, the *Tribune*, or the *Observer*. He wasn't a fan of the *Times*, but he liked the thought of her being in a powerful paper, a national paper. She didn't want to work for the regional mainstream papers, and she wasn't interested in the new, slick *Texas Monthly* magazine—she joked about the magazine, about how it was concerned with "designer sheets" and how its creators were earnestly trying to ape things being done by Clay Felker and other New York editors. Besides, she wanted to be nationally known, and it was still hard to do that from Texas. "You know, she said some things to Kaye, more than me, that being famous was very important to her. That she wanted to be famous, that that was a goal for her," says Sara Speights. "She told Kaye very directly it was a goal of hers."[18]

Throughout the summer of 1973, her relationship with her father remained inflexible, even with her growing reputation. The friends saw it and wondered what impact it was having on her. They knew she liked to shut down, to get far away into the distant, lonely parts of Texas—she was going on those floats down the rivers of Texas with Dave and Ann Richards, university botanists and archeologists, in seventeen-foot aluminum canoes. It was a far cry from her father's sailboats.

Some friends also decided that, early on, she had developed an ability to compartmentalize. It was that way with recreation, her drinking, her work. They were in different zones; she didn't allow them to overlap, to conflict. And there was a special compartment reserved for her father. She could go toe-to-toe with Bullock and even knock him to the ground, but her father still had a lingering ability to shake her. Her friends, especially Sara Speights, thought the family had an enormously complex dynamic—that her father might simply have resented her for not being born a boy:

> This was The General, you are supposed to do it his way, everything, you are supposed to do it his way. They were out at sea, something weird happened, a storm came up and he broke his arm and he sailed all the way back in without complaining of a broken arm. Molly's greatest sin was not being a male. And finally they had Andy. And all eyes were on Andy. Andy could do no wrong and he [the father] could never quit criticizing Molly and Sara. Andy could just crash 48 cars

> and it was all okay. It's just boys being boys. Molly loved Andy. They were good friends, they were really very fond of each other, they both remember walking to school every day, stuff like that. It was just that Molly couldn't do anything right as far as her father was concerned.

And if she complained to her mother, or sought her backing, it often wasn't helpful: "I will tell you what Molly told me, what hit her. After all this . . . her mother's response after all this was 'well, you should have set the table correctly.' All that would have been hard to live with, can you imagine. Here you are becoming the belle of the ball, you are becoming famous in a very positive way and your parents are still doing this to you."

The sticking points in her relationship with her mother, who would still scold her for smoking, cursing, and not behaving more politely, seemed to linger as she hit thirty. "It was one of those things that she couldn't solve and she knew that intellectually, but it was still painful for her," says Speights.[19] Her mother made sure to send out Ivins family Christmas cards decorated with little national maps showing where everyone was living—and she peppered her notes to Ivins with thoughts about men who might be suitable for her. Her mother was also sending her letters written while she and Jim Ivins were on long sailing trips, telling her that "there is a very nice young man aboard, aged 25, and I keep matchmaking . . . he is earnest and so nice and so kind. I do wish you were here because he's so nice. I know you'd be bored stiff but it's better to be bored with a kind person than entertained by a misunderstood jackass know-it-all."[20] She mentioned that as part of their sailing trip down the Eastern seaboard, headed to the Bahamas, they were stopping in a variety of cities, including Charleston, South Carolina:

"It doesn't seem to have the harsh decadence or the queers that New Orleans has."[21]

⋯

By her second legislative session in 1973, Ivins had gained weight; she was pushing toward 180 pounds and trying to lose some of it. She was, still, really the only woman in the room: "Molly made conscious decisions on who she wanted to become—and she became who she wanted to be—so yes, she wanted to be a writer, she wanted to be famous. How do you get recognized? Well, humor—that worked for her and so she honed it and honed it and honed it. But she also wanted to be gracious, all these things she wanted, and she became it and she did it. In spite of everything, in spite of her family, in spite of everything, it was pretty impressive," says Speights.[22]

She began to support Frances "Sissy" Farenthold, who, with Barbara Jordan, had opened several doors for women in Texas politics. At first Farenthold, more than Jordan, seemed accessible. Jordan, the first black woman to serve in the Texas senate and the first black woman from the South to serve in the U.S. House of Representatives, scared Ivins until they got to know each other better. On freelance assignment for the *Washington Post*, Ivins went to see the commanding Jordan right after she was sent to Congress in the early 1970s.

"God, Congresswoman, have you ever thought about running for statewide office?" Ivins asked her.

Jordan stared at her and boomed in a deep voice: "Barbara Jordan run for statewide office? A black woman run for statewide office in Texas?"

Ivins recoiled and said: "Well, you know, Sissy Farenthold ran for governor, and she almost won and she is a woman."

Jordan retorted: "Sissy is a white."[23]

Farenthold served as a state representative and then launched two campaigns for governor. She and Ivins bonded almost immediately when Ivins met her at the State Capitol: "I always felt that Molly held her own. She gave that impression. I gained the notion that if women stayed in the same place, you could be a pet. I think that's Southern. For example, I was in the legislature, the only woman. They worried about what to give me as a favor—they gave me a bowtie instead of a long tie. And on Valentine's Day, they read a poem to me. I could have had a little niche as a pet, but I didn't go that way. Molly and I had that in common."[24]

Farenthold also suspected, especially in later years, that there was an inherent loneliness to Ivins. She was extraordinarily generous, she always seemed to remember to bring a gift to someone's child, she hosted slumber parties for reporter Dave "Moose" McNeely's daughter, she lavished attention on older people—but maybe being a writer had made her lonely at some core level. By 1974, other friends were concerned. Ivins was well on her way to being a highly functioning alcoholic, someone recognized for an ability to drink hard and crank out endless reams of copy. She was standing in the back corridors of the capitol, in the Quorum Club, near the well-stocked private bars the legislators kept in their state offices. "Molly was very disciplined. . . . I can remember guys being incredibly impressed that she had drunk them under the table, but it was also, all that social interaction is where she got a hell of a lot of her ideas, it's where a lot of her good lines developed."[25]

⋘⋙

At one of the campouts held by liberal politician Bob Armstrong, Ivins had started drinking early. It was getting cold and she was already drunk when she crawled into Speight's station wagon with another six-pack. She and Speights drank some more while they turned the car on and tried to stay warm. Suddenly, the door flew open. Northcott was staring at them. She had bolted over to the station wagon, maybe fearing the worst—that Speights and Ivins had passed out in the car and asphyxiated.

"Well, fuck you two!" Speights heard Northcott shout.

And Ivins and Speights turned to each other: "What did we do now?"

They convulsed in laughter as Northcott stormed away. Speights knew that Northcott would get mad at her and Ivins for drinking. And with Ivins, Speights was often laughing until it almost hurt: Ivins was beginning to try out lines for her stories and speeches on her. Somehow, a lot of it was bound up with alcohol:

> Oh, I had lines tested out on me so many times, and then a lot of my own lines ended up in her stories, but she did a good job with it. I mean, I guess one of the things they used to say about alcohol is: If you're an alcoholic, alcohol is your lover. Those years when Molly was sober, she was still too damn shy to get in a relationship . . . it [being sober] didn't change things.
>
> The times the alcohol horrified her was when she embarrassed herself in a social situation, but it never interfered with her work.[26]

⋘⋙

In 1974, Ivins applied for the Harvard Nieman Fellowship again, this time with a letter of recommendation from David Broder, who by then had won his Pulitzer for political reporting. She was rejected again (this rejection letter noted that it was a "pleasure for all of us to talk with you in Washington"). After this latest failed attempt to get to Harvard, she threw herself into freelance work. She became a frequent contributor to the *Civil Liberties Review*, thought about a standing invitation from *New Times* assistant editor Frank Rich (who would later become a *New York Times* columnist) to be their Austin correspondent, and fielded offers from *Harper's* to do some work there. Larry Burns with *Harper's* sent his inquiry to the *Civil Liberties Review*, after seeing one of her articles. An editor at the *Review* promptly wrote Ivins a note: "Fuck them! If you're going to do any occasional writing, do it on civil liberties themes and give it to us."[27]

She wrote a note to herself on her thirtieth birthday, August 30, 1974:

> It's raining but that's not depressing. I really think I shall quit smoking today, but if I manage to find this essay on Aug. 30, 2004, I should like to think the biggest mistake I have made in the first 30 years of my life was to start drinking and keep drinking. . . . Still feel that my life is not set as I certainly expected it to be when I was 20. I wonder how much one forgets? About the way one feels or felt. Shall I not be able to remember what it was like, this being 30? . . . If I'm not hungover on my 60th birthday, I should like to do some comparisons. I suppose I really do feel like an adult. Responsible for myself, got to clean up my act and fly right.[28]

She did another 6,000-word piece in November for the *Times* Sunday magazine, a profile of the city of Austin; it was, again, essentially a straight piece, with the requisite he-said–she-said journalism. She quoted her friends and she talked about crime, music, recreation, and the university. It was standard-issue reporting with just enough of that Timesian arching overview to suggest that Austin affectionately embodied a part of America that was eternally young, Peter Pan–like, never wanting to grow up.

The next month, her name resonated both with journalists and with members of the Christian right when she and the *Observer* were sued for $5 million in libel damages by preacher Lester Roloff, based on work she had done covering his controversial children's homes in Texas—and Kaye Northcott would later write that he was probably going to sue if just for the fact that Ivins had called him a "stud hoss evangelizer." She told friends she knew she had her story right, but that she was worried about the way a libel trial might go in Texas. As the case dragged on, she called Terry O'Rourke for legal help, and the suit was eventually settled out of court for $2,000. In some quarters, the net effect was that Ivins was seen as a crusading heartland journalist who had gone through the nagging but honorable libel wars with reactionary forces deep in the heart of Texas. The *Observer* was saddled with legal bills for almost $50,000, which put a shadow, for a while, over the publication's finances.

Meanwhile, Northcott wondered whether Ivins was watching her own money, or spending it too fast. She was, in fact, giving away her money—reaching for the check, buying small gifts for friends, somehow remembering children's birthdays by bringing an adventure book, a book of poems, a picture book. She never seemed to have any money left over. "She was doing features and speeches from the minutes she got here. I lived fine on our salary and Molly couldn't. I wondered if she overspent and that was her excuse for freelancing. But she always wanted to write, she was always pressing forward. If the *Washington Post* called, she was always going to answer."[29] And there was an inside joke welling up among her friends as they gathered under the stars at Scholz's for another beer blast, that she was just waiting for the *Times* to call her, to make a full-time offer—that she was like Delta Dawn waiting, with her bags packed, for the phone to ring, the knock to come at the door. The star *Times* reporters were still asking for her when they visited, including R. W. "Johnny" Apple, Jr.: "She felt obliged, I think, to work at the *Times*. She had come out of Smith. There was this sense of inevitability about the *Times*. Johnny Apple would want to take her to dinner. It was, somehow, just bred into her. You know, you had to get away, I mean from Texas. There wasn't anything else to do here. The *Times* was the paper to be on," says Northcott.[30]

In May 1975, Ivins had a blow-out story in *The Atlantic*, a long piece about the legislature, "the fun house" in Austin. (Her mother wrote to her that she had seen the piece and approved of her presence in the magazine.) In the summer, she began working on a piece for the *Times* about John Connally and his many conflicts—and she almost immediately began a back-and-forth exchange with editors about cutting the story, changes in tone, and a new ending. In November 1975, she wrote a sidebar in the *Observer*—a companion piece to a lengthy, critical story that Northcott had done on the University of Texas journalism program. She talked about her memories of Columbia, of being in New York, of how she got started: "We were good and knew it; thought of ourselves 'the best and the brightest.' God knows, a little more humility wouldn't have hurt. But I still think journalism is a profession sadly in want of change. I still can't tell Bodoni Bold from a sans serif, but when I get hold of *The New York Times*. . . ."[31]

The next month, through her allegiances to Faulk, Dave Richards, and other people whose lives and work had touched on First Amendment issues, she flew to San Francisco to speak to the ACLU at its Bill of Rights Celebration. She was touted on the front page of *ACLU News* in a story that began with a description of her as "one of the funniest writers in America." Before her speech at the Sheraton-Palace Hotel, she was interviewed by the *Oakland Tribune*: "Being a left-liberal in Texas is a little like being an early Christian. . . . I decided that if I was going to be a liberal, I would be the worst kind, a bleeding heart. My heart bleeds quite frequently, I must admit. . . . Objective reporting is a pernicious concept, a holy grail, a myth."[32] During her trip to the West Coast, she stopped to interview Ericka Huggins about a community school started by members of the Black Panther Party.

And when she got back to Texas, she told people that she was going to accept a job if the *New York Times* offered one to her. "Maybe she could never please her father. There was just still a bias toward the East Coast. New York was the place. That was where all the good journalists were. And there was no value in regionalism—if it wasn't published in New York, it didn't count for anything," says Northcott. Some friends were wary, wondering if she'd be able to do in New York what she had done so gleefully in Texas. "She was naïve enough to think they were going to let her continue."[33]

Some other friends were coalescing into the Horse's ASSociation and holding forth at Scholz's, carrying pitchers of beer across the hardwood planks of the old bar between the university and the capitol. Ivins swam at Deep Eddy Pool, another spring-fed marvel in the heart of the city, and when she was done, she would walk up the hill to Deep Eddy Cabaret and slip into the dark bar. She drove to the little towns like Winedale, LaGrange, and Luckenbach. One night, when Commander Cody and His Lost Planet Airmen were playing at the Armadillo World Headquarters—the shrine for all that was good and pure about music in Texas, and where you could hear Freddie King, Frank Zappa, Shiva's Headband, Gram Parsons—she found herself onstage. Jim Franklin, the cosmic Austin artist, was at the microphone, telling the crowd that he had someone in the audience who wrote stories for the *New York Times*. He introduced Ivins: She had dressed up in a stuffy, buttoned-down outfit—a *New York Times* outfit—and the mellowed-out crowd laughed and cheered. Texas, she told people, was almost too much fun. It was, in its way, stuck in a time warp. Disco wasn't dead in Austin; it had never really been born.

Whatever was happening in the bigger cities was indeed often bypassing Austin. It was still a college town in many ways; it hadn't yet morphed into a "high-tech" wonderland with massive suburban sprawl, though that was coming. It was very white; the minority population was still minuscule compared to Dallas and Houston. It was a music mecca, and people were following Willie Nelson there, fleeing the slicked-back Nashville sound and the California cocaine conceits. People in Austin played something called redneck rock; they liked to spend all day floating on the San Marcos River and to slip out to small towns to dance alongside old folks and stowaways from the city. Austin was also still very safe, a low-crime city, and it wasn't ever going to fall into the death grip of crack or develop a cancerous, rotting urban core. The Armadillo World Headquarters seemed to symbolize a lot—it brought the best musicians to Texas, it was filled with smoke and giggles, and the audience still wore headbands and beaded vests. It was a sort of high holy church in Groover's Paradise; there wasn't another scene like it in the country. And at concerts it was hard to predict who would come in the door—Dennis Hopper, Larry L. King, Billy Lee Brammer, musician Ray Wylie Hubbard, author Pete Gent (who had written *North Dallas Forty*), Willie and his posse. Austin left an increasingly indelible impression on Ivins, one that would resonate long after she moved to New York, one that would eventually lure her back.

She threw herself into getting Ann Richards elected as a Travis County commissioner, doing the kind of fundraising and politicking that would have made the editors in Minnesota insane. In November 1975 she suggested to Richards that she host a dinner party at her house. "Annie—I propose three events to get you started off here." She would invite reporters from the *Houston Post* and the *Dallas Times Herald* though "neither of them can do any good for you in terms of press coverage. It's their respective spouses you should meet."[34]

The spouses could provide fundraising assistance for Richards; they could help her hit up the people who lived in the fancy homes in Austin, and who could also walk her through some political infighting at the local level.

⋘⟷⋙

Ivins decided to apply for a Dobie Paisano Fellowship, named in honor of Texas literary patriarch J. Frank Dobie. The fellowship allowed writers to live for a few months at the bucolic Paisano ranch, set on a creek and draped by limestone cliffs, presumably to work on an important book. You had to be a native Texan, to have lived in Texas for at least three years, or to have written something significant about Texas to qualify. If you had literary aspirations in Texas, this fellowship was something you wanted to pursue, and it seemed that everyone who was applying knew each other. Billy Porterfield, whom Ivins had known in Houston and who competed with her for the editorship of the *Observer*, had won a Paisano.

In January 1976, she had just finished her last big freelance piece for the *Times*, a long take on Morris Udall for the Sunday magazine ("Liberal from Goldwater Country"). The piece was serious and sweeping in scope and it perhaps suggested to *Times* editors that she was more than just one of the "funniest" writers in America. Some of her original, edgier bits of writing were edited out and when the story appeared on February 1, it certainly appeared to be closer to what she ruefully called "objective" journalism. The piece, and the way she succumbed to the editing, might have reassured the *Times* that she would be a willing foot soldier. She had had a good run with the *Times* as a freelance writer. The stories were heavily edited, toned down, but they were about things she cared about, and they showed up as columns on the op-ed page or, occasionally, as literary-minded centerpieces in the Sunday magazine. The op-ed columns, especially, resembled what her *Observer* readers had come to expect. Her voice, though a bit muted for the *Times*, was still recognizable now and then.

The *Times* finally made her a full-time job offer, just as the Udall piece was set to run, but she told editors that she had to think about it, that the Dobie Paisano fellowship selection wouldn't take place until April. In February, the same week her Udall piece appeared, she got a letter from the *Times*:

> Dear Molly,
>
> We have discussed your situation and have decided that we are willing to wait until April 1 to see whether you have received that fellowship you mentioned. We think you're crazy not to rush into our arms now, but we are willing to wait until then and talk about a job. I would hope that if you did not get the fellowship that you would be free to move quickly, assuming you and we were satisfied on the terms.
>
> That was a good piece on Mo Udall.
>
> Hope you lose the fellowship.
>
> Sincerely, Peter Millones, Assistant Managing Editor[35]

CHAPTER EIGHT

The You Know What

The Times *has done its best possible to clean up my act.*

—MOLLY IVINS

In April 1976, Ann Richards sent out goodbye-party notices, arrangements were made for a cake, and a fake front page of the *Times* was designed as a parting gift. There were other little dinner parties around town. Ivins heard from people she hadn't heard from in a long time. She wouldn't get a Dobie Paisano fellowship, she wouldn't be staying in Texas, she was officially leaving the *Observer*. Most of the people who were calling her about her "New York news" were well-wishers, but there were a few skeptics, people who held or presumed enough friendship to suggest to her that going to the *Times* in the summer would be a horrible mistake—that the paper wasn't enlightened enough to tolerate someone as free-thinking as Ivins. Some suggested that it would be one thing for the paper to receive the "letters from Texas" that Ivins was sending, and that were maybe helping to reinforce some sense of sophisticated superiority among her New York editors, but it would be another thing entirely to have Molly Ivins—who smoked, drank hard, and had a dog named Shit—working at a place where more than one or two men still wore bow-ties and subscribed to a hushed, formal Ivy League air. She could talk DeGaulle and French history with anyone, but would she want to do it all the time? What about when she wanted to wear the denim work shirts that she and Northcott had worn to the State Capitol, or wanted to go barefoot in the office, or wanted to say whatever the hell she wanted to say in her copy? Her six years at the *Observer* were, she once said, "the happy golden period of sunshine, laughter and beer and living considerably below the poverty line."[1]

She drew up a list of things she needed to do: Write to the alumni associations at Smith and Columbia and let them know her address was changing. Do the same thing with the magazines she was reading—*Life*, *Newsweek*, *Ski*, *Harper's*, *The Atlantic*, *Foreign Affairs Quarterly*, *Bazaar*, *Esquire*, *Rolling Stone*, *Chicago Journalism Review*, *Columbia Journalism Review*. She packed up the letters she had been keeping, the ones she had written, received, and the ones she had never sent. She had remained a pack rat, a mole. She thought, long and hard, about what to do with Shit. The black beast was from a litter of puppies from Northcott's dog. She once had a little glob of shit on her and that helped to inspire her name—along with Ivins's suggestion that the dog wobbled when she walked, that she looked shit-faced drunk. The animal had become, in her way, the office mutt and she decided she would take her to New York.

Her friends passed around a piece of paper at the goodbye party, filling in their names and phone numbers and putting at the top a note that said "when you need a little solid conversation, call collect." The first names on the list were Dave and Ann Richards. Farther down was Congressman Charlie Wilson, someone Ivins was fascinated with.

Not going to the Dobie Paisano ranch was softened by the news that she had won the 1976 alumni award from the Columbia Graduate School of Journalism. It was one more thing that leaned her toward New York, maybe some sense that she was appreciated there. Ivins's award noted her "fight against corruption, ignorance and indifference without losing either her sense of outrage or her sense of humor." In May, she was looking at apartments on Morton Street in Greenwich Village and trying to figure out why her Toyota—she called it Hiroshima's Revenge—had been towed and impounded during her first week in the city. She was going through orientation, officially preparing for the city desk at the *Times*. Broder had sent her a letter saying, "I'm glad you are branching out. I wish it was our paper. You will be a smash, I'd forget the sleeping pills."

Her goodbye column appeared in the *Observer*:

"I'll remember sunsets, rivers, hills, plains, the Gulf, woods, a thousand beers in a thousand joints, and sunshine and laughter. And people. . . . Mostly I'll remember people."

⋘⋙

Her first story that summer as a full-time *Times* staffer was a breaking news item: "More than 300,000 gallons of tar-like fuel oil that spilled from an oil barge grounded yesterday in the St. Lawrence Seaway spread slowly today through the Thousand Islands resort area, but cleanup crews were beginning to contain the spill."[2] Her next story ran three days later: "John Lowenthal, Rutgers University law professor who has acted at times as Alger Hiss's lawyer, asserts that newly released F.B.I. documents show that the agency covered up evidence helpful to Mr. Hiss concerning the date of the manufacture of the Woodstock typewriter in the case."[3]

It was a plunge back to her early days in Minnesota and far different from the personal-pronoun essays she had written for the *Times* editorial page, or the long balls she was hitting for the Sunday magazine. Her stories for the next month were about preparations to restore the U.S. Custom House for the big American bicentennial celebration; Democrats meeting at a Shirley MacLaine show; a history piece about vice presidents; New Yorkers hosting soirees for Democratic national convention delegates; an obituary for sports writer Paul Gallico; a show devoted to cows and cow sculptures at the Queens Museum in Flushing Meadows; federal public works money that was owed to New York City; how Westchester was mobilizing against dart-gun attacks. And, finally, on the last day of July, she was assigned to a straight-ahead story about the conservative Young Americans for Freedom convention.

She was prolific, writing the short daily stories at the same pace she had done them at the *Tribune*: a piece on politicians who were pissed off about "electronic flagpoles," firemen riding out some bad weather, the long wait that fans of pop singer Peter Lemongello had to endure before they could get his new record. There were moments when she did work that cut closer to the *Observer* pieces she'd done on the racial divide: She went to Staten Island and wrote a late-August 1976 piece about a black family whose home had been broken into by a gang of white youths. The next month she was in Washington, writing about Milan's La Scala Opera making its American debut: "Milan's renowned La Scala Opera made its historic debut in America here last night before an audience that was both glittering and demanding."[4]

Her friends in Texas—ones who had grown fiercely loyal to her, and, in part, had rallied around her as a tireless drinking buddy, civil libertarian, Hill Country camper, and voice of the only liberal-progressive-populist publication of any influence in the Southwest—were not so much dismayed as they were concerned when they picked up the paper. In August, *Editor & Publisher* wrote a 500-word piece for its "News People in the News" section and featured her. The article asked whether a "woman journalist from Texas who likes to drink Lone Star beer can really be happy as a *New York Times* reporter."

She answered: "Yes sir. The place is more fun than the law allows."

She added: "I thought I would meet pompous people everywhere at *The Times*. But instead I've run into some pretty regular folks."

The writer asked about managing editor Abe Rosenthal. She said: "He's not what you'd think of as a company man. But a man who loves the *New York Times*, and its dedication to excellent journalism."

She wondered about the way she dressed at the paper: "I really didn't know if the blue work shirts that I was used to wearing at the *Observer* were going to be acceptable dress at *The Times*. But I've decided to compromise, and so I make certain they're pressed before I go to work." She was also concerned about the uniformity of the internal memos: "I recently sent a memo to three editors, addressed to their full names, only to have it returned, indicating that the memo style was Mr., Mr., Mr. . . . " She said working at the paper was like a scene in a play: "The butler was announcing to the lady of the house that two reporters, and a gentleman from *The Times*, were waiting to see her."

And she was concerned about the meetings, the endless number of them: "There are editorial meetings going on all the time. The paper is so dedicated to accuracy that they will meet to question whether a story has enough facts to justify using a certain word in the lead."[5]

Years later she would talk about how working there was like being in the court of Queen Victoria, who was not amused. She was mocking the *Times*, and Rosenthal had to know it—and had to wonder what the smart-ass reporter from Texas, smoking cigarettes and laughing her head off, really meant when she talked about him and his paper.

On it went for the rest of 1976. Stories about the Commission on Federal Paperwork; demonstrations in the Hamptons about condos being built in the rich resort areas; profiles of New York's Croatian community; the new head of Queens College; Soviet college students touring City Hall; city charter revisions. She tried to import some verve, some writing. In a piece about Atlantic City, she began: "Sometimes, decaying resorts develop a certain rich, plummy, Tennessee Williams decadence. But in order to have decadence, some elegance is required."[6] She was assigned political stories—gentle overviews on the history of political patronage in the city, visits with pols like Paul O'Dwyer and Abe Beame.

By the end of the year, she was getting her stories red-penciled, edited, chopped. She essentially had a six-month probationary period on the city desk, and then she was sent to the Albany Bureau, ostensibly so that the paper could take advantage of her skills covering state capitols. She joined E. J. Dionne, Linda Greenhouse, and Francis X. Clines. She was writing: "The opening of a legislative session is very like the first day of school, and one of the freshest freshmen in Albany yesterday was Assemblyman Clifford E. Wilson, a 30-year-old Democrat-Liberal of Queens. His mother cried, he buttoned up the vest of his new brown suit wrong and his wife got very nervous about meeting the Governor." The editors in Manhattan continued to sanitize her copy, over and over again.

She knew there were immense behavioral gaps between the politicians in Albany and Austin—certainly there wasn't anyone like Bullock, there wasn't that blatant game of grab-ass, there wasn't the locker-room sense that in between passing laws the lawmakers were talking about broads, barbecue, and bourbon. She tried to spike her stories with some jokes: Governor Hugh Carey's general counsel had a "belly so large it quivered like Jell-O"—the editors changed it to a "deceptively bland countenance." They gave her permission to say "he looks sort of like a large version of Bashful in a *Snow White* movie." The state's budget director was experiencing "a moment of madness" and a now-skeptical freshman lawmaker was a "quondam Candide from Queens." The Army was moving a training camp to upstate New York "because of the superior miserableness of its winter."

But, for the most part, there were the dutifully delivered, grinding, process stories about the Big Machinery in Albany, stories about the state budget and how "the State Board of Regents is considering a revised school calendar that would require all schools to close for five weeks next winter to conserve fuel." And, to her, it wasn't just that the issues were almost dead on arrival. The messengers were like emotionally flatlined solons from the uptight school of public affairs. Maybe it was the heat, maybe it was the tequila, but Austin was in Technicolor whereas Albany had that drab sense of snow that had turned from crystal white to dirty gray. She told Larry L. King that "[t]hose guys in Albany may be as dumb and as crooked as some of our Texas solons, but they are duller than a butter knife. At least in Austin our malpractors are good for some laughs."[7]

After the session, she was summoned back to Manhattan and the city desk, where she worked on more spot news stories, including a heist in the diamond district. Ivins was writing to her friends, sending along what she called "Happy San Jacinto Day" greetings on April 21, 1977, in honor of the final battle that Texans had fought to win their independence from Mexico. She said she was "now the entire general assignment staff of the NYT" and that her job was to "cover jewel thefts and neat murders and nursing home strikes and stuff like that. In between times, I fantasize about ways to disembowel the city editor. Life at the NEW *New York Times* ('It's More than Just News') is existential. Some of us are cooperating on a novel. . . . Actually, I think my porn novel, which I am co-authoring with a state senator, a television anchorperson, a member of the Carter administration and a Columbia lit. prof. has better sales potential."[8]

Sydney Schanberg, who had won a Pulitzer for his coverage of Cambodia, sent her an internal memo: "I just want to tell you that I thought the Albany Bureau's coverage this year was superb and your contribution was very much appreciated. The Albany maze may have been new to you, but your copy didn't read that way and you certainly uncovered some of the spice and shenanigans up there."[9] But she saw no spice, no shenanigans, none of the guffawing good ol' boys who came to Austin in their one suit every legislative session and drank so much Jack Daniels and Coke that their skin was turning the color of Mercurochrome. And back on the city desk in Manhattan, it wasn't initially much better. She did a story about a City of New York "garage sale"—but, then, more significantly, the first stories about a "deranged gunman," later dubbed the Son of Sam, who was shooting people with .44-caliber bullets. Throughout the spring and summer of 1977, she rode the Son of Sam saga—taking time out to write about the sausage vendors at the International Food Festival, the Taste of The Big Apple food fair, the Salute to Israel parade, squabbles over parking spaces in midtown Manhattan, how to beat the smoking habit through hypnosis, and "American chess is finally pulling out of its post–Bobby Fisher depression."

Kaye Northcott and Sara Speights visited her in the summer of 1977, just when Ivins was assigned to fly to Memphis to cover Elvis Presley's death, where she wrote about mourners "waiting to see the plump corpse." She did reaction pieces and book-ended the breaking news with an essay meditating on why Memphis attracted hundreds of thousands of mourners: "Memphis was awash with genuine emotion for three days. It is too easy to dismiss it as tasteless. It is not required that love be in impeccable taste."[10]

In mid-August, the *Washington Post* ran a small item saying that Molly Ivins had been contracted to update a previously published book by Hollywood writer May Mann on Elvis. The revised work, "*The Private*

Elvis—torn from the intimate diaries of May Mann . . . from first kiss to the death that rocked the nation! Including never-before-published photos!"—was released by Pocket Books with a yellow banner above the title that read "Including *The New York Times* Obituary." In September, she received an in-house envelope with a note from Arthur Sulzberger, the publisher, noting that she and John Rockwell were to share the "publisher's merit award" for writing under deadline pressure on the death of Elvis. The reward, $150, was going to be added to her paycheck.

Sara Speights put her feelings about Ivins's career path into a letter:

> I think at times I've pretended or thought I understood how tied in your progress could be with the *New York Times* direction, but I think after visiting with you, I see it a lot clearer. Wow! The pressure to conform, to be a *New York Times* team member, is really stiff. Which again, is not all bad, but now I'm doubting whether that is what Molly the person and Mol the writer really needs. Don't invest too much in a NYC wardrobe. You may not need it. . . . Molly, my dear, I do think about you. What a ridiculous scene you are in. Yet we all spend our tenures in such places, and I do know that you'll make the most of yours. Texas-style independence and other maverick thoughts aside, however, I think it could be a mistake for you to get too caught up in the whole *Times* scene. I think you can adjust and please them just dandy, but in the long run, I just don't want that to please you too much. I doubt that would be the best of Molly or the best for Molly. You, like myself, know damn good and well that somewhere along the road, the likes of us have got to get our excesses under control, if nothing else, because we'd feel so much better about ourselves. I think you still have to hold out for that.[11]

At her parent's home there were arguments, and Ivins could see the marriage moving toward a bad end. At one point, her father informed her mother that she would have to drive home alone from a Tenneco function. The children thought she looked shell-shocked and that the marriage had dissipated into an existence that wasn't worth continuing. In a handwritten note, her mother said that they had visited Andy in Austin and he had earned two C's, two D's, and one E, and that he "must be" on scholastic probation. She talked about going to the Bahamas on a ninety-two-foot boat. And she signed off by saying, "Daddy & I are off booze."[12]

Ivins filed the letters in now-bulging folders and headed to 5th Avenue and 13th Street for a canned fix of Texana at the Lone Star Café, still going strong a year after it had opened. The place wasn't as bad a caricature of Texas as she thought it would be—though few people knew how to sing along to the outlaw country lyrics "up against the wall redneck mother." She hadn't pulled up all her Texas connections: She called friends like the journalist Sam Kinch in Texas, she spent time with writer Larry L. King, who had written for the *Observer*, when he visited New York. She had dinner parties and when Nancy Dowd came to visit, they talked about David Susskind, Roman Polanski, and Dustin Hoffman. The weather was still making her miserable; she told people it made Houston seem like Aspen. She liked to duck into stores that had good air conditioning, and she spent more hours in the Daitch-Shopwell grocery store than she normally would. She took Shit the dog for walks in Central Park, the joggers occasionally veering away from what she said was a Texas blackhound; she let Shit linger with another dog named Zac, who seemed to hump everything in sight.

And she grew closer to a circle of friends at the paper, people who would be with her until she died—especially Eden Ross Lipson, an editor at the book review section and a former director of policy planning for the New York City Parks, Recreation, and Cultural Affairs Administration. Lipson became a constant ally and supporter at the *Times* and throughout Ivins's life, helping to promote her work in New York and guide her through a variety of medical issues. They had met at the elevator on her first day at work, when Lipson had asked if she could help her get settled and Ivins said "find me an apartment," which Lipson gladly did. Lipson would become the long-time children's book editor and someone whose counsel Ivins would seek regarding career development, health issues, writing projects, and even books to read—in her way, Lipson became the "New York" presence in Ivins's life, and their friendship would be deep and lasting. Charles Kaiser, who had gone to Columbia College, was another reporter who became part of Ivins's world. He would go on to be a founder and president of the New York chapter of the National Lesbian and Gay

Journalists Association. There were other good friends, too—especially John Leonard, the book and cultural critic. And she got to know Clyde Haberman, a City Hall bureau chief she worked for; Joe Lelyveld, a *Times*-trained reporter who would be foreign editor, managing editor, and executive editor (he thought Ivins was generous when she helped him with a list of contacts in Texas);[13] Charlotte Curtis had welcomed Ivins and stayed in touch with her; Marcia Chambers, another reporter, grew close; and Adam Clymer, the Harvard-educated reporter who had worked at the *New York Daily News* and the *Baltimore Sun*, became close to Ivins after he joined the *Times* in 1977. Clymer would make news years later when a microphone picked up President George W. Bush saying to Vice President Dick Cheney, "there's Adam Clymer, major league asshole from *The New York Times*"—to which Cheney replied, "Oh yeah, he is, big time," assuming that no one would hear him.

Clymer says of Ivins:

> *The Times* in those days was concerned that their writing was dull. They had a theory that they could hire some great writer from some place or other, and then just polish them, just sand them down a little, and they'd be fine at the *Times*. Molly was one of the most spectacular failures of that theory. I mean, Molly doesn't sand down. She once had a marvelous proposal. The metropolitan desk in those days was not a very happy place. And she once suggested that what they ought to do was publish the official shit list each week—because probably more people thought they were on it than actually were, and this would be reassuring.[14]

She complained about the ludicrousness of writing about Elvis as "Mr. Presley" in the *Times*.[15] She smoked, cursed, wore a buffalo-hide coat, and ladled on the "Hello, sweet pea" accent when she greeted someone. She joined in the after-work bullshit sessions over drinks, when the reporters bitched and moaned about management, Rosenthal, the Sulzbergers, and about how the well-chosen words were lopped from stories. She rounded up more friends and took them back to the Lone Star Café, especially when she knew that Kinky Friedman and The Texas Jewboys were playing—Kinky had the same ability she did to mimic and mock the Texas stereo-

Baby Mary (center) with sister, Sara, and mother, Margaret Milne Ivins, during the war years (Courtesy of the Ivins family)

he was a Brownie and attended the ame camp where Lyndon Johnson ent his daughter (Courtesy of the vins family)

The Ivins and Holland families grew up together in Houston. As a child, Molly pretended she would save the world. Back row (left to right): Frank Holland, Molly Ivins, Ann Holland, Hank Holland, and Sara Ivins. Front row (left to right): Andrew Ivins, Baxter Holland, and an unidentified friend (Courtesy of Ann Holland Dow)

Their father taught Molly and the rest of the family to sail at The Houston Yacht Club (Courtesy of the Ivins family)

She maintained a lifelong passion for sailing, inviting friends aboard her father's boats (Courtesy of the Ivins family)

Molly as a St. John's student (Courtesy of the Ivins family)

Seated on the right, she joined her mother, Margaret, sister, Sara, brother, Andy, and father, Jim, at Houston functions (Courtesy of the Ivins family)

During high school, she traveled with other students to France and studied language and culture (Courtesy of Kaye Northcott)

She said mercurial Yale student Hank Holland was the love of her life (Courtesy of Ann Holland Dow)

Hank Holland, left, standing behind his sister, Ann, just before his doomed journey to Washington (Courtesy of Ann Holland Dow)

: *The New York Times* she was at war with her
:ecutive editor (Courtesy of *The Texas*
bserver)

Her merrily writing that a New Mexico festival was a "gang pluck" led to her departure from *The New York Times* (Courtesy of *The Texas Observer*)

'rom 1970 into 1976, she helped run *The Texas Observer* with her close friend and ally,
<aye Northcott (Photo by Alan Pogue)

Dancing with lifelong friend Carlton Carl at the 1971 inauguration party for Texas Governor Preston Smith (Photo by Bill Malone; Courtesy of Carlton Carl)

Covering the Texas legislature was like running with the bulls (Photo by Alan Pogue)

At *The Texas Observer*, she was free to develop her voice (Photo by Alan Pogue)

She had, a friend said, an iron constitution (Courtesy of *The Texas Observer*)

Camping on Austin streets in 1996, with musician Steve Fromholz, to protest treatment of the homeless (Photo by Alan Pogue)

With Barack Obama and Carlton Carl at the 2004 Democratic Convention (Courtesy of Carlton Carl)

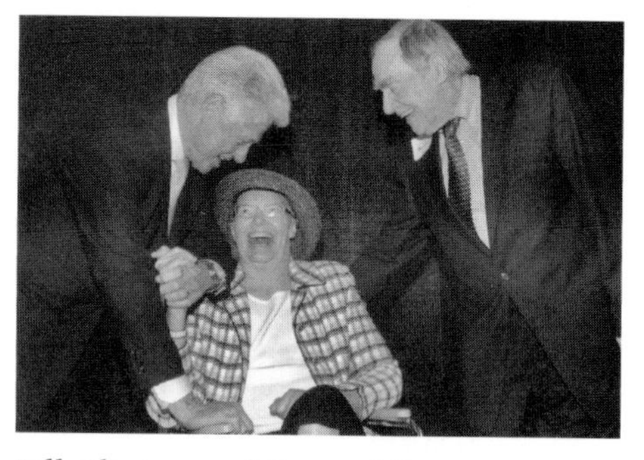

Bill Clinton and Bernard Rapoport came to her aid during her illness (Photo courtesy of Chris Caselli.com)

(© Thomas McConnell)

types all at once. She brought Shit to work and that didn't go over too well. When she hit the streets of New York, she would occasionally show some decorum and call the dog "Sitter." In the newsroom, she liked to wear jeans and debate the copy desk about the pillorying she was trying to insert into her copy. It was a push-pull affair, often about matters of writing and personal style, and it simply continued to escalate until it became a fait accompli with executive editor Abe Rosenthal. People like Charles Kaiser saw it coming:

> Well, she was this larger-than-life figure who had enormous self-confidence, and was already a famous person in her own right in Texas before she got there. And basically her whole life was a monument to iconoclasm. This was a person who succeeded almost everywhere she went by not conforming. And so she arrives at the *New York Times*, which was, I mean all big-city newspaper newsrooms in the 1970s were pretty conformist macho places—where it's true that the men, you know, wielded most of the power, even though I still don't think that her sex was the main reason she didn't fit in. It was that she was not a person who ever made much of an effort to fit in. Although at the same time, she was very popular within the newspaper among her colleagues. I mean she was certainly a beloved figure with other reporters. But anybody who wants to get ahead or even just to stay in one place at the *New York Times* as opposed to getting demoted, you have to spend at least 50 percent of your time playing politics and 50 percent of your time doing journalism and this was not a person who was going to spend 50 percent of her time playing politics, you know, to get ahead. That's just not the kind of person she was.[16]

Like her other friends, Kaiser thought she was enormously generous, always reaching for the check, even when there was a crowd that had run up a hefty dinner bill. They laughed over the fact that when she was apartment hunting in New York, she didn't know that "wbf" stood for wood burning fireplace. He admired the idea that there were only two people who got away with padding barefoot through the newsroom—Ivins and Arthur Sulzberger, Jr., the publisher's son. And Kaiser saw the battles over her copy:

> You know, it was all the things that she tried to sneak past the copy desk, and this was an era where there was virtually no writing freedom whatsoever. It was the most heavily edited newspaper in America. I suppose it probably still is, but you know, nothing got into the paper without two, and usually at least three editors getting their hands on it first. And if it was something that was for the front page it would go through, you know, five, six, seven, eight different editors. So something almost all of us tried to do is sneak in phrases or double entendres or jokes that they wouldn't understand. She probably did that as often [as] or more often than anyone else.[17]

And it rarely worked—in a chain-of-command operation like the one at the *Times*, her peccadilloes and her insistencies were being noted, not just in the collective memory bank but in internal memos floating up to Rosenthal's office:

> This, you know, kind of outrageous hilarious, iconoclastic Texan was never going to fit into this incredibly uptight political buttoned-down institution, where people got ahead by, you know, licking the asses of the people above them. None of this was a fit. On the other hand, she still managed to do quite a few good stories, and I think she had a good time some of the time, but I think it was clear to everybody including herself that this was a ticket she was punching. . . . This was not going to be where she was going to spend the rest of her life as a journalist. . . . She was going to go back, I guess back to Texas, and become the person that she became.[18]

⁂

She was liking the New York Yankees and it was bothering her to some degree—but she was intrigued by Reggie Jackson, his bravado, the way he was the self-acclaimed straw that stirred the drink. She was in a sublet co-op apartment and the people who ran the building were mad at her and Shit, because Shit had shit on the living room floor. A man from Malta was her superintendent, and at least he and she got along. The heat in the summer of 1977 was bad, but so was the humidity, and she felt boxed in. It was, she told people, as far as you could get from watching Willie Nelson play at Floore's Country Store, watching the Pedernales River curl in Central Texas, smelling the perfectly charred brisket on the huge oil-drum smoker that somebody had magically airlifted into the middle of the bluebonnets and Indian paintbrushes. She was glad to see friends from Texas when they arrived in New York.

Northcott was there: "I think she talked sometimes like somebody from the East Coast. Eden Lipson took her under her wing and tried to make her dress well, and every once in a while, she would. She wore a work shirt a couple of times at the *New York Times*—and you know that was as intentional as can be. She was creating her own history through the things that she did. She was pushing back." At lunches, Northcott would listen to her friend and the other *Times* staffers. "You know, at those lunches, everyone was concerned, who was doing well—total, total *Times* stuff, very career-oriented. As soon as she got there, all she would do is talk about the *Times*. I would visit her and she and her friends would only talk about *Times* politics. She had a dinner party group, Eden, her husband, Charlie Kaiser, Donna Shalala, Ellen Fleysher, John Leonard."[19] And, "in New York she was very proud of her connections."[20] She had told Northcott that she had been mentioned in Roger Angell's Christmas poem in *The New Yorker*.

Norman Isaacs, the editor and journalism professor, had stayed in touch with her through Columbia University and her proud allegiances to the National News Council. (Isaacs served, for a while, as the chair of the nonprofit organization that monitored bias in the news industry. Abe Rosenthal, the executive editor of the *Times*, loathed the NNC, thinking it was intrusive and "a bad idea to start with"—and his reaction was no doubt one more strike against Ivins in the *Times* firmament.) Gene Shalit, the film critic, contacted her. She visited her old professors at Columbia. James Brady, the editor of *New York* magazine, asked her if she wanted to write columns about city politics. The president of the Manhattan Chess Club sent a letter to managing editor Seymour Topping at the *Times*, complimenting her. She also began drafts of short stories and novels, typing them on long sheets of paper, editing them in pencil, and putting them aside. One is about a heated, charged encounter with an intense professor; one is about a newcomer to New York hopelessly ensnared in the city's bureaucracy as she tries, over and over again, to get her car out of the pound and her rent paid; one is about newcomers to New York who are both lost and hopeful.

She was writing letters back to Northcott, long ones, and Northcott would post them on the wall at the First Friday parties in Austin—house parties for like-minded liberals from all walks of life that had been started by Sam Whitten, a professor of library science at the University of Texas, and his wife Virginia. Northcott described the group as being like connected tributaries, people intertwined through their relationships with Ann Richards, Bob Bullock, *The Texas Observer*, Ivins, Ronnie Dugger, and John Henry Faulk. The First Friday tradition, a potluck-and-beer salon where people would sing, debate, rant, recite poems, and share political intelligence, would trade hands over the years in Austin and finally, once Ivins had settled back in the city, find her home as its headquarters.

The *Times* kept her busy, but the stories had no predictable pattern in terms of a beat—she was part of the Metro desk pool, on call for anything. She kept getting the one-liners pulled from her column, the things she was playing for laughs. She had gotten good notes ("From: Sydney Schanberg: Molly, My personal thanks for a great job on the hurricane") and she had gotten cautionary notes from anonymous allies at the paper ("Big Editor is watching you").

On the first Wednesday in September 1977, the Lone Star Café was packed with friends who had come to the city for an *Observer* fundraiser that she organized. The new editor, Jim Hightower, was there. Larry L. King. John Henry Faulk. Somehow Ivins had secured seventy dozen tamales and people were grabbing them along with the Lone Star beer. Writer Nora Ephron was there, along with the legendary West Texas trial lawyer Warren Burnett and former LBJ aide Bobby Baker. Faulk roamed the room, telling Texas stories and summoning up his characters and caricatures while people danced under a giant Texas flag. Faulk told people his cousin Fanny Rollins had said, "God wouldn't have put Texas where it is if He didn't mean it to be the center of the universe." The scene was captured by a young reporter for the *Austin American-Statesman*, Ben Sargent, who would later become a fiercely liberal Pulitzer Prize–winning editorial cartoonist and remain one of Ivins's lifelong friends.[21]

A memo went out to the staff two days later, on September 8, 1977, from national editor David Jones: "I am pleased to announce that Molly Ivins, who has been a reporter on the metropolitan desk for the past 15 months, will join the national staff as Denver correspondent later this month." There was none of the usual "Let's join to congratulate her" bonhomie in the memo. She would be running a one-person bureau covering several states. She knew they were trying to exile her, to get her out of the newsroom. When she got the news, she composed a letter to a friend in Austin and mentioned, in passing, "Mr. Chidsey," her old headmaster at St. John's in Houston:

> My term in N.Y. City is also passing, to my glee. I have just been named the Rocky Mountain Bureau Chief of the *New York Times*. Reason I am chief is on account there ain't nobody else in the bureau. There will be NO fucking morale problems in MY bureau. I get to cover New Mexico, Arizona, Colorado, Utah, Wyoming, Idaho, Montana and both Dakotas. I keep wandering around the city room with this tactless grin pasted on my kisser, saying, "I'm leaving. Bye."
>
> This here move is considered very Big on the *Times*'s part because it has become known that I have a Bad Attitude. I believe Mr. Chidsey was the first to note the fact. Much passes, little changes. I am specifically charged with A) walking around the city room in my bare feet B) laughing too loud C) not dressing right D) making fun of editors E) showing insufficient enthusiasm for the *Times* and all its wonders and F) just generally coming on too strong. What can I tell you? As Gary Trudeau once wrote: Guilty, guilty, guilty.
>
> *The Times* has done its best possible to clean up my act. They had no more luck than Chidsey-boy. 33 years old and an irredeemable smart ass. Too old to be cute, too old to change. I could tell you that pompous self-righteous motherfuckers bring out the worst in me. I think I will. Shall.
>
> 14 months in the Big A. have not been good for me. *The Times* has made me unhappy which is not my wont: I believe I am a congenitally cheerful soul. *The Times* has done its corporate best to ruin my

style. And it has capped that performance by demanding to know why I do not love it truly. Fuck *The Times*. Very bad attitude. All I want is out and they have finally given me that. For that much, God bless the *New York Times*.

This city is a great place to visit. One would have to be dead to be bored here. If I were a foreign correspondent for the *Nairobi Daily Jump Up and Hallelujah*, I would love it. So many wondrous subcultures. I met people who live in the Hamptons and drink boysenberry daiquiris and play backgammon. I met beautiful people who said when they make the film of my life, I should be played by Lauren Hutton. I love my super who is Maltese. Sometimes I hate the city because it is dirty and noisy and anti-human. Sometimes I love it because it is 90 percent other, and it is healthy for children and other living things to know that the world is mostly made up of people who are other.

I just got back from Salt Lake City. No one in Salt Lake city is other. They are all Sames. That's what ails Salt Lake City.

I have to get rid of my sublet. A man on the board of the coop apartment where I live brought someone in to see the place without warning me. Shit, my dog, had shat on the living room floor. The thing that amazes me about my dog Shit is her sense of presence. I believe she has a heavy rep as the most worthless dog in the Western world. She does not fuck up everyday, just any old time. . . .

I am becoming a Yankees fan, that's how low I have sunk. I figured, if I live here, I should root for the home team. It has not been easy, but Reggie Jackson, store-bought though he is, makes it almost o.k. If you have not read Roger Angell's "baseball companion," you should.

Four days in SLC [Salt Lake City]: My rule No.1 about covering the West—always eat the parsley. No matter where one goes for meals, what kind of restaurant, what time of day, there is always one sprig of parsley served on the side. It is the only fresh vegetable to be found west of the Divide: all else comes canned. If you do not eat the parsley, you will get beri beri. This includes the sprig on the side of a plate of blueberry pancakes at Denny's in the morning.

I guess I could tell you some of the other serious stuff but I don't think I will. Just how mellowed out are you getting in beloved Austin? My friend Fletcher Boone claims that no one ever does genuinely valuable work in Austin because it's too pleasant.

Lotus land.

Her close friends, the ones who had been through her tenure at the *Times*, thought it to be a bad marriage, one of colossal proportions. Said Myra MacPherson:

> Perhaps the worst marriage ever in journalism was when *The New York Times* hired Molly. Whatever prompted this career choice, Molly should have received the Purple Heart of journalism. The first indication that life was not going to be just swell in the corporate headquarters of the ever-so-beige *Times* was when she was rebuked for taking her shoes off, the better to concentrate on her prose. As Molly always told it, she had endured such copy changes as "bosoms and buttocks" for her phrase "tits and ass" [even then the acceptable-to-everyone-but-*The-New-York-Times* title of a song in *A Chorus Line*]. Like many of us who wrote for the *Times*, tears could fall at the breakfast table when we read for the first time the published results of an editor's scalpel. On one such occasion, Molly saw her phrase "beer gut" changed to "protuberant abdomen."[22]

Clyde Haberman at the *Times* felt the same way. It was well beyond an oil-and-water mix:

> Somebody like Molly was going to make Abe crazy . . . you know one can argue if Molly was ever right for the *New York Times*. I think not. Normally, because everybody likes the rebel, or most people do anyway, it's usually seen as the *Times*'s fault and Abe Rosenthal's fault in particular—that it couldn't find a way to accommodate Molly. But it's very possible that certain organizations just cannot accommodate everybody. It was just a poor fit. You'd be hard-pressed to argue that the *New York*

> *Times* is not a great newspaper and having Molly or not having Molly didn't change that. I don't mean to be unkind. I'm just being realistic. It was not a good fit and in particular not a good fit with Abe.[23]

On September 20, 1977, her friends threw a going-away party and gave her a joke present—a copy of *Pentecostal Hymns, Number Three, A Winnowed Collection of Evangelistic Services, Young People's Societies and Sunday Schools.* It was inscribed "To Molly—A Spiritual Guide for Her Temporary Sojourn in the Wild West" and was signed by thirty people, including her *Times* colleagues Charles Kaiser, David Jones, Eden Lipson, and John Leonard. One friend wrote: "Ivins, this is the first time anyone has taken Shit out of New York." Another, possibly her Columbia classmate Cary Winfrey, wrote: "Counting on you to uphold the class of '67's highest values—whatever they may be." A note, apparently from Roger Wilkins at the *Times*, simply says: "Well, shit." And David Jones, who would be editing her pieces, wrote: "NY's loss is my gain." Ellen "Flash" Fleysher signed the card—she had been a TV newsperson in New York and was on the verge of becoming the deputy commissioner for public information for the New York City Police Department. She would visit Ivins over the years, go on rafting trips with her, stay in close contact.

As she did with thousands of mementos, documents, papers, and pay stubs, Ivins filed the hymnal away. She told friends like Terry O'Rourke back in Texas that she thought she would prefer being in the West as opposed to the bureaucracy in New York. She thought about the best way to transport Shit.

In Denver she worked out of her home, a well-worn yellow farmhouse near Cherry Hills, on East Stanford Street. She liked it, instantly. Her house had land around it, the mountains were close by, and you could see the sky. For the first several months she barely unpacked boxes. She traveled the region, met contacts the national desk had steered her to, worked at her kitchen table, made arrangements for someone to board the dog. Throughout the spring of 1978, she dutifully proposed stories but, for the most part, she was assigned pieces. She was allowed to hire a part-time secretary; she smoked as much as before and seemed to drink more than ever. In Austin she knew everybody in the extended *Observer*-Armadillo-Scholz's crowd of cultural outlaws, literary types, liberal icons. In New York, she had found a like-minded crowd of young journalists, and a few older, savvy veterans, who resisted the conformist, institutional aura at the *Times*. But in Denver, there wasn't really a similar crowd or culture to turn to. She told a local writer:

"The transition was not a completely easy one. Denver is a city without a center where everyone goes home at night. The first thing I did when I got here was to ask where the bar was that all the reporters drank at. I was told there wasn't one. I think every city but Denver has one."[24]

She found one kindred soul in Gaylord Shaw, the Rocky Mountain Bureau Chief for the *Los Angeles Times*. He was two years older, from El Reno, Oklahoma, and they bonded quickly. He wasn't like the Ivy League–educated reporters at the *Times*; he had gone to the University of Oklahoma. He was also a serious investigative reporter, at work on a series of stories on unsafe dams in America. His work on these so-called time bombs led President Carter and federal regulators to unleash money so that the major dams could finally be inspected. In 1978, Shaw won the Pulitzer for national reporting. In Denver, Ivins and Shaw decided to start the "First Annual Grand International Rocky Mountain Correspondent's Association Chili Cook-Off"—an excuse to rein in new friends, schmooze with rainmakers they wanted to invite, and offer up their versions of the kind of food they liked to eat in Oklahoma and Texas. She had floated down the Rio Grande in years past and attended the famous, sometimes raucous "international" chili cook-offs that were held in Terlingua, Texas. Regional pols, from governors to Senator Gary Hart, were invited to the Shaw-Ivins events.

She was still listed as a contributor to *The Texas Observer*, and if she had a break, she would fly to Austin to hang out, visit Deep Eddy, and eat Mexican food at Matt Martinez's restaurant. Jones, on the national desk, seemed to want to work with her, in that he let her open her style, pursue meatier stories—but, in some ways, it was a glorified version of what she had done in New York. She was on call for anything, at any time. She did sports stories, covering the U.S. Open golf tournament close to her home. She was writing a story a week, at least, and was dipping into those panoramic stories that the *Times* loved so well—the fate and future of water in the American West, whether there were boundless energy sources buried out there, whether certain animals belonged on the endangered species list.

She wrote about Aspen's concern that its ski slopes were being taken over by foreign corporations. An outbreak of Russian flu at the Air Force Academy. The opening night for the new concert hall in Denver. Uranium mines in Wyoming. Grasshopper plagues in four states. The Christian Bookseller's Convention. The American Medical Association conference on rural health care. IBM's business plans: "Frank T. Cary, chairman of the International Business Machines Corporation, reported today that I.B.M. now has the largest backlog of orders in its history and expects to add 10,000 people to its manufacturing divisions."

In the summer of 1979, she flew to Austin and spent several days there visiting friends and working on stories. She wrote about the bloody battle over the presence of Vietnamese immigrant shrimp fishermen on the Texas coast. She dropped in on the drug-smuggling trial of Jimmy Chagra. And she wrote a long homage to Scholz's, introducing it to *Times* readers as the latest place to be put on the National Register of Historic Places. It was the perfect peg to mention her pals in the story—the artist Fletcher Boone, whom she immortalized in the piece for once being locked into a boozy, fifteen-beer, five-hour debate with another liberal-leftist friend, Martin Wigginton, all while under the watchful eye of another good friend, library science professor Sam Whitten. "Although Texas is widely supposed to be whiskey country, it is actually a state with a beer culture," she noted. She wistfully suggested, at the end of the piece, that the place was famous for its assemblage of liberal legislators who cooked deals and policies on the outdoor patio—but it was now on the outs with the "liberal crowd."[25]

Most of her Denver bureau stories appeared as straight news pieces when they were published. Sometimes a word, a phrase, that was a tad edgier wound up in the final version: "Five hundred fools stood freezing their feet off in the snow in the dark by an obscure highway Monday morning, every one of them as happy as a swilled hog in the sunshine," she wrote in a story about people in Big Sky, Montana, watching a solar eclipse.

Topic-wise, there were glimmers of the things she had done in Minnesota and Texas—covering a protest at the nuclear weapons plant in Rocky Flats, an alleged sex discrimination case at the Santa Clara pueblo in New Mexico, the fate of union workers at the Coors Brewery, militant Hopis organizing and protesting. She was proud of the work she did about Rio Arriba County in New Mexico and the undercurrent of a major marijuana smuggling culture—but she was afraid her sources would blink at the final version that ran in the *Times*, wondering if their cooperation was worth the short, toned-down piece that eventually ran.

⤛⤜

Friends heard that her father had told her mother he was going out sailing—and that he went out one day and never returned. That he had met another woman, named Virginia. Jim Ivins's relationship with Molly, always complex, took on a steely distance in his letters. He was still admonishing her, telling her to leave a better greeting on her answering machine. Still telling her about his sailing adventures around the country, including "Venetian Night" at the yacht club in central Wisconsin where he and Virginia were looking for real estate. He would eventually move to Sarasota, Florida, to be closer to better yachting opportunities.

On June 28, she took out a yellow legal pad and started writing:

> On June 22, I had several beers and then went to the liquor store, where I lost my dog Shit. Because I was drunk, I did not notice she was not in the back of the car, and because I was drunk, it took me three hours to notice her absence.
>
> The night before I got drunk and passed out in the bathtub. When I woke up, I got into bed [writing indecipherable] and almost ruined my new mattress. A few days before, in Idaho, where I got drunk every night, I passed out in the tub reading. I ruined a fine new history of *The Times*.
>
> Two nights ago, I got drunk and made a fool of myself by calling Sam Kinch and babbling forever.

Alcohol is a drug. It is destroying my brain and my life. I have said horrible things to people when drunk. I have [been] rude, thoughtless, hurtful. I bore people. But mostly I just make an ass out of myself. It is time to get professional help.

On a camping trip in The Big Bend, I had been so hard and dominating and horrible—like Sara—that Ann Richards told her husband she couldn't stand me.

I am fat from drinking. I have let wonderful dinners burn up from drinking. I have jeopardized my job from drinking and failed in my responsibilities as a journalist.

I have wasted so much time by getting drunk. I have wasted so much time hating myself for it the next day. I have broken and burned things because of alcohol.

The opinions of countless people of me have been lowered or worse because of my behavior when I drink. . . .[26]

CHAPTER NINE

"Molly Ivins Can't Say That, Can She?"

Dallas, that's the meanest town I know.

—JOHNNY WINTER

She had actually found some semblance of Austin in Boulder, where she was a frequent participant at the annual Conference on World Affairs put on by University of Colorado sociology professor Howard Higman—justly famous debates and panels that featured a crazy quilt of speakers: Buckminster Fuller, Ralph Nader, Brian Wilson of the Beach Boys, Henry Kissinger, Marshall McLuhan, Arthur Miller, and plenty more. She found the conferences entertaining but sometimes meandering and exasperating. She told friends she wanted to get away from work, from the demands, and she tried to find some time to explore the outdoors: In the summer of 1980, just before her thirty-sixth birthday (and close to when she wrote her painful meditations on her drinking), she decided to organize a rafting excursion for fourteen women down the main fork of the Salmon River in Idaho.

She said she was working seven days a week, often fourteen hours a day, and wanted a break. Before the river trip, she traveled to Corrales, New Mexico, on July 12 to cover "the annual" chicken plucking and slaughter festival—a beer-tinged event in the town of 3,000 where people literally gathered to cut the heads off of chickens, hang out, and swap stories. Her childhood friend Margaret Sher was in New Mexico; so was former U.S. senator Fred Harris from Oklahoma, who had run a populist platform campaign for the presidency in 1976 and was deeply tied to that old extended network of southern progressives. Harris had become a professor at the University of New Mexico, and he would eventually marry Sher and draw closer to Ivins.

In Corrales, he joined in on the festival and gave her some quotes for her story—suggesting he had a chicken so large he was going to try to get it a basketball scholarship. When she filed her story, Ivins wrote that the whole affair looked like a "gang pluck"—and the debate on whether it was appropriate language or not wound its way to Abe Rosenthal's office.

Rosenthal had tried to make some sort of peace with her, and had even reconnoitered with her a year earlier in Austin, so he could see firsthand what Texas was all about. She took him to a party at Dave and Ann Richards's house and the future governor of Texas answered the door dressed as a Tampax. The drinks flowed and Rosenthal mingled with Ivins's other friends, including sportswriter and novelist Bud Shrake, who was dressed in an Afro wig and pretending to be Julius "Dr. J" Erving, the legendary basketball star. Rosenthal, according to Dave Richards, also donned an Afro wig, enjoyed some cool beverages, and seemed to be shedding his tight *Times* skin. If there were any lasting, warm feelings inspired by his trip to Austin, they were over by the summer of 1980.

Rosenthal ordered the "gang pluck" line deleted from her story and the affront was added to her list of sins at the *Times*. And he also ordered her to a dressing down in New York. She arrived in the city the day before the meeting. She was tired, hungry, hungover, and staying with her pregnant friend Eden Lipson.

"What are you going to wear?" Lipson asked her.

"What I've got on, I guess," said Ivins.

"But Molly, what are the blotchy brown stains all over your dress?" asked Lipson.

"I dunno. Oh, yes I do. Blood. Chicken blood," said Ivins.

She went to take a shower and Lipson told her she would lend her some clothes. She rummaged through a bag and found a demure grey dress with a dainty white collar. At the *Times*, in Rosenthal's muted office, Ivins took a seat. He suggested she was trying to inspire readers to think dirty thoughts and dirty words by putting "gang pluck" in her story.

"Damn if I could fool you, Mr. Rosenthal," Ivins told people she had said.[1]

⤛⤚

She ordered pink T-shirts with the word "Salmonettes" on the front and invited a mixture of friends from all phases of her life, most of whom had never run the Salmon River before. Donna Shalala, a professor of politics at Teachers College at Columbia who had just become president of Hunter College, and who would serve as Secretary of Health and Human Services in the Clinton administration. Nancy Dowd, her friend from Smith who had won an Academy Award for the *Coming Home* screenplay. Alice Rivlin, the director of the Congressional Budget Office. Marcia Chambers from the *Times*. Ellen Fleysher, who had gone back to TV news at ABC. New York City Council president Carol Bellamy. Anne Crittenden, a business writer from the *Times*. Margaret Sher, her old friend from Houston. Elizabeth Roistacher, a deputy assistant secretary for Housing and Urban Development.[2] There would be other trips, bonding moments, over the years, with some of the same women.

A month later, she held another chili cook-off and invited the governors of the states she was covering. Governor Scott Matheson of Utah sent his regrets for not being able "to attend your infamous" event. She had found a few kindred souls in Boulder, people she felt comfortable with, but she was still more closely bound to her friends in Texas. She told them that the area she was covering was diverse, in its way—there were miners, lumberjacks, Native Americans, energy barons, real cowpunchers, Mormons, and people who still believed in some chinny sense of Manifest

Destiny. But Denver was still not like Austin, where things were still comfortably settled into that Groundhog Day groove, constantly repeating themes from the '60s. She drove to Austin, flew to New York, for business meetings and to see friends, and thought more about leaving the *Times*. Kaye Northcott saw the end coming, and she also saw the way Ivins was drinking:

> As long as you are under the thumb of the *Times*, and you are drinking on and off, which is not something the *Times* is going to be real happy about, then they are not going to give you too much leeway. She was drinking quite a bit at certain points. I didn't understand about alcoholism. I didn't confront her. There was no such thing as an intervention. So I wasn't the one to do it, since I wasn't a drinker. I was too goody-two-shoes to be able to say "Molly you have overdone it." It was amazing what her constitution was.
>
> It was a bad fit from the beginning. She had the capability of a Johnny Apple, but she couldn't play the politics. I don't know what she thought she was going to get there. . . . *The Times* was her father, I really think that. She was back living with her father. She couldn't put up with it. It was not in her to put up with it.[3]

During one of her visits to see Jim Ivins in Maryland, he had taken her out on the best boat of his life, a thirty-six-foot Morgan Out Island. It was the one he would sail up and down the East Coast, to the Bahamas, to Martha's Vineyard. She was drinking a beer and suddenly put the can on the deck and squashed it hard. Her father went crazy, cursing and screaming. *It was his goddamned boat.*

⁂

She filed several more stories—on radioactive waste spills, heat waves, fights by the Sioux to redress crooked land deals with federal agencies, and the rescue of wild burros in the Grand Canyon. She kept adding to her collection of favorite quotes, jokes, one-liners. When she was in graduate school at Columbia she kept them in a spiral notebook. Now she was keeping them on blue index cards and filing them alphabetically, either by subject or by writer. She tried them out on friends and they laughed, and she wrote down which ones really worked. Friends knew she loved John Henry Faulk and they believed her when she said that there was more to the humor, that she wanted to do something to push it, to make it useful in her stories, in her work for the ACLU.

She was being paid more than she had in any other newspaper job, and it seemed as though she was also still always giving it away—making donations to the *Observer*, to the ACLU, probably breaking even more rules at the *Times* about not wearing your politics on your sleeve. Friends her age who were having babies, some of them dropping out of the journalism game, would find letters, cards, packages from her—with children's clothes, picture books, little toys. When she traveled, she bought the local oddities—the stuffed armadillo that was reclining and drinking a bottle of Lone Star beer—and gave them to friends. She left her house open to her family, and to anyone from Texas or New York who wanted to visit. She invited them to go skiing with her in Aspen; it was a place where she forgot about Rosenthal and the *Times*—and she would offer to pay the way for anyone who wanted to come along

At night, sometimes in the early morning hours, she would reach for the phone in her home and call people in San Francisco, in New Orleans, in Austin. She was laughing uproariously about something in the news, she had remembered some story she had heard, she had to describe some blowhard politician she had just met. She would shout out "fabulous" and cackle and ask about their families, remembering the children's names, even those of the pets. More than one of them wondered if she was too isolated in Colorado, recalling that she had always worked hard to have parties, to be around as many people as possible—and maybe some of that was harder to do in Denver. And she told stories that had them laughing in the middle of the night: Ivins going to a restaurant in the heart of the West and ordering the chicken-fried steak and having it served to her with a lone sprig of parsley, which she knew was going to be the only green thing she'd see on her plate. She gobbled it up. The waitress watched, then drawled: "Honey, if I'd a known you was gonna eat that thing, I woulda washed it." When she finished her yarn, she would laugh, seemingly for an entire minute, and the people on the other line couldn't help but convulse in chuckles.

Two months after the Salmon River trip, she was told that her tenure as Rocky Mountain Bureau Chief was over. She was being reassigned back to the city desk, to cover City Hall and local politics. The consensus among friends and colleagues was that she hadn't been serious enough—that the *Times*, ever concerned about its image, wasn't being represented very well by her and her copy. Her competition in Denver, Gaylord Shaw from the *Los Angeles Times*, had won that Pulitzer Prize for national reporting. She had flummoxed the copy desk, and lower-rung editors, by sending in stories that had the word "crap" or used the analogy "like a fart in a whirlwind." If it was true that the *Times* was her father, she was tired of pleasing him and Abe Rosenthal. "Somebody like Molly was going to make Abe crazy, and I guess the gang pluck thing was the final straw," says Clyde Haberman.[4]

She reported back to New York and made a point of going to see the dictation staff and thanking them for their efforts—she told Northcott that the overlooked dictation people were glad to see her because she was one of the few who ever thanked them. She greeted the cleaning people, the ones she had befriended during her earlier stint in Manhattan. And she began slogging through stories that bored her, but would have thrilled other, less jaundiced staffers. "She was rebelling against them, like a child, like she would against her father, and they had to watch her every step of the way—which made for some great stories. I think she did some stuff just because it would make great anecdotes."[5]

Haberman knew that "she had basically been yanked out of Denver."[6] He was the City Hall bureau chief when she was reassigned and he became her immediate supervisor. It was a three-person bureau and normally it "would be considered a plum assignment in many ways, but with Molly it was clear she was being sent down there as punishment."[7] He watched a pattern develop. After she filed her stories, they were always far more heavily edited than the pieces he turned in. At one point they joked about seeing what would happen if they put his byline on her stories—they assumed the stories would be treated more kindly. Haberman noted:

> Where things really went wrong, though, was that Metro in those days . . . was something of a gulag in the *Times* structure. It was disproportionately populated with people who were very young and ambitious and just starting out but had their eyes on other things—you know, foreign assignments and God knows what. And people who were superannuated and were kind of riding out the string, in the twilight of their careers. And then there were a fairly large number of people who were in Abe's doghouse for one sin or another, real or imagined, on his part. . . . And Molly fit the category of those who were in Abe's doghouse, so she was sent down to City Hall. It was made clear to me quite early that they didn't want her to get any good assignments. . . . We had a long heart-to-heart talk one day or night, because she perceived me as, I think she told some people, that I was hogging good stories. Now, I mean, not because I was the bureau chief and naturally I had every right, the right and even the obligation, one would say, to take the major stories. When I tried to give her good stories, I was screamed at from the bosses on 43rd Street, which was where the *Times* was headquartered in New York.
>
> It was a very difficult period because I respected Molly tremendously. And I didn't have to explain to her during this chat, I just mentioned that she didn't appreciate the great pressure I was under not to assign it to her. I said anytime I did assign her a really good story, I got yelled at. . . . They were constantly messing with her copy in the office. You would have thought this woman didn't know how to write. It was just painful to watch. It was clear they were going to try to drive her out.[8]

The bureau had plenty of ribald material to work with, maybe not like the Hee-Haw Gone to Seed Scene at the State Capitol in Texas, but there were tempting targets such as Mayor Ed Koch to consider. Yet she was consistently steered away from the meatier stories, and certainly away from covering the mayor. "She wasn't happy. . . . She was in purgatory and probably on her way to damnation fully," says Haberman.[9] She spent her last year at the *Times* writing about city budget hearings, redistricting battles, neighborhood meetings, the city planning commission. Her last piece for the paper was about Korean émigrés and their search for peace and happiness in the Big Apple.

The story was headlined: "To Find Success Amid the Stress of New York."[10]

⊰⊱

In the early 1980s, the *Dallas Times Herald* and the *Dallas Morning News* were engaged in one of the livelier, even more highbrow, newspaper wars in the country. It was one of those enlightened moments when competition in Texas actually led to something approaching healthy, quantifiable improvement. While the San Antonio papers sometimes seemed to be fighting in the gutter, trying to out-sensationalize each other, and while the Houston papers had settled into an almost mutually laconic partnership, things were heating up in Dallas. The two major papers there—the *Times Herald* and the *Morning News*—had for years largely ignored minority communities, systemic corruption, and the insidious tendencies of the police force. But that was changing as new editors were being imported at both papers, ones who hadn't necessarily been slaves to the dictates of the old guard in Dallas. It was also a sort of golden period in growth, in the sense that the city was filling with Northern émigrés, and major corporations like Exxon and J.C. Penney were relocating to the greater Dallas area to take advantage of the boundless office space, the suburban housing for employees, and the friendly arrangements at every municipal level imaginable. The net effect was that both newspaper advertising and circulation were bounding, and though the *Times Herald* generally lagged behind the *Morning News*, there seemed to be enough to go around—and the parent company, the *Times Mirror*, was viewed as the solid, forward-thinking mainstay that would keep the *Times Herald* well lubricated and humming. The paper had, by Dallas standards, a certain sense of itself as the hipper daily—and it sometimes tried to woo away *Morning News* staffers by suggesting there was a huge culture clash. One writer from the *Morning News* was called, at his desk, and invited to a quiet meeting a few blocks away in the office of a high-ranking *Times Herald* editor. "You don't want to work for a fascist newspaper," he told the *Morning News* writer.

The *Times Herald* had had a series of new publishers and editors who increasingly moved the paper into direct competition with the *Morning News*. The *Times Mirror* chain steered journalists from its other papers to Dallas, bumped up the travel budget, redesigned the pages, and improved the Sunday magazine. The *Morning News* tried to keep pace. The result was some of the best journalism ever produced in the state—while the papers competed into the '80s and '90s, the *Morning News* won Pulitzers for national reporting, investigative reporting, explanatory reporting, and feature photography. The *Times Herald* won two Pulitzers for feature photography. Both papers were ranked on the lists of the top papers in the nation and went back and forth in nasty, accusatory circulation battles. To a large degree, the editorial fight took place on the high ground, with each paper pursuing its own process and agenda. The *Times Herald* was presumed to be more liberal, the *Morning News* far more conservative—perhaps as an outgrowth of the fact that it was locally owned and closer to the older vanguard of political and financial might in the city. Reporters from around the nation were increasingly applying for jobs. Dallas had become a goal, and the papers simply added more and more staffers. Ivins's friend Gaylord Shaw, the Pulitzer Prize–winning reporter from the *Los Angeles Times*, was typical of the *Times Mirror* synergy—he had left the Denver Bureau to come to Dallas and was now moving from assistant managing editor to managing editor of the *Times Herald*.

He and the other editors made Ivins an offer in late 1981, telling her she could write a column about anything she wanted. She quickly agreed to start in early 1982. The *New York Times*, in a fit of generosity, informed her that they would allow her to do freelance pieces for them.

⤛⤜

She had never really liked Dallas, at least compared to Austin. But there were a handful of people she knew, and she got in touch with them right away. Billy Porterfield, her old colleague from her internship days at the *Houston Chronicle*, was there—like a lot of reporters in the state, he had bounced around from one city to another. He had an early handle on what Dallas seemed to be in the early '80s: "Houston was like a huge, vulgar city. It had dead people floating in the ponds. And the cop shop was real busy all the time, fishing these bodies out. But that was Houston. Dallas was Neiman Marcus, you know?"[11] The sense was that Dallas was miles of high-end stores, new highways, suburban sprawl, shopping malls, and the headquarters of Neiman Marcus. It was the era of the TV show *Dallas*, mega-churches, Coca-Cola Cowboy chic, and the idolatry extended to the Dallas Cowboys and their inflexible, taciturn coach Tom Landry. Dallas, people in Austin sneered, had come to symbolize the very essence of excess. It wasn't just going disco; it was where the slick cocaine businessmen would roam, like Gordon Geckos set loose on the Porsche Prairie. Dallas was only a straight 200 miles north of Austin, yet the distance between them in terms of lifestyle and culture could have been as long as the Silk Road. Ivins used to tell people that Houston was like "Los Angeles with the climate of Calcutta." If that was true, then Dallas was like Studio 54 tricked out to look like Southfork Ranch. Still, she was glad to be back in Texas, glad to be working for the most liberal big daily in the South, and especially glad that she could make it to Scholz's in three hours if she kept her foot on the pedal. There were still some campouts to get to, and periodically she would come to another one put on by Texas politician Bob Armstrong.

In Dallas, she settled into a city where the reporters would invariably run into one another on assignments or at watering holes. The town was small enough, and the social circles sufficiently intertwined, that it was easy to see her, hear her. At Joe Miller's bar, you'd find courthouse reporters talking to judges and silk-suited attorneys, and occasionally you'd see eye-patch-wearing R. D. Matthews—aka The Patch—who scared the holy hell out of people as he stared at them. Matthews was always rumored to be in league with the dark forces that ran the city in the old days—the people behind the people who were behind Jack Ruby. Some journalists reaching for another bowl of free peanuts would talk in hushed tones about whether Matthews was one of the "mystery tramps" who had been seen congregating near the spot where Kennedy was killed in 1963.

There was Belle's Green Glass, where some of the writers went and would get so drunk they'd walk into pillars and knock themselves out—she liked to go there. The Green Glass was dark, and it was a solid place to sneak into for *Times Herald* staffers. You could tell the city-desk receptionist that you were going out to buy a pack of cigarettes, veer off to the bar, and no one would really seem to notice or mind. There were other places, too—Sol's Turf Bar ("home of David Berg's famous corned beef" said the sign over the front door), where a black man named Israel made the pizza and the Solomon family had, in the back, the original front door to Ruby's Carousel Club. There was the nearby Oyster House, with its secret upstairs bar called The Shell Room. There was the Unique Steakhouse with its indoor phone booth and the gamblers curled up with *The Racing Form*. And if reporters wanted to really feel the chilled frisson of danger, like they were close to the beating heart of the devil, they could go to the dive bar where the cops would drink—The Idle Rich—and the reporters would stare, cautiously, at the bullet holes in the ceiling where the cops had shot their guns. At The Idle Rich, right into the '80s, there was whispered talk by some of the off-duty police about "niggers" being blown away. One night outside The Idle Rich, there was a scuffle, some muffled noise—and an off-duty cop went outside, fired his gun, the noise settled, and he came back inside to finish the drink that the bartender, an ex-cop in a bolo tie who was named Snake, had just poured for him.

Ivins also quickly arranged to meet *Dallas Morning News* columnist Maryln Schwartz, whom she had first met in Memphis while covering Elvis's death—they used to laugh about sharing their "first corpse." She was also in contact with Blackie Sherrod, the legendary sports writer and editor who had worked with or had a hand in the careers of any number of people Ivins knew—particularly her Austin friend Bud Shrake. Texas, in a way, was a small circle when it came to journalism. People started in one city in the state, moved to another, sometimes returned to where they began. Houston, Dallas, Austin, San Antonio, and Fort Worth were filled with reporters and editors who had put in time at various publications, lived in different Texas cities, and welcomed newspaper pals who wanted to crash on their floors. Meanwhile, her friends in Austin recommended people in Dallas whom she should look up. In many ways it was harder to be a cheerfully wide-open progressive-populist-liberal-leftist in Dallas than in any other big city in the state. In Austin there was Scholz's, the Armadillo

World Headquarters, the big university producing the next generation of leftists and idealists. Dallas had Southern Methodist University as its academic anchor, but its campus was almost like a gated community inside the wealthiest neighborhood in the city.

The underground in Dallas had always been forced way underground, close to the center of the earth, and it was more difficult to find your fellow travelers there, but Ivins followed the connections—through the *Observer* supporters, the John Henry Faulk supporters, the American Civil Liberties members—to her new allegiances. She liked Schwartz at the rival *Morning News*—even though she told people "pigs would fly" before she ever thought of working there. She felt that the *Times Herald* had "the guts and the writers" and the *Morning News* had "the money and the circulation."[12] Schwartz was droll, liked to laugh, and had a handle on the history of the Southern mores for women. There were Ken Gjemre and Pat Anderson, ardent environmental activists who co-founded Half Price Books and were linked to the set of civil liberties organizations and peace movements that had quietly coalesced in Dallas. The same with attorney John Albach and his wife Susan. Ivins hung out with Bryan Woolley, a son of deep West Texas, who had written several books and was one of the feature-writing stalwarts at the *Times Herald*. John Bloom, more famous for his invented alter ego "Joe Bob Briggs," the crazed drive-in movie critic from Texas, was there. And there were legendary women in the city, ones who had skipped back and forth between news careers and high society and work doing public relations—and seemed to embody, perfectly, the way that Dallas sometimes wanted to do business. Patsy Swank, who used to write under the pen name "Patsy Peck" and had been a correspondent for *Life* magazine during JFK's doomed visit, made a point of including Ivins on her social whirlwind—inviting her to lavish parties, introducing her to movers and shakers, letting Ivins crash at her house when necessary.

And initially the *Times Herald* let her run free, with the editors assuming they could find some middle ground between her work at the *Observer* and her work at the *New York Times*. She'd write a column, newsier and funnier than what Dallas was used to, and the editors hoped that it would underscore the differences between the two newspapers—that the *Times*

Herald was the better-written publication, more irreverent, infused with a bit more brio.

⊰⊱

She almost instantly took to mocking Dallas, and though she would spend only three years living there, friends were surprised she lasted that long. She wrote about the way people dressed, the way the city seemed hell-bent on growing in a manner that would have pleased the advocates of un-zoned Houston to no end. She also had her way with the local pols. In 1983, she wrote that Republican Congressman Jim Collins—who had served as a lieutenant with General George Patton—had said that the current year's edition of the energy crisis could be avoided if "we didn't use all that gas on school busing." Ivins wrote that if Collins's "IQ slips any lower, we'll have to water him twice a day."[13]

The story hit the fan, the paper got some angry calls and letters, and some businesses canceled advertising for several days. The episode, amplified in various retellings over the years, led to discussions in the glass offices off of the newsroom about how to better market, hype, the paper. The *Times Herald* had long been viewed as the afternoon edition of the working class, more of a blue-collar publication, and now it was undergoing a wholesale transformation under the aegis of various reporters and editors brought in from Los Angeles and Washington and the extended *Times Mirror* network. The marketing staff suggested that it promote Ivins as a professional iconoclast—as the plain-speaking Texan who was a must-read because you never knew what she would say next. The idea was to capitalize on the notion that the *Morning News* was ploddingly covering power in its über-objective way—or, worse, on bended-knee to Perot and the others—while the outside-owned *Times Herald* had an actual voice, an opinion. Billboards and bus signs went up touting Ivins's Metro section column, and the slogan was a riff on one of the complaints the *Times Herald* had received: "Molly Ivins Can't Say That, Can She?" The marketing department was told to push it hard. It was one of those rare moments in modern newspaper history when the competition drove things and the writers were marketed, touted, and sold—it was a TV conceit, but transferred to the percolating newspaper war in Texas. And, given that they were marketing her audacity, she suspected that they could hardly edit it out of her columns.

Her work was an extension of what she had done at the State Capitol for the *Observer*—but this time she was writing about the city at large, about the people who ran it. Dallas, growing exponentially, was still trying to find its identity: One of the reasons it became home to the largest churches in America, and also the highest divorce rate, had to do with that rootless quality. People were coming to it, looking for a way to get anchored, and instead wound up adrift. She ran free in her depictions of Dallas—and more letters came in. The editors tweaked her now and then, shifting the section where the column would appear, finally moving her into a slot on the op-ed page.

By the mid-'80s, though, it had become clear to the people who knew the numbers that the *Times Herald* was constantly slipping behind the *Morning News*. There were murmurings, from on high, that Ivins should think about hitting it down the middle a bit now and then—especially when it came to describing Dallas or describing some of its potentates. She had already drawn a line several years earlier, in *The Nation*, when she referred to the *Dallas Morning News* as being "to the right of Ethelred the Unready," and her thinking about the city-at-large hadn't changed that much in 1983.

As often as she could, she traveled back to Austin. She liked the fact that it had all but enshrined Willie Nelson as its patron saint—and that Willie was giggling in a smoky haze out along the Pedernales River, skinny-dipping with his posse, playing rounds of stoned golf on his private course that took all day long because people were laughing their asses off, singing songs, drinking more beer, and lighting up fat doobies. What Dallas celebrated, truly, were its "Big Bidness" heroes: elephant-eared Ross Perot, stern builders like Trammell Crow, the old money czars from the Hunt family. Dallas, she had decided, placed its faith and stock in those can-do gladhanders who mingled at the power breakfasts in the penthouse clubs downtown, bowing their heads as a soft-skinned preacher read the invocation and the black men brought the scrambled eggs. The citizen-kings of Dallas were those Big Bidness folks, especially Perot, who seemed to want to weigh in on city matters as if he were the High Lord Mayor.

At lunch, she regularly ate at Neiman Marcus; it was a short stroll from work, and she could see a certain side of Dallas laid out before her. It was not like Scholz's beer garden in Austin; at Neiman's there were well-dressed socialites talking about charity balls, their husband's careers, and life in the exclusive neighborhoods of the city. Sometimes Stanley Marcus, the famous owner of the fanciest store in the South, would be out on the floor, mingling with customers.

Dallas, as definitively documented in the classic work on the city called *The Accommodation*—written by Jim Schutze, one of Ivins's colleagues at the *Times Herald*—had always been overseen by the business cabal, for both very good and very bad reasons. The cabal milked the city for profit, sometimes gave some of the money back late in life, and for decades had set about enforcing a de facto socioeconomic segregation that kept the minority community "accommodated." Those citizen-kings basically paid minority leaders to keep a lid on unrest, to make sure that Dallas never blew up in the '60s and '70s the way so many other cities did. It was a plan, and it worked exactly the way the men who created it intended for it to work.

In Austin, some of her friends were digging in against the rising yuppie tide. In Dallas the tide had already washed over the whole damned place. It reached a certain apex when the city began preparing, seemingly for years, to host 1984's Republican National Convention. Whatever she thought about Dallas, it was only made worse by the exultant welcome it was forever extending to all the Reagan Republicans. Nancy Reagan, wearing a bolo tie, was showing up in town—and so were a grinning Ronald Reagan and George H.W. Bush, each of them sporting strangely feathered cowboy hats that real Texans like Willie Nelson wouldn't wear at gunpoint. She thought the city was hopelessly boosterish, searching for an identity—New South Powerhouse, New West Wonderland, New Something Big. If Austin was self-congratulatory, then Dallas was self-conscious, checking the mirror, always trying to measure itself against Phoenix, Houston, or wherever, like it had a case of Edifice Complex Royale. It was, really, too close to the mad scramble that her father had been locked into for decades, lurching from one corporate deal to another, moving the family and destroying his marriage. She had specialized, all the way back to Smith College, in serving up Texas stereotypes and Dallas played right into her hands.

Still surrounded by men, she put the hot sauce and cornpone back in her voice, in her writing, and applied it to a city that desperately wanted to be taken seriously. If she was going to prosper back in the land of Lyndon Baines Johnson and the Bush Dynasty—in the rattlesnake boil of the Dallas Cowboys, Big Oil, Mega Churches, Lee Harvey Oswald, Friday Night Lights, NASA, The Alamo, Ross Perot, Howard Hughes, and Bonnie & Clyde—she needed to write with a pointy cowgirl boot rising to meet some pontificating fat ass's pressed pants. It was Sam Clemens satire, speed-laced and circa the Reagan-Bush era.

She had seen doctors about her drinking and was prescribed Antabuse, the first medicine ever approved by the FDA for the treatment of alcoholism. She opened a spiral composition book and wrote at the top of the page that this was "My Summer Vacation 1983."

"Mon.—fly in from S.A., o.j. and coffee on plane. Horrible hangover. I wish I were dead all day long."

She wrote about a diet and exercise regimen, trying to eat pasta, fruit, vegetables, and trying to stop smoking. She swam some laps in a pool in the evening. She ran three laps in the evening. She snacked on green beans and Triscuits with butter. She missed an appointment with Dr. L on Monday, "maybe part of depression," and when she called him, she learned he was unavailable for weeks. She had insomnia, tried not to smoke or drink. When she weighed herself, the scale said 172 pounds, "which pissed me off a lot." She wanted to be under 160 by her thirty-ninth birthday. She noticed that she was singing around the house: "Which I haven't done for a long time. 'I wish I was dead' becoming rarer and rarer—now only comes when I'm hungry."

On Saturday, August 13, she wrote that she'd been hanging out with *Times Herald* friends and then had gone drinking at the Green Glass and "came home and deliberately started drinking. I think it was simply the conformity. I wanted so much to be like the others, one of the gang. Boy there is a lot of 'we all drink' pressure. . . . I feel good about having people over, 3 in a week, and seeing more of people."

During the week of August 14, she tried some self-hypnosis to stop eating, smoking, and drinking. She wrote some more in the composition notebook:

> Last night I sat down to dinner—of a fine salad. I decided to have a glass of wine as well. And bread and butter. I then drank the entire bottle of wine, a little less than half a bottle of sherry and almost half a bottle of Grand Marnier. . . . Only by accident had I not called anyone or seen anyone and made a horrible fool of myself. . . . I do not want to drink ever again. I don't want the calories. I don't want the amazing expense. I don't want the depression, I don't want the awful out-of-control, leaving pots on the stove, lights on all night, doors open, files scattered about. I don't want the danger of driving drunk. I don't want to make an ass of myself in front of people I care about. I don't want to call Helen & Ollie twice in one night with the same story. I don't want to gross out David Richards, Ann Richards, Mitch Green, Sheila, Kaye, Eden & Neil, Charlie K—Christ the world. I do not want to drink. I am going to accept the contradiction of wanting to drink when I'm with young reporters in the Green Bar (and avoid the Green Bar—no reason to be there unless asked). I now have $1.68 in my bank account from a tax return check of almost $4,000. A lot of that has to do with booze, at least half.

The following Tuesday, August 16, she wrote:

> Hurt car on way home. Could easily have killed someone. Understand Charlie Wilson entirely. My problem, my fault, my way of life. This morning I find a bottle of Scotch out. A bottle of Grand Marnier out. . . . I have no recollection whatsoever of how the evening ended. . . . Shit, who was in my room. Nothing. This is it. I will not drink again. If I drink again, I will go get professional help for my problem.

On Thursday, August 18, she wrote:

> I think we're back under control again. Tuesday was beyond belief . . . an entire day of suicidal depression. Wed. morning, went to see Dr. L. Did feel better after "confession." Although I was sarcastic about it. . . . Still dealing with some self-hatred and suicide, but much better. I plan to go back on Antabuse for a couple of weeks.[14]

One afternoon, she had danced round-and-round with the editors about her column and she decided to skip out. She found Porterfield, who had also been given a column, at his desk.

"I can't stand this shit anymore. Let's go early and have a hamburger and get drunk," she yelled.

They left the paper, like the old days in Houston, and went looking for a place to drink and maybe eat some food. All around downtown, if you looked carefully, you'd see the pseudo-Bohemian shuffle of a reporter or two or three, out "taking the pulse of the city," smoking and headed for a hidden place to drink for a few hours in the afternoon. She was wearing a sparkly dress that day, a tight one, and she and Porterfield headed to Green Glass two blocks away from the paper. They drank several shots of Jack Daniels.

"Living in Dallas is like living in corruption. It's all around us," she said to Porterfield.

And he told her that he wanted the same thing she did: "I was just a reporter but I wanted freedom."

They laughed about the way some people in town would swoon when "celebrities" came to visit for some symphony gala, museum opening, or charity event at the fancy hotels: "What about the time Sophia Loren was here and somebody from Neiman Marcus dropped his head right into Loren's sweet dolce vita tits?" Porterfield was not part of the deep, deep Austin crowd, but he could be trusted, he hadn't changed, and he still had the somewhere-beyond-skeptical view on things.

They drank their Jack Daniels and stepped back and began the crawl to the paper. They stopped at a downtown intersection. They waited for the light to change—in Dallas, police routinely gave out tickets if you crossed the street when it was red. Alongside them were some tall, well-dressed men—members of the Harlem Globetrotters who were in town, checking out the city before their game. As the light changed, everyone stepped into the street, and one of the basketball players suddenly reached out and pinched Ivins on the ass. She thought it was Porterfield. She assumed that a big-time writer in Texas had pinched her ass, on a downtown street in Dallas, and she wheeled and cold-cocked him, hard and intense right in the face, his blood and his front teeth spraying right out of him. He tried to explain, she didn't want any of it, and they plodded back to the paper, the blood soaking into his shirt.

"We're both Scotch-Irish. I'm the Amazon part of the Scotch-Irish . . . and if you EVER fuck me over, I'm gonna bash you in the head," she shouted. And then she laughed and laughed.

Porterfield flashed his missing tooth back at the paper and it made a good story for years to come. He had decided that Ivins was the greatest journalist he had ever known. And, he knew she really hated Dallas.

"Austin is the Athens of Texas—and Dallas is nothing more than a goddamned Neiman Marcus city," she told him. "Let's get the fuck out of here. Let's just get the hell out of this goddamned crazy place!"[15]

⟶

She knocked down garbage cans when she got in her car and zoomed away from high-octane newspaper parties. And when she walked into a room, men and women popped to her like metal shavings to a magnet. She was on the radio, on TV, and she was increasingly appearing in national publications. She was writing her "letters" from Texas again, this time working with what she thought was her easy-to-find prey in Dallas. Her calendar was filling up with public appearances—the League of Women Voters wanted her to come to Houston, libraries wanted her to speak, the State Bar Association wanted her back.

As the Republicans began arriving for their national convention in 1984, both the *Times Herald* and the *Morning News* went into deep strategy sessions, trying to figure out how to handle it. There would be special news sections, newspaper-hosted parties, and editorial staff meetings to talk about how the publications were going to be on display, how this was a big fat coming-out party because the national press would be at the Hyatt, at the grand old Adolphus Hotel, and this was a moment to impress. The details were laid out, military-style, and reporters were assigned to cover every facet imaginable.

City leaders were scared shitless about protesters, outside agitators who might ruin the whole party and recast Dallas as the unhinged place that had once conspired to kill JFK. Some fevered mind suggested that the protesters be allowed to convene, but that they be "assigned" to an official protest area—a recommendation that was perniciously logical and very Dallas-like in its rationale. There would be an orderly protest, a confined and quarantined protest—and, further, the protesters would be given a diseased piece of land filled with hypodermic needles that rolled down behind the local jail toward the noxious banks of the fetid Trinity River. The *Morning News* assigned a reporter, before the convention, to camp out in the Trinity River bottoms and write a piece about what it would be like for the protestors down by the Trinity—where people used to joke that if you dipped your hand in the coal-black water, you would be missing fingers when you pulled it back. The reporter dutifully camped out in the wastelands, listening to the scum-coated creatures scrambling over the abandoned refrigerators and shopping carts sticking up out of the ten-foot-wide, polluted river—and to the entreaties of sex-crazed prisoners howling through the bars on the jailhouse windows. At night, there was a thudding crunch on the gravel and a cop drove up to tell the reporter he was an idiot and would probably lose his life.

Ivins was issued her press pass for the convention and was hired by several publications, including the *Washington Post*, to tell them what Dallas was all about:

> Let's face it, this is a white-bread town . . . it's the world's most self-conscious city in the world's least self-conscious culture. Dallas is an uptight town . . . the materialism is enough to make you sick, if you happen to be sensitive to it. . . . Dallas is the makeup capital of the universe . . . a city of earnest, energetic strivers, many of them millionaires many times over, trying to make Dallas great. . . . Dallas is

> set amidst some of the Lord's less impressive handiwork. . . . Dallas' full share of human folly, lunacy, and wonderfully ludicrous absurdity wouldn't be half as funny as it is if Dallas didn't try so hard to be straight.[16]

She liked the people she knew more than the job; she liked the people more than the city itself. Her editor was Jon Senderling, a respected newspaper veteran who had worked his way up through the *Times Herald* ranks and become editorial page head in 1981. He wasn't exactly like Ivins; he loved Frank Sinatra and horse racing and had the patience to immerse himself in a long game of chess. He would eventually go to work as the public affairs manager for Ross Perot's company EDS.

She was still giving speeches, moving outside the orbit of the editorial page—it was something that she had done before, even when she was in Denver, and she continued in Texas. She weighed an offer for $750 and expenses to talk to the Public Affairs Council in Washington but turned it down in 1984. She was the "roastmistress" at a fundraiser for family violence programs. She went to Austin to appear at the Texas Women's Literary Tradition conference; she and Northcott were put on a panel moderated by Liz Carpenter, Lady Bird Johnson's former press secretary. She spoke to the State Bar of Texas about ethics in journalism. At Texas Woman's University, where the newspaper was called the *Daily Lass-O*, she did a speech titled "Texas Women: They Used to Say Texas Was Hell on Women and Horses—Why Did They Stop?" Her talk was scheduled the day before one given by opera star Beverly Sills. And she went to the campouts around Austin, spent a weekend in September at the dog races across the border in Juarez, Mexico, and got notes from Carlton Carl about a news item that mentioned she had been spotted around Dallas looking chic in her white summer dress and sneakers. And she spent more time reconnecting and extending that network of *Observer* supporters, social justice activists, pro bono attorneys, liberal lawmakers, academics, and poets across the state.

In November 1984, her Columbia professor Melvin Mencher sent her a note: "Dear Molly, God what a disaster. But I see you are still at it down there, telling your readers about people like Phil Gramm. Ugh. . . . The school . . . well, it is still here. It stands at 116th and Broadway and has a physical presence. Period."[17] She corresponded with other people she had met in New York, including author and educator Catharine Stimpson, who had written extensively about the roles of women in culture and society. And there were late-night calls, sometimes at 2 A.M., with Myra MacPherson in Washington—who sent her a note card printed with the words "don't ever change" and writing "Ye Gods, growing up is hard to do" and "you are too wonderful as it is now, gives us all an inferiority complex."[18]

Friends in New York asked her if she would be godmother to one of their children, and the two would eventually correspond. Ivins recommended books to read—including *The Diary of Anne Frank*—and she also encouraged Kaye Northcott to mentor the girl. Her own father was in touch, writing more often about his new relationship with Virginia and the debate they were having about taking a barge trip in France. And friends were calling her about her appearance on the *MacNeil/Lehrer* show on PBS—telling her they laughed out loud when she talked, on air, about rednecks liking women with big "garbanzas." She received a note from "Ray" in the summer of 1984 telling her that he was leaving the *New York Times*, that he had heard that her work was always being sanitized—and that he could relate to her, as his stories were being scrutinized for any liberal views that might "taint the big mother."[19]

Friends continued to wonder if she would ever get married. It was, in some circles, a bit of a parlor game: The more famous she became, the more speculation emerged about her sexual preferences—was she gay, straight? Her best friends knew that she had had a series of short-term relationships with a number of men (after Hank Holland and Jack Cann) who were immensely successful in their respective careers—and who were also married. Her archives are dotted with evidence that suggests quiet, perhaps secretive, affairs with various men at distinct junctures in her life. A globe-trotting, award-winning photographer. An influential author on the East Coast. Various political figures in Washington and Texas. One thing was clear: She had no shortage of suitors. Several powerful men—lobbyists, lawyers, writers—pursued her with cards, letters, calls, and drinks.

With her friends, she talked about the rumors that swirled around her—why she never seemed to have a steady man in her life and that must mean that she was gay. She told the same joke, over and over again, that she would be a lot more interesting if she really was gay. More than one friend said that Ivins was too committed to her work to ever engage in a long-term relationship. And more than one friend said that she simply never wanted to slip into the world that her mother and father had constructed for themselves—a marriage that, at least from her father's perspective, didn't deserve to last. And, of course, there was at least one friend who believed that with her intense workload, with her renewed commitment to sobriety programs, she had no time for anything, or anyone, else. Besides, she had friends, hundreds of people who would summon her to parties, who liked to be around her, who made her laugh, who passed for her extended family. At holidays, she liked to invite to her home the people who had no family to celebrate with. Her generosity, as always, seemed almost unbounded and unnatural. When she wanted to be friends with someone, she stared hard at them, asking them questions about their background, education, interests. And sometimes at the parties she had at her house, some other powerful politico or celebrity-seeker would arrive, wanting to meet Ivins. She would tell her friends that the men were almost clawing, pursuing her around the house as if she was some sort of prize. It was, she told people, as if nothing had changed in Texas since she first began covering the State Capitol—and the yahoos from Texas were reaching for her tits. The men she was interested in, the ones she preferred to spend time with, the ones she embarked on relationships with were almost a bit like her—workaholics, well-read, liberal, somewhere north of sarcastic and south of cynical. Someone who eventually went to work for her said that she only slept with men who were her equals.

Reinventing herself as a Texas Mark Twain was still an ongoing process, an increasingly purposeful project. Many of her friends talked to her about it in the context of her relationship with her father. It was, she admitted to some of them, a constructed persona that allowed her to feed off her anger at her father and the values he represented. As her work began to be distributed through the *Times Mirror* chain, as attention turned to Dallas because of the Republican National Convention, editors around the country started asking her to do what she had always been willing to do—interpret Dallas, and Texas, all over again. Her freelance opportunities multiplied and she fielded numerous TV and radio requests. It was the dawn of what one of her employees would call "Molly Inc." She was still a columnist for a regional paper—and arguably often measured against one of the best reporter-columnists in the city, her colleague Jim Schutze, who frequently linked the intimate, acute details of life on the streets of Dallas to the bigger policy imperatives. He often spoke of the Big Picture debates in Dallas through the prism of ordinary people. His column ran right under hers on the "Opinions" page—and there is a possibility she worked to distinguish herself from his approach and pushed even more toward her dialect-laden send-ups on people in power, leaning heavily on personal pronouns, writing in the present tense, writing in first person. "I believe that laughter heals almost anything, including bigotry, and if you need some, try reading Oscar Wilde," she once wrote for the *Times Herald*, on a day when Schutze was writing a somber, aching story about the lost dreams of the Asian refugees who had been sent to live in the near–East Side slums of Dallas.[20]

But as it became more clear that the *Times Herald* was really losing the newspaper war, the editors were taking stock of her collective legacy of torching the people who basically ran the city: She had said Ross Perot was a "man with a mind a half-inch wide" and businessman Eddie Chiles was a "loopy ignoramus." People were calling the paper to complain. Not just subscribers but advertisers, too, and they were telling editors that she seemed to hate the city her paper served. As one writer observed the scene: "Eventually the city fathers stopped getting the joke, especially when her leads began with 'It's been 10 years this month since [legendary community organizer] Saul David Alinksy died' and 'Happy May Day, comrades.' The bust was settling in. Pressure was put on the paper's owner, the *Times*

Mirror Corporation. It was felt, in the words of then editor Will Jarrett, that 'Molly was not in love with Dallas and Dallas was not in love with her.'"[21]

But her freelance work, writing about the conservative West that had spawned Ronald Reagan, writing about the Houston-based Big Oil Wonderland that had bankrolled and promoted the Bush Dynasty, simply led to more national venues. Texas seemed as complex, as crammed with sinners, as ever before. It stood for something, it was easy to caricature. And in many ways the distances between what old Austin represented and new Texas had become were now even more polarized, set against each other. With the green-lighted business growth, with the holy allegiance to capital punishment in the Lone Star State of Death, with the haunting reminders that violent racism was still entrenched in long stretches toward the Sabine River, with the Rio Grande Valley all but forgotten, with women still being held under the thumb of major institutions, it was clear that she had more than enough bittersweet work to cull. Her scope had broadened; it wasn't the characters at the State Capitol all the time. It was, really, the entire State of Texas, from Amarillo to Brownsville, from Texarkana to Marfa.

By the end of 1984, as the *Times Herald* kept slipping in Dallas, there were changes at the paper, a creeping, barely articulated sense that the paper needed to do more to fight the *Morning News* on a local level and take back the city in some way. There was a sense that she might be better at doing what she had started at the *Observer*, and what she had increasingly been doing for other publications and in her speeches—ripping Texas and its politicians, and doing less of her condemning takes directly on the culture of Dallas. Toward the end of the year, she was told that she had the "opportunity" to relocate back to Austin, to work out of the *Times Herald* bureau. She had just bought a house in Dallas, so she knew it wasn't really her bosses giving her a reward. She had tried to fit in—even agreeing to play a little toy drum with the Dallas Chamber Orchestra in its Christmas show. But there was all that barely disguised loathing. She liked some of the people, but she said she couldn't camp out alongside the Trinity River. That's where they put the protestors. And that's where the cops found dead bodies folded in the reeds, not far from the blinking neon of the twenty-four-hour bail bond offices. That's where the treated city wastewater flowed. All that shit in Dallas.

According to Kaye Northcott, "She was moved down here [to Austin] from the *Times Herald* because they wanted to get her out of the office. . . . They said, 'Wouldn't you like to go to Austin.' It was not a reward. If she wasn't wandering around Dallas, she wouldn't offend so many people."[22]

CHAPTER TEN

Molly, Inc.

My newspaper died the other day.

—MOLLY IVINS

She was laughing about the "glassholes"—the nickname the reporters had given to the editors back in Dallas, the ones who worked in the cloistered glass offices and seemed to be bending more and more in the battle against the *Morning News*. The *Morning News*, to her, was like a conservative version of the *New York Times*—dying on the altar of objectivity, earnestly accumulating national awards but not doing the kind of work that Newfield and others espoused. She talked about it around the office—how there were a dozen or more versions of reality, how you could report a story to death and find yourself knowing even less than you did when you started: That ultimate objectivity was bullshit and it could freeze a reporter in the grey zone, wallowing around and trying to "be fair" when there were larger points to be made—when systems, when people in power, had willfully abdicated their responsibilities and nothing was more important than just unloading on them.

Back in Austin in 1985, she reconnected with John Henry Faulk and his wife Liz. Her friends in Austin watched the relationship grow even more than it had before—and some decided that on the short list of people who "created" whatever Molly Ivins had become, Faulk might be at the top. Bullock was still there, waiting to see her, trying to stay sober. Richards, of course, was there too—throwing welcome-home parties, seeing her at the campouts. In the years that Ivins had been in New York, Denver, and Dallas, Richards had honed her own political ambitions, slicing deeper into the numbing, endless protocol of attending galas, functions, benefits, board meetings, and the seemingly every-weekend gatherings at the homes of wealthy Democratic kingmaker-lawyer-philanthropists on the west side of Austin, in Montrose in Houston, in King William in San Antonio, in Lakewood in Dallas. She wasn't drinking with Ivins anymore. And Ivins was seemingly successfully staying sober. She told friends she was happy to be in Austin.

According to Ross Ramsey, who worked with her at the *Times Herald*:

> Austin was where she wanted to live. Austin is politics central. There were two kinds of editorial reactions to her. There was always the group of editors who got Molly, totally. You know, "This is a political raconteur and entertainer and this is more about opinion and the subjective vibe of politics than this is about fact." We were an Austin bureau, for hard, factual stories about politics and government and Molly is the seasoning. And the other editorial reaction was "She's a journalist and the standards are the same for journalists"—and you had a whole group like that. You know, "Let her go off on her opinion stuff but she should be on a relatively short leash." And she'd report back to her editors, and group one always won.
>
> Molly was the kind of person you put on a billboard to draw people to the paper because they wanted to hear her voice, and they wanted to see what she had to say, even when she pissed them off. Sometimes especially when she pissed them off. Some of the people that we talked to over the years, they'd call the bureau, you'd be talking to them, you'd have some conversation with some Republican or whatever and you'd say, "So, do you read Molly?" [They would reply,]

"Yeah, I don't agree with a thing she says but I read her every time she comes out." She reveled in that.[1]

In early 1985, she learned she was on the list of the *Washington Journalism Review*'s best in the business. She took out a pen and carefully underlined the names of everyone she knew on the list—the people from Minneapolis, Houston, Dallas, Austin, and New York. She was a finalist for the Pulitzer Prize in commentary for 1985. But there were still hardcore *Texas Observer* supporters who wondered what she was still doing at a mainstream paper. Some chalked it up to money. During her first year back in Austin she wrote, with increasing frequency, for *The Nation*, *The Progressive*, and *Ms.*—and, ultimately, for at least twenty other publications, including the *New York Times*, *Time*, *Savvy*, the *Washington Journalism Review* and, of course, *The Texas Observer*. She was making $1,000 for speeches, except the ones that she would do for free—especially for the ACLU and its offshoots. The ACLU board members knew that she was available at almost any time, that she would never turn down an offer to speak—she had promised Faulk. He wanted her to continue his work, his appearances, and she told him that if there were opportunities to help the ACLU, she would. Throughout the '80s she constantly traveled doing ACLU work—and almost always received letters from the grateful presidents of local chapters because her appearances had raised more money than ever before. According to Ramsey:

> She was being pretty carefully mentored by John Henry Faulk. To the point where he would take her to speaking gigs and sort of show her how it was done. I don't know how structured it was, but it was obvious some thought had gone into it on both their parts. Molly struck me . . . as shy in front of audiences, not shy at all in print, but shy when you put her in front of a microphone or when you shined a spotlight on her. And I think Faulk taught her a lot about how to do this. And I think one of the things that happened, or that developed, it might have already been there, was the two-voiced Molly. There was the Molly, if you were just talking to Molly, that was thoughtful, intelligent, well-educated, extremely well-read. She was a blast to talk

> to about "What have you read?" That kind of thing. And then the sort of, the public Molly, which was the kind of "How y'all doing? Oh, how are you?" All that kind of stuff. Talking Texan the way no Texans actually do. Sort of over the top. But that was the public Molly and people liked it.[2]

She would insist that the other reporters go with her to see Faulk, to watch him sign copies of his book, work the room, and be greeted as the legendary survivor of the blacklist wars—a "freedom fighter," as she increasingly called him. Ramsey says:

> There's always a political circuit in Austin. There's always this group who's having John Henry Faulk talk to their group. And his deal was about the First Amendment, about the blacklist and all of his experiences. And so she would grab you and say, "Hey, let's go listen to this." It was obvious she and Faulk were having a conversation about it at a different level—which was sort of a "Here's how you do this and here's how you do that." They weren't overt about it but they were—he was training her. There was a mentoring relationship. She obviously had the touch in print but it's different when you are speaking, and she picked that up and she got really good at it.[3]

⁂

Ramsey liked Ivins. And she wrote notes to herself wondering if he would ever be someone she could be close to. She was a star at the paper, one of the people the paper promoted, but she still picked up the check, bummed cigarettes, and liked it when the reporters gathered for lunch, dinner, or beers at Scholz's, El Azteca on the east side of town, the old Greek diner downtown. She moved, for a while, into a place on Waterloo—a street honoring Austin's original name. She was given her own office inside the newspaper's Austin bureau, so when lobbyists, glad-handers, and politicians came bearing press releases and election-time spiels, it was like two operations—the Molly Ivins Section and the other three or four reporters. "The people who came in to visit her were often completely different than the people who came to visit us," says Ramsey. Her friends were dropping by, trying to cajole her into taking a break to go swimming in Barton Springs, to go hang out somewhere down by Town Lake. "She was a separate force."

And the reporters, the people who really hadn't known her very well from the old days—or knew her only as operating in some other orbit above the collective gene pool in Austin journalism—learned to guard their sources and secrets. Ivins never believed, as she frequently told other reporters, that anything was really off the record. "One of the first stories that everybody told when you went to work in the Austin bureau was . . . don't ever talk about stuff that is off the record or that you're trying to hold close for a while, around Molly. Because she's basically a magpie, and if it is bright and shiny she'll take it and put it in her nest. And you'll burn a source and your story will be broken, and it'll screw things up," says Ramsey.[4]

She strolled from her office, puffing on a cigarette, even though the people who ran the bureau building frowned on it: "What are you working on?"

The reporters would fudge. "Ah, nothing. Nothing."

It was also what she did outside the office—working the room: "People weren't as handled as they are now. And your chances of calling up a governor or a lieutenant governor and saying, 'Hey, let's go get a burger' were better, it wasn't an outlandish thing. . . . She was really good at that kind of social reporting, of being around people and soaking things up."[5]

She would often protect Bullock, Richards, and some select others. She could have told stories about Richards's drinking, about Bullock's insane escapades—but she didn't. Others, usually the pontificating plutocrats she disagreed with, were not so lucky. She didn't traffic in gossip in her columns, but she was not afraid to write in dialect, to recreate conversations in her columns, to have her way when she described someone's girth, smirk, or attitude. She told people—even her closest friends who suggested that she had drunk too much of John Henry Faulk's down-home tea and started polishing the stereotypes and even recycling her lines like Ann Richards—that it was necessary to make the stories palatable, readable, effective.

It was increasingly effortless, it was not a far stretch to call it Samuel Clemens–like, and it was becoming more than a cottage industry. Publications were clamoring for her work—even the *New York Times* had decided that it was safe to hear from her again, perhaps as long as she wasn't writing about City Hall, Albany, and sewer board hearings in lower Manhattan. It was, as it evolved, a uniquely American Franchise—a business move that her father, if he'd only took the time, would have understood. Her father had an unending attraction to the wealthiest people in Texas—and she had an unending distrust of it all that only drove her to be more successful. One of her best friends said George W. Bush and Molly Ivins were actually the same in one way—that they were out to prove to their fathers that they were better than their families perceived them to be, that they could succeed at something on their own. The difference, of course, was that she wasn't just rejecting his legacy, she was rejecting what he stood for.

Shoes off, feet up on the desk, she was wearing a Hawaiian shirt and singing Patsy Cline songs with someone on the phone. Some reporters in Texas knew she was still backing away from straight news paradigms—the standard journalism practice of calling people for opposing views, calling "experts" who could provide a careful, almost academic analysis of both sides of an issue. She also wasn't really doing intricate investigative work.

Dallas had helped coalesce a thought in her mind: She didn't want to have to really work for anyone again. In a city like Austin, where the politicians all know each other, where the spin doctors all knew each other, it was easy to immerse herself in the political scene. By the late 1980s, she was easily one of the best-known journalists from Texas. When the doors to the Texas senate or house swung open, people paid attention and almost instantly rose to greet her. The lawmakers liked the frisson of celebrity that she carried. There were more women in the room—more female officials, aides, and reporters—but she stood out because her very presence suggested that what was going on in the State Capitol might be written about for a national audience. Her very presence suggested a proximity to the *New York Times*, the *Washington Post*, all the places she had written for—and it suggested that the crap, the drudgery, and occasionally the issues being finagled under the big dome of the capitol actually mattered. Ross Ramsey says:

> She was one of those presences in the press corps where you could all be sitting around, all of us who were covering the legislature every day, wall to wall—you'd be sitting there slaving your ass off in the 130th day of the session—and Molly would walk in. And the whole place would stop and go over to see Molly. She was an eminence in that way. And they always wanted to know what she was thinking about, what she was talking about. There would just be a big crowd around her. She was a real magnet. This is a non–TV celebrity. She didn't get famous on TV. She didn't get famous on the radio. That's a writer.

He studied her, thought it must have been extremely satisfying to have that kind of reach, that impact, as a writer. "I always got the impression that she was doing exactly what she wanted to be doing."[6]

⇺⇻

Three days after Thanksgiving in 1985, she wrote some personal notes about her drinking and about the news she had just received—that her uncle, Bud Crawley, had committed suicide. A sculptor and photographer who taught at the university level in North Carolina, he took a boat out on a lake in Greenville and shot himself in the head. He had taken photographs of children to use in connection with his sculptures and police had barged into his studio and confiscated the pictures. Molly was livid, fearing that her uncle, who also had wrestled with a drinking problem, had been unjustly accused and then driven to suicide. She wanted the family to file a lawsuit, and she offered to contact the famous trial lawyer Gerry Spence to take on the case. Ivins wrote this to herself:

> The second anniversary of my sobriety and I am pleased with myself and proud of myself and still getting better. Went to AA tonight, I think just to share, tho I did not speak. When at first I couldn't get into the room, I walked away feeling sulky and hurt, but Bob ran after me down the street. Told me about the back door. AA at its best. Also heard today about my uncle Bud Crawley committing suicide. This is

> a ghastly story. . . . I think they ought to sue the blue bellied hell out of the pd [police department] and the postal inspector. There is apparently no complainant in the case, no child, no parent of any child, no one Bud ever dealt with.
>
> I believe all suicides have had it in them for a long time. Bud used to drink too much . . . but this is eerily like the Ingmar Bergman case and the Kafka case for that matter. Bud must also have had a horror of the groundless accusation you think you cannot disprove. . . . I consider him a victim of the mullahs, perhaps the first Jew in this pogrom, and the reaction is not just "I am not a Jew" but "He was not a Jew." Deny, deny, deny. It's the Jewish reaction to threat—deny it ever happened, cover it up. I'd like to see Gerry Spence try this.[7]

Despite the sad events occurring in her personal life, she was making more money than ever before—and, unsurprisingly, giving it away as soon as the paychecks arrived. She donated money to causes—to civil liberties groups, to anti-poverty agencies, to legal defense funds—and simply pressed dollars and personal checks into people's hands. She continued to send books to the children of her friends; she had sleepovers for kids, including her nephews. She kept tabs on her brother and gingerly tried to offer advice on life, jobs, his health. On weekends she rode the back roads that filtered out from Austin—in 1986, a fifteen-minute ride outside the city limits would bring you to some places that heaven had gratefully frozen in time. Small towns with quiet watering holes, cold beer, and barbecue smoking in the back of an old shack. Country dance halls where the rednecks still danced alongside the cosmic dropouts from Austin. Tiny towns where the ancestors of the German settlers still operated their own one-lane bowling alleys, served up homemade bread and curling ropes of smoked sausage. Some things had vanished—the Armadillo World Headquarters, where she had once dressed up as a stuffy *Times* reporter during a Commander Cody and His Lost Planet Airmen concert, was gone. So was the Soap Creek Saloon, where Doug Sahm and his musical entourage had done their best to hold old Austin together, to really keep

Austin weird, to really keep it Groover's Paradise. The heart of the old city was changing; it was the beginning of what some people would call Silicon Prairie—or, in a nod to the rolling land to the west, Silicon Hills. The buzz was all about the incoming software companies, the emergence of Dell Computer Corporation, the way the city was becoming a high-tech center.

There was more than a creeping sense that the people who had defined a certain scene in Austin in the late '60s and '70s were about to be lapped by the new thing—this massive infusion of techies, venture capitalists, and California realtors. The die-hards fretted about the Californication of Austin; too many McMansions, they said, were being built over the aquifer and the cedar-studded limestone cliffs, and the funky places where you could get an enchilada as plump as a baby's arm were being chased by the chain restaurants. At First Friday, the rolling party in Austin where Ivins became a fixture, a lot of that cultural churn was checked at the door. Inside, there was still an unlikely freak flag ensemble—dough-faced liberal lawyers mingling with someone who had played for The Uranium Savages, farm worker activists up from the Rio Grande Valley and huddled in the corner with runaway poets from Houston, a young man who would write her a letter saying he hadn't really been comfortable being gay in Austin until he came to her parties. Someone would put Stevie Ray Vaughan or some other blessed soul on the turntable and the music itself was enough to temporarily keep out whatever was creeping into Austin—probably something sent, many people assumed, by the Great White Devils in Dallas. Those parties at her house, like the smoky campouts, were reinforcing moments for her in Austin—being around the wing of people who were going to push her to write what she wanted.

⤛⤚

She spoke to the Texas Institute of Letters banquet in February 1986, prophetically reading from Larry McMurtry's book *Moving On*. The next month she flew to New York to speak to *The Nation*'s one hundred twentieth anniversary and fundraiser—with Joan Baez, Studs Terkel, George McGovern, Jesse Jackson, and Rosario Murillo, the Sandinista and a member of the National Assembly of Nicaragua. Victor Navasky, editor of *The Nation*, wanted to offer her a job as the magazine's Washington correspondent:

> In that capacity, you would be you. Which is to say that you would (or wouldn't, your decision) cover the White House, the Supremes, the G-men, the Fourth Estate, fifth column, sixth sense, Seventh Day Adventists, presidential politicks, Congress, the Congressional Record (Izzie Stone division), etc., etc., etc.[8]

He offered to pay her what she was getting at the paper, $84,000, and see if he could get her columns syndicated and also talk about helping her do a book. She'd get an office across from the Supreme Court. She thought about it, especially since everyone could hear the death rattle of the *Times Herald.* Cutting its losses in the losing battle over classified ads with the *Morning News*, *Times Mirror* sold the paper to Dean Singleton, whom some critics considered the enfant terrible of the newspaper industry. In the '80s, he began buying papers and either putting them out of business or sometimes watching them slowly die. His detractors said he was a mortician: his supporters said he was an efficient businessman. When the conference call came to Austin to alert Ivins to the sale and the fact that the paper was no longer going to be linked either to the war chest or to the high-road culture that some associated with *Times Mirror*, she grabbed a notepad and took careful notes. She was told that she was an "asset" and would be protected.

The newspaper's dissolution did little to slow down her outside endeavors. She was still attending the annual Conference on World Affairs in Boulder, Colorado, mingling in 1986 with writer Whitley Streiber, reporter Jonathan Kwitny, Roger Ebert, and others. She joked that there should be an Anti New Age Panel at the conference—to talk about how dumb pyramid power is, how awful sushi tasted, how barbecue smells better than incense. In Texas, she was still invited to be a guest speaker at high-profile events—she told one-liners at a roast for attorney Warren Burnett, the famous trial lawyer from Odessa. And on the family front, her father told her that he was moored at the Longboat Key yacht club and planning to permanently relocate to Sarasota, to be close to the water, to have a larger yacht that he could sail to the Keys and beyond. He added that he was a big fan of Senator Robert Dole—because he was a "Kappa Sig." Her sister wrote her in 1986, declining her offer to have her kids come to visit because in Austin "that would be like putting a kitty in with a lion."

Austin had become the perfect place for Ivins to begin teeing up on the Bush Dynasty. George Herbert Walker was pushing for the presidency in 1987, and James Baker III and the petroleum potentates in Houston were cracking open their vaults to help him. She had seen them all in Houston, and writing about them was a short, easy stroll in the orchard. She had helped explain LBJ-era Texas to America, through her work for the *Times*, the *Washington Post*, and the *Observer*. And, as the George H.W. Bush presidency loomed, her work was almost acutely personal. She knew people like the Bushes, she had gone to school with people from their army. She grew up in the same zones as the Bush family. It was easy for her to write about the Bushes; the people who worked for Ivins said she never really minded calling it class warfare.

She had always wanted to write a book, maybe something that touched on those Big Power people in Texas. Maybe something that touched on the Bill of Rights, the Constitution, the broader notion of freedom of expression in the United States. Something intensely serious, outsized. Maybe even a better, contemporary, version of Billy Lee Brammer's thinly veiled novel about politics in Texas—maybe the book that he would have done, the follow-up, if he hadn't been eaten alive by drink and speed. She told people at the *Times Herald* that she sometimes had reservations about writing a book, that it might be beyond her reach. It wasn't a crisis of self-confidence, one friend explained; just hard to envision how to do a 100,000-word book that had a consistent theme—and would be written in that by-now-recognizable, on-demand voice. It was one thing to do it in short form, in 800-word bites in a newspaper column. It was another thing to sustain the voice, the attitude, for several chapters devoted to one theme.

She was watching George H.W. Bush on TV and scribbling little notes to herself: "The fatuous bonhomie of Bush, the banality of his programs." And she thought about herself on TV: "If they can teach Mr. Ed to talk on TV, they can teach me." That spring she held out hope that she'd win a Pulitzer for commentary, but she was again named a finalist.

In the summer of 1988, she was invited—along with many of the women who had also gone down the Salmon River, including Donna Shalala, Alice Rivlin, and Carol Bellamy—on an eighteen-day trek to India, to Kashmir. She took notes: "India is living in several different centuries at the same time. New dimensions in sensory experience for these feet. Amazing, I was feeling quite perfectly miserable and certain this bug was [a case of] developing pneumonia. When I started doing yoga, I now feel 10,000 percent better." The trip was rough, in its way, with primitive facilities and Ivins popping some Cipro to ward off any lingering illnesses. When she returned, she talked to various producers about doing more regular radio and television work, especially the *MacNeil/Lehrer* program on PBS. She flew to San Diego to accept an ACLU award for "civil libertarian of the year"—and she nominated John Henry Faulk for a Hugh Hefner First Amendment Award. She had met Hefner, liked his commitment to freedom-of-speech issues, and communicated over the years with his daughter, Christie. Faulk won the $3,000 award—she was as close to him as ever and worried about his health. He was in his mid-seventies, battling cancer, and the expenses were mounting. As 1988 came to a close, she was devoted to keeping the *Observer* financially afloat—and Faulk's legacy intact—by donating money to the publication and speaking as often as she could to civil liberties groups around the nation.[9]

In Austin, she conferred with Ann Richards about Richards's gubernatorial campaign. Richards had moved her way through the ranks, becoming an expert political tactician, then state treasurer, and had her breakout in 1988 when she went to the Democratic national convention and ladled on the Texanisms by saying she pitied George H.W. Bush: "Poor George, he can't help it. He was born with a silver foot in his mouth." It was exquisitely deadly and delivered with drop-dead, droll perfection. Richards was kicking Bush's gilded ass in a national forum, and people said it was something that Ivins had already been doing in print for years. As Richards ran for office, Ivins's obvious allegiances to her—all those camping trips, the mutual struggles with alcohol—were only cemented. Ivins felt a palpable sense in Austin that Richards was going to take back the State Capitol, and Ivins was planning to join a "people's march" up the steps of the building in case Richards was the unlikely winner against Big Oil Man Clayton Williams.

Richards had sought help for her alcoholism in the early 1980s; her marriage to Dave Richards had also ended. She was fighting rumors about her personal life—GOP-inspired whispers that she was a cokehead, that she was a lesbian. It was, really, something else she shared with Ivins. The gossip mill in Austin was whispering the same things about Ivins. The thinking went like this: Nobody was that funny, or could stay up that late, unless she was drug-fueled. It became a sort of sub-specialty in the slimy corridors of Austin, the all-purpose accusation leveled against political figures—Ivins, Richards, and even George W. Bush. One prominent defense attorney in Odessa called up a reporter in Austin and suggested he had some solid leads that could show that Bush was snorting cocaine out at the Midland polo club—but that he certainly wouldn't provide any of that solid evidence or go on the record. A syndicated national cartoonist suggested a reporter check into rumors about Bush importing prostitutes from Mexico so his friends in West Texas could have a party. Meanwhile, Richards was constantly being scorched by the outer edges of the Karl Rove–inspired political machine in Texas. And if Richards had dirt in her background, then Ivins must have some too. She wasn't running for office, but she was famous enough, politicized enough, for people to spread rumor after rumor about her—that she was addicted to drugs, that she and Richards were lovers, that Ivins slept with Congressman Charlie Wilson, that she had once been best friends with George W. Bush. The stories piled up to the point where a reporter from *People* magazine called Texas to ask about Ivins's sexual orientation.

Ivins told friends she thought the gossip was laughable. And she told them she simply wanted Richards to win. She was unabashed in her public and private support: "Republican nominee Claytie Williams was a perfect foil, down to his boots, making comments that could be construed as racist and sexist. Ann was the candidate of everybody else, especially women. She represented all of us who have lived with and learned to handle good ol' boys, and she did it with laughter. The spirit of the crowd that set off from the Congress Avenue Bridge up to the Capitol the day of Ann's inauguration was so full of spirit and joy."[10]

⁂

John Leonard, who hired her to do freelance book reviews for the *Times*, might have been the first person to understand the bigger political expediency in Ivins's work—not just the items or agendas she advanced in her columns, but the thought that she was emerging as a political force at an opportune time for Democrats and liberals. He marveled at her work, thought it somewhere beyond unique—a mixture of Lenny Bruce, Rabelais, Lily Tomlin, Mark Twain. He came to call her style simply "Molly." To him, there was no match for her, at least in terms of columnists who were mocking the right with such eternal glee. She had Ronald and Nancy Reagan to work with: "His mind is mired somewhere in the dawn of social Darwinism and she's a brittle, shallow woman obsessed with appearances, but then it was that kind of decade, wasn't it?" On the first George Bush: "Calling George H.W. Bush shallow is like calling a dwarf short." More on Reagan: "Ronald Reagan is so dumb that if you put his brains in a bee, it would fly backwards." And on the CIA: "The CIA should start a chapter of Nun Killer's Anonymous."

She and Leonard bonded over their addiction to alcohol. They spent Thanksgiving together in New York and searched for an AA chapter; she cracked people up at the twelve-step meetings they attended. Later, they took a ride in a white stretch limo out to Long Island, just to have fun. He had decided that she had more than the usual following for a newspaper columnist: She had a singular voice *and* a political following.

It was increasingly clear to the friends who came to see her in Texas, or who grilled her on the reportorial process, that she had had to slog through some lonely moments in the State Capitol, in the musky barrooms where

Bob Bullock and the others practiced their cowboy necromancer dances, in the small towns where women were simply still not welcome at the police station, the judge's chambers, or the county commissions. As her friends filtered her work, her career, through the landscape and the history, through what Texas still had ties to, her career arc began to appear even more of a feminist triumph. She had done work in Texas that people in New York hadn't done, even with all the endless, welcoming venues for their work. There were writers at *The Village Voice* and some op-ed columnists who hammered hard on the people channeling Boss Tweed, but Ivins in Texas wasn't just railing against her targets, she was usually alone as she made fun of them in their own backyard.

Her loyal friend Eden Lipson said: "I finally realized that it was us, the cosmopolitan New Yorkers in the media capitol, with our literary and political gossip and hermetic chattering who were, in fact, provincial. Molly was the one who saw America large and clear, who out-reported the mainstream media from Austin, who had a balanced and ultimately optimistic view of the world. Molly's generosity was legendary, but in addition, she was brave."[11]

If reader response was any measure, the letters she was receiving suggested that there was now a dedicated national audience that liked the polemics leavened with humor. A readership that didn't want to be preached to by a dour soul quoting Emma Goldman, that wanted to laugh at the condition, the opposition, and have someone hopefully make it all a bit less painful. With right-wing radio simmering and headed to full boil, with Big TV and mainstream newspapers muted by corporate ownership, Ivins was picking up more readers. As Leonard would say, a constituency. And, with that surge in popularity, she also drew people who loathed her. In 1990, she received a letter:

> You are so arrogant that you are insulting even when you try to be reasonable. The way I see it is this. I suspect I am brighter than you, better educated than you, more worldly than you, contribute more to charity, have dealt with more minorities and more with those at the poverty level than you.

She sent the letter back with a note scrawled at the bottom:

> May be, but my manners are far better than yours. Sorry you are so angry, you would spill this kind of nasty bile on someone you've never met and about whom, obviously, you know nothing.[12]

⇜⇝

Her name was resonating in the right publishing circles in New York. John Leonard and Eden Lipson from the *Times* championed her, and her work was appearing in even more magazines. *Esquire* sent her a note in January inviting her to a Manhattan banquet honoring the magazine's list of the "Women We Love." By 1990, she also had an agent in New York. Dan Green had pursued her after one of her appearances on National Public Radio. She told him she already had a deal with a small Texas publishing house. But after she grew dissatisfied with the publisher, she talked to Green and he secured a two-book deal for her with Random House—to do a collection of her shorter pieces and also to do a longer book about the Texas legislature. He urged her to do the anthology first, even though publishers sometimes fret about whether journalism collections can ever sell well. Green felt she had something different to offer: "She was not part of the Washington–New York punditry." And that fact might give her a bigger audience—one composed of readers who were tired of the predictable, and predictably boring, talking heads and print pontificators.[13]

Ivins told Liz Faulk that when she had flown to New York to cement her book deal, she met Random House editor Peter Osnos at an expensive French restaurant. She felt self-conscious, thinking that Osnos might view her as a hick from Texas. (They actually had met years earlier when Ivins and several journalists from around the country had traveled to Moscow as part of an exchange program. Osnos had been a correspondent for *The Washington Post* in Moscow).

She had kept all those old notes from her drinking bouts with Bullock, during which he dictated story after story about bagmen, holier-than-thou governors, and the profane scramble for lucre in Austin: the kind of material that might form the backbone of some intense examination of the howling acts of illusion in the Texas legislature. But Green was still keen on her putting together a collection of her stories from *Ms.*, *The Nation*, *The Progressive*, *The Atlantic Monthly*, *Mother Jones*, *Savvy*, and the *Washington Journalism Review*.

During a visit to her home in Austin, Osnos spotted one of the *Times Herald* posters: "Molly Ivins Can't Say That, Can She?" He suggested that the slogan be the title of her book. Green thought that, at the very least, it would be a bestseller in Texas.

While she was away from the office, someone in the *Times Herald* bureau dropped a note on her desk on April 9: "From Kaye Northcott, Please call. John Henry died this evening."

Ivins had known, weeks earlier, that he didn't have much longer to live. She had gone to see him and said: "John Henry, I don't want you to worry about the First Amendment. I'm gonna take care of it." She tried to fly back for his funeral, but got stuck in the airport in Dallas. She wrote down some thoughts about Faulk: "Do not ever doubt that the man was a radical. . . . [W]hen it came to politics, Johnny Faulk believed in, acted upon and lived out one of the most radical political creeds to show up in the course of history."[14]

She appeared at a memorial tribute, and two months later his widow wrote a letter to Ivins:

> Thank you for being there for me during the difficult times during John Henry's illness. And thank you, too, for being there for him. He was always delighted in your visits and was, as you know, quite spirited—certainly saying what he believed right up until nearly the end.[15]

Ivins offered some work to Elizabeth Faulk, or "Liz" as everyone called her. Friends thought that Faulk would bring some efficiency, order, to the cobbled-together existence that had engulfed Ivins. She had been jotting down speaking gigs on the back of scraps of paper, forgetting to pack things for trips, agreeing to appear at one benefit when she had already agreed to another on the same day. She was still worried about her battle with alcoholism, she was still prone to being depressed, she was still astounding people with an almost boundless, un-tethered generosity. People who knew her in Minnesota, who knew her in France, who had come to an ACLU event in San Francisco or listened to her speak at the Conference on World Affairs in Boulder, were all inclined to call her before they came to Austin for their book tours or speaking gigs, and she arranged dinner parties for them that lasted for hours—and then she'd invite them to crash at her house and take whatever they needed to eat in the morning. If someone was in Austin—Roy Blount, Jr., and others—they invariably wound up seeing Ivins.

Faulk began to forcefully rein things in, organizing Ivins's rambling files, negotiating bigger speaking fees, making travel arrangements, screening calls, making doctor's appointments. She was doing the things she had done for her late husband—bringing order, clarity, to a haphazard process. Ivins would write a dedication to Faulk in one of her books: ". . . and to the indispensable Elizabeth Peake Faulk. As members of the Lizzie Fan Club nationwide know, she's pretty fabulous folks her own self, but you should never leave her on hold for long." Faulk was blunt and had a low tolerance for bullshit, for the hangers-on she assumed were around only to gorge on Ivins's celebrity and generosity. Faulk hated East Coast pretensions, and she loathed the people she thought were using Ivins as if she was a commodity. She would come to Ivins's house—a home in South Austin that was set on a hill that afforded a nice view toward the rising downtown skyscrapers. Faulk waded into the papers, books, notebooks, ashtrays, and leftover food. Ivins might have skipped out to meet with reporters at The Broken Spoke, the old, low-slung honky-tonk not far from her house; when she came back, Faulk had restored order.

The surge simply never stopped. Ivins's column was being syndicated. The *Times Herald* editors cooked deals with papers in El Paso, Corpus Christi, Odessa, and other small cities. The *San Francisco Examiner*, *Detroit News*, *Philadelphia Daily News*, and *Houston Post* also quickly picked her up.[16] That year she asked her Dallas editors if she could reduce her workload to one column a week so she could start selecting and editing her old stories for the Random House book.

⋞⋟

For the book-cover photo, she put on boots and a blue-denim Western shirt and reclined, with a typewriter nearby, against a backdrop of grass and a cluster of trees. She asked Governor Ann Richards to write a blurb: "Molly Ivins has birthed a book and it is more fun than riding a mechanical bull and almost as dangerous." And, she asked David Broder to write one too: "If there is a shrewder, funnier observer of the American scene writing today than Molly Ivins, I do not know her. This is unconventional wisdom with no inhibitions. Bless her and don't let her change." The book lurched onto the *New York Times* bestseller list at No. 12 on November 17, 1991, a few notches below books by Oliver North, Shirley MacLaine, Katharine Hepburn, Bill Cosby, and evangelist Pat Robertson. And then it spent the next twenty-nine weeks on the list—gusted along by an especially high level of exposure in newspapers around the country. Journalists had been following her work for years and they did countless stories and reviews. It all dovetailed with the fact that her speechmaking was seamless; she had locked into an engagingly paced delivery that played well almost everywhere she went. The book simply kept selling and selling.

Osnos was surprised. He came to a conclusion: that Ivins had dedicated followers at each of the newspapers and magazines she had written for. In a way, those sets of readers had coalesced and turned into a constituency—a large one that pushed the book up the bestseller list. She had developed friends and followers as a result of being so prolific. And at every one of her publication venues, she had a zealous fan base. Liberals were eager to hear more from her. "She said things that journalists across the board didn't think they could get away with," says Green.[17]

As her book was climbing the list, the newspaper war effectively ended in Dallas when the *Morning News* crushed the competition. In 1991, the *Times Herald* was sold again, this time to the company that owned the *Morning News*—and the paper was promptly shut down in December. She wrote a goodbye piece about the paper in *Mother Jones*: "My newspaper died the other day. I'd worked for the *Dallas Times Herald* for ten years, and its death was a kick in the gut the like of which I cannot recall ever having experienced." Some reporters had already bailed out, anticipating the closure; others angled for work at the *Morning News*. Given Ivins's constant, open attacks on the rival paper, that was not an option for her.

She was good friends with Dan Rather; they had regularly crossed paths on stories and especially in Texas, where they intersected with the *Observer* crowd, including Ronnie Dugger. CBS News was, maybe, a place to go—doing commentary, having her own field producer, and trying to figure out how to meld her voice, humor, and politics for television. There were the stand-by freelance outlets—*The Nation* and *The Progressive*. She could rely, exclusively, on freelance—*Playboy*, *Time*, *The Atlantic Monthly*, and her contacts at the *Times*. She could also, maybe, go to work doing a bigger book—not a collection of her shorter newspaper and magazine pieces, but a book on the Texas legislature, or a larger take on LBJ's legacy, on Ann Richards, on Barbara Jordan.[18]

When the *Times Herald* folded, she was quickly contacted by the *Fort Worth Star-Telegram*, which had almost quietly been gaining its own reputation as an improving regional daily. "It was serendipity. She was well-known, they called her the most sought-after unemployed columnist in the country," says Ken Bunting, deputy managing editor.[19] Shortly after the *Times Herald* collapse, *Star-Telegram* editor Mike Blackman asked Bunting to relay a job offer to Ivins. An interview was set up and in January 1992, Bunting and Blackman traveled to Austin for a lunch at The Oasis, an often-crowded, trendy restaurant almost precariously set on a big cliff overlooking Lake Travis. As they settled in and ordered cheeseburgers, the whole restaurant began rocking with intense fifty-mile-per-hour winter winds. Blackman's stomach was churning and he had the vague feeling that the whole place was going to cascade down the rocks and into the water. Blackman had been warned by various editor friends inside and outside Dallas that hiring Ivins would be a massive mistake. She had written that famous Fuck You story about her editors in Minneapolis. She had basically gotten fired by the *New York Times* for trying to put a word that sounded like "fuck" in a story. She had been expelled from Dallas by her editors at the *Times Herald*.

"She closed one paper, you trying to close yours, too?" Blackman was told. And he heard this: "Fort Worth readers won't stand for a columnist like Ivins—they're convinced she's a pinko commie-lover."[20]

Blackman and Bunting saw the numbers, the way her book had anchored itself on the bestseller list. They told the publisher Ivins was worth it. And they told Ivins they wouldn't mess with her column, that she would be able to use her voice, write the way she wanted. They danced around the topic of money; she said it was more important to be able to run free. Her book had been on the bestseller list for nine months and publishers were clamoring for something new. She was being offered as much as $10,000 for as many twenty- to thirty-minute speeches as she wanted to do. Blackman felt obliged to talk about libel and the local sensitivities, suggesting that Fort Worth was different from New York.

"I always liked that town," said Ivins. "Good folks."

The winds still swirling, the editors picked up the check and felt good that, even though she wouldn't take the job, they had at least gotten a company-paid lunch out of it.

"When do I start?" Ivins said.

She said she didn't want to leave Texas, she liked having a routine, a regular column. She liked the fact that Blackman was wearing a motorcycle jacket.[21]

⊶⊷

Bunting pushed hard to have her column appear on the front page. He told the publisher and various business-side people that it was the right thing to do, that it was one way for the *Star-Telegram* to bulk up its readership—since it was now embarking on its own head-to-head battle with the nearby *Dallas Morning News* for circulation and advertising in the sprawling, so-called Metroplex region. Several people above him in the food chain wanted Ivins to relocate to Fort Worth, but Bunting knew she wouldn't do that and he pushed back on her behalf. Having expended a lot of political capital trying to get her hired in the first place, then to keep her in Austin, he and Blackman knew they had to be careful. Bunting told Ivins to immediately call the paper every time she faxed her latest column to Fort Worth.

She wrote her first column for the paper in February 1992. It was close to 5 P.M. After the fax went through, she called the newsroom.

"Hon, this is Molly Ivins. I'm making sure my column is there. And hon? Can you talk to Ken Bunting? I'm not sure he wants me to say dildo."

She had written about archaic Texas laws involving "lifestyle accessories" and whether or not you should be charged with a crime for owning a certain number of dildos. Bunting brought the column to Blackman. Blackman told people that he saw his newspaper career flashing before his eyes.

"This is crazy, this can't run this way," said Blackman.

Bunting decided to change the wording in the lead to "phallic sex toy." He and Blackman called her and told her they were making the change.

"Molly, I just want to be sure we want to say 'dildo' in the lead. I'm a little worried," said Blackman. She didn't argue. Blackman assumed the worst was to come—that Ivins would ultimately resign, that he would get fired, that several other heads would be chopped once the readers came with the torches and sticks.

The new column read this way: "Should you happen to contravene a law made by the only politicians we've got, this too will become a matter of some moment to you. For example, if you happen to possess six or more phallic sex toys, you are a felon under Texas law. In their boundless wisdom, our solons decided that five or fewer of the devices make you a mere hobbyist."[22]

⤙⤚

Blackman and Bunting flew her to Fort Worth to meet the publisher, editors, and reporters. As a joke, and maybe as a test, Blackman picked her up at the airport and drove directly to a car dealership where the right-wing mayor of Arlington, one of the cities covered by both the *Morning News* and the *Star-Telegram*, was working. Ivins and the mayor hit it off, talking for twenty minutes. Blackman felt better.[23]

Another time, he came to visit her in Austin, driving around in her pickup truck, taking tours to the clothing-optional swimming hole known as Hippie Hollow, eating at small Tex-Mex dives, and going back to The Oasis restaurant where they had their handshake agreement for her to join the paper.

She filed her columns to Bunting and he thought she was actually an easy edit, that she would bend when there were things that simply made no sense or that would ultimately cause more harm than good. She was also a fast writer. If there were changes, new deadlines, she filed new material very quickly, often in just a few minutes. If a news wrinkle developed that changed the fundamental thread of the column, something he relayed to her, she would tell him that she'd call back and rewrite the 800 or so words in several minutes. In between, she and Bunting talked about their upbringings in Houston. He was black and had grown up in a working-class, moderately diverse part of the city. They talked about Barbara Jordan, who had spoken at Bunting's high school graduation. They talked a lot about race, but usually in the context of some politician who did something stupid, or in the context of specific policies coursing through the legislature. She told Bunting that thinking about race had changed her, that the legislature still had a blind spot when it came to aggressively addressing racial matters, that the lawmakers didn't seem to grasp the context, the history.[24]

It wasn't that there were hoods and sheets at the State Capitol, but that the state's leaders lacked some overarching sense of how things had evolved over the years in Texas, how certain things were settled, ingrained, and how a de facto segregation still existed. It was an unhealed wound that she would revisit for years—that things had surely changed a bit by the '90s, that overt racism or injustice was less common, but that the people in power simply lacked the will to make lasting, palliative moves. She felt that way about George H.W. Bush. That not unlike her father, he hadn't really been all that interested in the plight of the disenfranchised—and if he occasionally spoke on the matter, it was in a paternal, patrician way, reflecting that old notion of noblesse oblige. Like Katharine Hepburn talking about the little brown babies in *The African Queen*.

She was beginning to feel that disconnect again as the George W. Bush campaign to oust Ann Richards as governor of Texas began in 1992, just as she began writing her new column. She knew he was once a bad drinker. He had embarrassed the hell out of himself by getting shit-faced drunk in a Mexican restaurant in Dallas—and verbally accosting, cursing, journalist Al Hunt and his family as they quietly tried to eat a meal. Bush had cleaned up his act in some way, tried some stumbling efforts in the oil patch, borrowed money from banker friends in Texas and finally bought a fractional piece of the Texas Rangers baseball team—with his friend Karl Rove insisting that Bush be called the "owner" even though he owned only 1.8 percent of the team. Rove desperately wanted Bush to be known as "owner"—it sounded better, especially considering the fact that Bush had no civic résumé of any consequence. He hadn't been elected to anything, he hadn't shown any real interest in studying, enacting, overhauling, or suggesting public policy. Richards told Ivins that Bush couldn't be a threat, that he was an empty suit. The old man had simply taken the silver foot out of his mouth and handed it to his son.

In 1992, she had a column again, one that the Capital Cities Communications executives, who owned the *Star-Telegram*, were promising to help promote through bigger syndication. She agreed to serve as a Pulitzer Prize juror. And she didn't have to leave Austin. The Bush for Governor campaign was beginning in earnest, and all the shadowy spin doctors in the city were making their midnight creeps, meeting for drinks with seasoned old-school journalists at the Texas Chili Parlor or luring the newer, preening breed of metrosexual reporters to chi-chi coffee shops downtown. Opposition researchers—young, feral political wannabes or graduates from the public affairs division at the university—were photocopying secret documents, studying police reports, and dredging up, or making up, whatever slimy shit they wanted. And then they would cart it all back to the well-fed Austin spin-masters padding around their "political consulting" offices, each of them smugly suggesting that they were all on the right side—as they rolled out, really, the latest evolution of the political chicanery that LBJ and his cronies had started up in Texas fifty years earlier. But, by the clawing 1992 standards, the old shenanigans had an almost rascally quality to them. In 1992, political theater in Austin had reached some sort of blood-game level. The paranoid political operatives, and sometimes the reporters they courted, were like harsh insects twitching and colliding under a numbing cloud of adrenochrome. Richards and Bush were muscling each other for national headlines. The heavy-hitter spin doctors were in from Washington, crowding the lobby of the Four Seasons Hotel, jabbering into cellphones, and leaving lousy tips. Big Power was in play. Austin felt like it was occupied by a jangly army. And sometimes it seemed as though there was time for only one last languorous dance down in Groover's Paradise.

CHAPTER ELEVEN

The Kind of Pressure

Girlfriend, we are walking in high cotton, aren't we?

—MOLLY IVINS

Her book was a staggering success, a liberal book that confirmed the worst fears and assumptions people had about Texas. Back in the '60s, her friends had joked about the "wastelands" in Texas. Now, she was writing about the political wasteland, sometimes the sociocultural wasteland, as she saw it. And the massive success of the book changed everything. Linda Bloodworth-Thomason, the producer of the TV show *Designing Women* and a close friend of Bill and Hillary Clinton, called Ivins. She was in the final stages of producing the political promotion video *The Man from Hope* that was airing at the 1992 Democratic National Convention. Bloodworth-Thomason told Ivins that she wanted Judith Ivey, the actress from Texas, to play a character on *Designing Women* modeled after Ivins. She had already fielded offers from producers who wanted to turn her book into a one-woman play, or maybe some kind of movie. Creators Syndicate picked up her column for national distribution. And Kaye

Northcott, as close as anyone to her, saw the way that people wanted Molly Ivins to perform for them: "They put the cowboy picture on the cover of her book—and that became her persona."

Peter Osnos, her Random House editor, says that Ivins had made a decision. "The shit-kicker, the good ol' girl, was a choice that Molly made. She chose a persona. It was what Molly chose to be." And, over time, "the persona became stronger, the character became stronger." There was a conversational element to it, a storytelling component, and when it was coupled with the homespun one-liners—and the photos that showed her beaming, unthreatening countenance—she seemed to breed a certain familiarity with some readers: "The kind of person that everyone wants to lean in to," says Osnos. "People felt that they knew Molly. And they always expected her to be 'on.'"[1]

Osnos echoed what some other colleagues and admirers would say about Ivins. She was overtly gregarious, friendly, and able to mingle at various ends of the social spectrum. She was warm to newcomers and could make people feel like she was their new best friend. But she left him with the impression that she was holding something in reserve, that the effusiveness should not be confused with intimacy. "She was gregarious, but at the core, she was hard to access."[2] And, if she was that way, then it might have had a lot to do with the choice she had made to adopt that Dame-from-Texas persona.

Ivins talked to Northcott about being in California, going to a function at a museum, and being notified that Warren Beatty wanted to meet her. Dinner was arranged for Beatty and friends and "it was as if they were waiting for her to perform. They were fans of her, liberal, and they were waiting for her to perform."[3]

⁂

Her friends knew she had worked to stop drinking. At home, she composed letters to family and friends, admitting she had a problem and talking about her "disease." Richards had called Ivins and told her to stop drinking. Over the years, friends heard the phone ringing, well after midnight, with Ivins on the other end, sometimes slurring about the pressure, about her self-image, about money.

Meanwhile, Liz Faulk did more work for her, trying to make the trains move on time, essentially now as her full-time aide, caretaker, scheduler. Her answering machine was almost always loaded; when Faulk checked it in the morning, there were forty, fifty messages. The requests were ubiquitous and eclectic. *People* magazine was calling for a quote about Ann Richards; the Alaska Press Club wanted her to fly to Anchorage and give a speech; TV newsman Sander Vanocur wanted to take her to dinner; a writer from *Harper's Bazaar* wanted to talk; a professor at the University of Texas Lyndon Baines Johnson School of Public Affairs needed her; a producer in L.A. was calling about a new idea for a show, riffing on *Golden Girls*, that would include Molly Ivins, Ann Richards, and Austin-based atheist leader Madalyn Murray O'Hair; someone from the Senate Hispanic Farm Bureau wanted to confer; a reader was calling collect; an independent TV producer in NY wanted to talk; a producer from CNN was doing a report on "civility" in America; her rafting and trekking friend from New York, the politician Carol Bellamy, wanted to talk.

⁂

At a banquet in New York, Maya Angelou introduced her. Angelou had never met Ivins before. Ivins bounded on stage, walked up to the famous poet, wrapped her in a bear hug, and then told the audience:

"Maya Angelou and I are identical twins; we were separated at birth."

Angelou, like everyone else, laughed. It was outrageous. Ivins had a franchise going in America—it was the "Molly Ivins Can't Say That, Can She?" franchise. It was something Ivins never thought it would be—a self-perpetuating engine coupled to a welling mythology. Ivins had become famous. She had become a quotable character. She had a bigger following, a bigger constituency, than many of the people she wrote about. At the banquet, Angelou looked at Ivins and couldn't help but say: "Our hearts beat in the same rhythm. Whoever separated us at birth must know it didn't work."

Ivins whispered to her: "Girlfriend, we are walking in high cotton, aren't we?"

Her growing fame, some of her friends suggested, might have had a perverse boomeranging quality: The satire, the lampooning, the laughter in print and in her speeches, might have led conservatives to ape her style, to try their hand at it, instead of using the usual glowering or snooty–patrician–William F. Buckley, Jr. approaches or the creepy macho of G. Gordon Liddy. Talk-radio zealots were responding directly to her—she was one of Rush Limbaugh's original "feminazis"—or trying to suggest that they too were bypassing the usual corridors of power, that they were talking to and talking like Everyman, USA. Either way, her influence, through the emergence of a book of unfettered liberalism, populism, and left-leaning essays about a dog named Shit, about John Henry Faulk, about the madness of King George Bush, was unparalleled.

"I think all of us here didn't quite understand the impact Molly was having wherever she went," says Northcott.[4] The artist Judy Chicago sent a note asking Ivins to sign her book. Dan Rather asked for return calls, as did Clinton White House operatives and press aides to various senators. There were messages from people she hadn't heard from in years, from friends who were frustrated by the fact that she didn't call them back, didn't return their letters, and that they had to "go through" Liz Faulk to get a message to her. Faulk had a resolute sense that Ivins needed to be protected, that her head would probably explode from all the demands. As she booked Ivins for trips, she learned that it would make no sense for her to stay with friends—the people in that old, extended network of *Observer* subscribers, liberals, and leftists who used to hang out with Ivins when she passed through town. Better to have whoever was paying her for a speaking gig also pay for a hotel room. Faulk reasoned that Ivins needed down time, that she would be better off left alone in her room, reading the books she had packed.

In a nod to the time she had spent at the Houston Yacht Club, sailing with her father, she read Patrick O'Brian's series of novels about nineteenth-century seafarers. She read Agatha Christie murder mysteries. She read trashy romance novels. And she accumulated more serious fare. "She loved to read history her whole life. She was a serious reader. She would say she was really into a particular century in France. She had buddies to talk to about the Middle East. She was looking for column ideas, and she was reading history." But she also turned back to some of the cheaper books for particular reasons: "She was a murder mystery addict. When she was down about something, she read murder mysteries. And when she was really, really bad, she would read romance novels. She liked to go someplace else in her murder mysteries, where you go to a foreign country."[5]

Ivins had told Northcott after she joined the *Star-Telegram* that she "wasn't going to put up with anyone telling me what to do." By 1993, she didn't have to. Whatever leverage she had before—based on the *Star-Telegram*'s awed reaction to landing the former *New York Times* reporter who had been one of the star columnists at the respected *Dallas Times Herald*—was multiplied tenfold. She was the best-known print journalist from Texas. The syndication numbers kept growing, beyond 200 newspapers. Northcott vowed to not add to the pressure: "I vowed never to ask her to do fundraisers, give a speech. My whole life as I knew her, I wanted her to slow down. She did have her values right, if there was some hoity-toity person who wanted to talk to her for not much reason, or someone's daughter who had spina bifida, she went with the right one. It was very important to her that people not think she had become a big ass."

Ivins grew to loathe the routine, the endless travel. "She hated flying. She just spent so much time flying. She always had her bag packed."[6] And, by the mid-1990s, so many of the speeches Ivins was giving seemed to Northcott like part of a traveling, polished show delivered by an indefatigable trouper. "By then, she and Ann Richards had practiced enough they could always hit it out of the park. That's why I know so many of her stories. She had an incredible constitution and she seemed to be oblivious to pain," says Northcott.[7]

Nadine Eckhardt had been married to two mercurial men—Congressman Bob Eckhardt, one of Ivins's political heroes, and Billy Lee Brammer, the doomed writer who wrote his defining book about Texas politics and then essentially self-immolated in the haze of old Austin. Ivins had given John Henry Faulk's widow some work; now she hired Eckhardt to work for her as well. Eckhardt, erudite and funny, was a good fit for Ivins—and someone who cared for her at a deep level, someone who also really understood the mounting pressures. She had seen politics from the inside, and she had been married to a writer who tangled with drug excesses and moments of self-loathing and fear:

> Molly was pretty much in the present. She wasn't one for introspection, or verbalized introspection. Also, since she drank so much, that kind of dulled her to whatever was going on. I'm sure that she had an awareness that she was really powerful. She knew how things were going. But she didn't have enough self-awareness to realize she was dying and she wouldn't take care of herself. It was terribly painful to see a person not take care of themselves. I think that child part of her—that wanted that cigarette, wanted that drink—was running her. She was a big child in many ways. "I'll do this if I want to."[8]

Eckhardt felt that there were people gravitating to Ivins so they could have some proximity to power, to fame. She had seen it before with each of her husbands, the way people could fall over themselves to ingratiate themselves with someone whom they perceived had some currency in New York or Washington:

> The thing is there were a whole bunch of people that I would call Molly's hanger-ons. They exploited her, they really took advantage of her kindness. They loved her, but the thing is they played on her dysfunction. And the thing was that she had all these other people she was co-dependent with. And she took care of them and did whatever co-dependents do. I've always thought it was really unfair of them to latch on to Molly, who was vulnerable with her feelings. She was generous. They were just sucking on her all the time. She was generous and they liked to hang around her house and do whatever. She picked up the tab.[9]

She thought it had a lot to with Ivins's upbringing, the way her relationship with her family, especially her father, had evolved. Molly had never stopped rebelling, in print, at her home, at work:

> She would finally get those columns done but she didn't have the self-control . . . didn't have that discipline. I don't know how her mother and father figured into this. It was somehow. . . . She missed out on the self-discipline. She would just burn herself out. I knew that Molly was just going to do whatever she was gonna do. She got more famous and more famous . . . and she had a real hard time saying no. Molly was always up for having a good time. She was so funny. She was hilarious. I just loved her so much. I respected her for her wonderful brain and her wonderful heart.[10]

⋘⋙

Faulk had gone to work for Ivins on a regular basis. "From my point of view, she needed me to take care of her. This is what I knew to do."[11] She had thought about why Ivins hadn't gotten married. Ivins's mother had written Ivins letters wondering if she would get married, suggesting that a woman wasn't really complete unless she was married with children. And Ivins laughed when people suggested she must be gay. Ivins came up with a stock response, describing herself as "a left-wing, aging-Bohemian journalist who never made a shrewd career move, never dressed for success, never got married, and isn't even a lesbian, which at least would be interesting." Friends who knew her earlier in life had decided that she could never be married, that her relationships with the super-charged Henry Holland and the activist Jack Cann were as close as she would come to some sort of lingering, permanent relationship.

Liz Faulk knew Ivins had had a handful of short affairs. And there were those rumors over the years—reporters insisting that she must have carried on a relationship with Bullock, that she had been close to a Pulitzer Prize–winning staffer at the *New York Times*. But she didn't have any long-range, public relationship from the moment she returned to Austin. Says Faulk: "I don't know whether she could have gotten married. I think that she felt that men were intimidated by her. Intimidated by her, absolutely."[12] Faulk and Eckhardt were women who had been married to powerful men in Texas. Friends who saw them as they worked for Ivins and got closer to her thought the two women certainly were bringing Ivins the benefit of experience—these two had seen things, and then some, in Texas.

And they weren't just answering her calls, filing her papers, responding to readers, and stonewalling people who demanded her time but also dealing with friends who needed help with back taxes—and with the seemingly endless number of people who needed money. Ivins wrote checks over and over again to people who were behind on mortgages, between jobs, or pissing it away on alcohol and other things.

"She spent a lot of money. She was very extravagant. She would say, 'Well, Liz, I want to buy this,'" says Faulk. And if Faulk told her that she had no money to buy the new TV for someone, for herself, she'd say, "Well, book me another speech." Ivins was getting as high as $15,000 for an appearance and her records show that she could have done one or two a week for an entire year. Faulk tried to limit it to a handful, maybe two a month, with one of those always being a pro bono appearance on behalf of the ACLU. She told people she was making under $100,000 a year at the *Star-Telegram*, less than some sports columnists, but she made up for it around the country: "The speeches were the money makers. She made a mint. She needed it. She wanted to spend the money. The money was there to be spent."[13]

Faulk tried to rein in the finances and also tried to stay away from Ivins's social orbit. She used to hear her husband talk about how he refused to visit some of the self-appointed doyennes of media in Austin, because they wanted him "to sing for your supper." She wanted no part of it with Ivins, and she thought, increasingly, that Ivins didn't want to have to put on an act for people and maybe was even fundamentally shy. There was, perhaps, a sense among some people close to Ivins that she had willed herself to be perpetually extroverted—that she simply had decided to not slow down, to take time for herself, to really meditate. According to one friend, Ivins said it was simply a matter of finding it difficult to turn anyone down. And when people knocked on her door, when they invited themselves to her house, when they wanted her to show up at a party, she was usually willing to be in the moment. Faulk said that Ivins had made a choice. "She may have had the capacity for introspection, but she chose not to be introspective."[14]

⤛⤚

Her mother was having financial problems. Ivins told Sara Speights that after her father had sailed out one day and never returned—and had left her mother for a younger woman—all kinds of credit card bills started showing up at her mother's home in Maryland. Ivins told Speights that the week her father had planned his disappearance, the family had called the Coast Guard—to look for the man who had been in the Coast Guard during WWII. It took years for things to become untangled, for the children to stem the financial hemorrhaging. Her mother, who had abandoned whatever career inclinations she might have entertained at Smith in order to follow her husband from coast to coast, was in many ways plucked from the only circle she had known. Her letters to Ivins were always dotted with references to the people they knew in River Oaks, to the people they had met through Tenneco, through the Big Money fandango in Texas oil and politics. She and her husband had traveled the world together—to pre-Castro Cuba, to France, to countless Broadway shows. Now, she was headed toward her eighties and struggling at times.

In Austin, Ivins's friends wondered if she was thinking of ways to avoid relationships with lovers, and to avoid what had happened to her mother. Some said that her solution was to be unrelentingly prolific, even during those periods when it seemed as if she was close to drinking herself to death. Too, she was hell-bent on maintaining some sort of unpretentious decorum, even if her health was unraveling and the pressures—deadlines, planes to catch, people wanting money and time—were mounting. Speights says, "Molly was incredibly disciplined. I think she was dead determined not to act nouveau riche. She didn't want to be one of those people. She wanted to be a genuinely gracious Southern lady. She made a conscious decision on how she would treat people and she lived by it. People would always come up to us in airports and she was always nice to people."[15]

The big media machine—the syndicate that published her column, Random House, magazines, TV—demanded more and more, and she sometimes found herself scrambling for material. The GOP rarely failed her: After hearing Pat Buchanan's diatribe against liberal culture at the 1992 Republican Convention, she suggested the speech "probably sounded better in the original German"—and it became, in its way, her version of Richards's "silver foot" line about Bush. It was quoted everywhere, and critics on the right foamed about the Hitlerian references.

She still filled binders and cardboard boxes with items she cut from newspapers. A David Remnick piece about Ralph Ellison in *The New Yorker*. A *Times* article referencing *The Bell Curve*. *Washington Post* pieces about Robert Caro's work on LBJ. She still tried out lines on people, including Speights: "Oh, I had lines tested out on me so many times. And then a lot of my own lines wound up in her stories."[16] She was working more and more from home, less often at the *Star-Telegram* office downtown where she would constantly smoke inside her cramped glass office. But she wasn't working the legislature like she used to. If she was strapped for a column idea, she asked Faulk or a researcher what they thought was worth writing about.

She arranged for a leave of absence to work on the second book for Random House, the "real book" that would take some long-form planning. She called it her "big book." But, at home, it never progressed. She was too busy fielding calls for the speaking engagements, talking to state lawmakers about how to get their bills passed, going to local television studios for interviews, going to the public radio affiliate and being linked to national shows. People in Austin, including those who would go on her payroll, thought that Ivins had increasingly compartmentalized some things and people—that she put them in defined compartments and then kept those compartments separate from each other: Her drinking friends. Her friends inside civil liberties circles. Her statehouse friends. There were the older liberals—the dwindling number of people, like Liz Faulk and Nadine Eckhardt, who had ties to Ralph Yarborough, Bob Eckhardt,

Maury Maverick, Jr., and John Henry Faulk. There were the folks in the aging art-music-literary-journalism crowd that had coalesced in the late '60s and '70s—she was bumping into one of them, Kinky Friedman, as he was refining his cantankerous Texan shtick. And there were the friends she had made in New York, the relationships she had with Eden Lipson and Ellen Fleysher. As she was pulled increasingly toward TV and publishing business in NY, she spent more time with Lipson. Friends in Austin said that Lipson worried about Ivins—about whether Ivins was taking care of herself, and whether the people around Ivins were taking good enough care of her.

There was another compartment and that was her family; her friends from New York and Austin had met her siblings, her parents, but few had grown especially close to them. Few of her friends realized how close Ivins had become with her brother Andy. He seemed to have absorbed Texas at a deep, real level—more than anyone else in her immediate family. He had worked for an investment firm in Houston, then become a lawyer, and he spoke in an authentic Texas accent most of the time. Andy thought she was a very good aunt to his children Drew, Dax, and Darby: "She was great with my kids, my God. We sent every one of them to spend time with her. She just bent over backwards to make sure they had fun."[17] When they were in town, during summers, she would take them to see the Dallas Cowboys training in Austin. And as Dax suffered through pressures that eventually led to his suicide, Ivins tried to talk to him and his father. When Drew went to Tulane, Ivins paid for half his education. She gave gifts to Darby.

As he watched his sister, Andy thought that her success and generosity were almost easy to understand. She had grown up disliking the pecuniary people who lorded over others, and she was determined to move in the opposite direction. If she made money, she would spend it, dispersing it into those various compartments. He thought, too, that her behavior really did trace all the way back to her relationship with her father: "I mean whoever was running the show was in her crosshairs. She was critical of leadership. I mean I had that impression about her from way early on and what that had to do with, was my father. I was always wondering why they were arguing. Why couldn't they just talk about it? I was wondering what are they getting in an argument about that for?"[18]

⁂

In January 1993, the KKK alerted the media that they were going to be busing in from Waco and protesting in downtown Austin, near the State Capitol. Ivins wanted to do a counter-protest. She met with musician Steve Fromholz at a bar a short drive from her house in South Austin and plotted out a move. Word spread to several hundred counter-protestors and they caravanned to confront the fifty Klansmen. The police were edgy; they had set up perimeter patrols and sent undercover officers into the streets. Then on cue, Ivins and the others suddenly lowered their pants and mooned the KKK members. People who were there said it resembled a sort of wave-like pattern.

The pulls and tugs were coming from every direction that year: Luci Baines Johnson asked her to do a book signing at a local store. Readers bitched that she'd incorrectly labeled Thomas Paine an atheist. After her failed attempt to work on that larger book, she had a black T-shirt printed up that said "DON'T ASK ABOUT THE BOOK." She wore it to work on her first day back in the newspaper bureau, and then she and Faulk turned their attention to culling more of her old stories and columns for another Random House collection, *Nothin' but Good Times Ahead*. But in the summer of 1993, she told a reporter from the *Houston Press* that she actually *was* still working on the "big book," a portrait of Texas as seen through the Texas legislature.[19]

She was also still exchanging notes and phone calls with Richards, urging the governor to resist pressures to repeal the Texas Homestead Act, which essentially protected a family's right to not be forced from their homes by creditors. Her legendary friend, the San Antonio columnist-activist-civil libertarian Maury Maverick, Jr., was threatening to put a bullet in his brain if Ivins didn't help put some heat on Richards: "If I were you, I would not appreciate havin' a friend layin' that kind of pressure on me."[20]

Ivins was preparing for a fall book tour and Richards knew that Ivins was going to be asked about the governor of Texas. She knew that Ivins invariably would tell stories, maybe one too many about hanging out on the San Gabriel River, about what Richards *really* thought about the Bush Dynasty, about how Richards behaved before she had gone sober. "Ann was socially close, but later on there was a little bit of rivalry on the book circuit—Molly would tell stories about Ann that she thought Molly should have the sense to not talk about. There were pressures like that. As Ann became more famous, it became more awkward."[21]

⊰⊱

The new book sold well but failed to make the *Times* bestseller list dominated by Howard Stern and Jerry Seinfeld. She flogged it in Houston, Dallas, Toronto, Chicago, Indianapolis, New York, Boston, Washington, Atlanta, San Antonio, Seattle, Portland, Los Angeles, and San Francisco—doing the *Today Show*, the *Tonight Show*, *Charlie Rose*, and a visit to Studs Terkel's radio show in Chicago. After the tour, she traveled in November and December to Australia and New Zealand for a few weeks on assignment for *Travel & Leisure* magazine. While she was still in Australia, Faulk called to relay the fact that an old friend, Sammilu Williamson Evans, had jumped to her death from her penthouse on the twenty-third floor of a fancy building in Houston. Ivins immediately filed a column from Australia: an homage, a bittersweet goodbye to a fellow alcoholic. Evans was what Ivins might have been—a sorority beauty queen from Houston, a former Miss Texas with both good manners and a sassy mouth. She was also a hopeless drunk who guzzled Stolichnaya and whose father also drank too much. Evans had checked into the Betty Ford clinic, and she had told Ivins only a few months earlier "thanks for taking me seriously." When the police found her body, she had a blood alcohol level of 0.50, the equivalent of more than a dozen drinks in an hour, more than enough to put most people into a coma. Faulk knew that Ivins was deeply disturbed by Evans's tragedy.

⊰⊱

Back in Austin, she learned that Amherst wanted to award her an honorary doctorate—and that Victor Navasky at *The Nation* had written a front-page piece calling for her to run for the Senate from Texas. He said she would do better than other Democrats, including Jim Mattox: She had written that Mattox "was so mean he wouldn't spit in your ear if your brains were on fire." She was still doing her columns on Sundays, Tuesdays, and Thursdays—and pressing her aides to help her with story ideas—when she got a phone call from her father in Sarasota: He had cancer. He was seeking treatment at a variety of hospitals in Florida; he had lost control of his bladder but was on medication and still sailing, still rowing. She asked Faulk to see if there were any speaking gigs in Florida, any that would bring her near him—and to see what it would take to use her frequent-flier miles to get him to Austin.

She had a new dog, a standard poodle named Athena, and she was putting some of the book money into remodeling her house. Her sister Sara was in New Mexico, and she thought about visiting her, maybe with her father—she had bought a necklace and earrings for Sara's daughter on a trip to Los Angeles. She worried about her sister, and her brother—about whether they would find peace from whatever personal issues they often seemed to be wrestling with. She was very worried that her father would die.

The pace was maddening: She received an invitation to a black-tie dinner at the White House. *USA Today* contacted her about writing an extra weekly column just for them. She gave a speech at Texas Tech University in Lubbock and said she loved to read the local paper because it was consistently wrong about everything—and she deemed Lubbock "the funniest place in the world." Lady Bird Johnson's former press secretary faxed over some blurbs she had written for her own book, ones that she hoped she could affix Ivins's name to.

Ivins also began work on a story for *GQ* about Congressman Charlie Wilson, a prescient piece about her old friend and drinking companion who would become famous for his role in secretly funding foreign wars. It was one of the first explorations of how he could somehow disarm the most powerful people in the world even though he struck many as a cologne-and-cufflink, pseudo-suave Hugh Hefner in the halls of power. Wilson was not far removed from the kinds of men she had lingered with in her life. Hate his politics or not, he was singular and single-minded. He liked to fuck with the system, he liked to drink when he wasn't supposed to. He had a kind of careening love affair with power, mocking it and wallowing in it. He was on her list of people who had always intrigued her, who had signed up to say goodbye to her in Austin, in 1976, when she left for the big gamble and her new job at the *New York Times*. In April 1994, he sent her a fax from his office in Washington with some information she needed for her article. There was a note attached: "You know Angelina County's a dry county. It's as dry as a dead dingo's— well you get the picture. Hope this info helps."[22]

There were moments when Ivins found some solace in more ordinary, lower-profile things. She was in a book club with friends in Austin, several of them journalists, and she hosted get-togethers at her house. She was still going to the springtime Bob Armstrong campouts. She was talking to Fromholz about running Texas rivers, about doing it on the Rio Grande in far West Texas. But she also told her best friends that this wasn't the time to slow down—that the job offers were endless and she had to answer them. When *Mother Jones* asked her to write a piece about Richards in 1994, she demurred, saying that she couldn't write about a friend. The magazine pushed her to write it anyway—"You'd cast aside journalistic objectivity at the get-go, so our readers would understand that what followed was biased and one-sided and written with total passion."[23] And, other people wanted something from her: That same spring, Donna Shalala's speechwriters were telling Ivins that the media were not writing about the Secretary of Health and Human Service's work on domestic violence, and would Ivins consider doing something along these lines in her column? Her days had a certain pattern, even with all the urgencies, deadlines, and travel. Faulk and Eckhardt would comb the correspondence she was receiving, often in giant accumulations of regular mail and email. They knew which ones she would want to consider, which ones she would have no time to deal with. There were letters arriving from Harry Whittington, the Austin attorney who would one day be blasted in the face by future vice president Dick Cheney; he was telling her to read some stories in the *Wall Street Journal* about the need for more prisons. She read his missives. And of course anything sent by her father was a priority. As he slowed down, he wrote her more often. Small notes about something he had read. Neutral comments about having seen her on TV. He sent her a copy of a letter he had written to Tina Brown at *The New Yorker*, telling Brown that his children concur with his decision to cancel the family subscription: "The blatant and frequent use of obscenities and just plain vulgarity has cheapened and spoiled the magazine to say nothing of the gross covers and repeated emphasis on homosexuality both in the writing and the cartoons."[24]

Faulk and Eckhardt also knew to make sure that any letters from Ivins's mother were quickly given to her. Her mother wrote that she was excited when Ivins wound up as a clue in a *New York Times* crossword puzzle. She also sent several messages hoping that Ivins would join her at the Smith College reunion in 1994, so she could "show you off."

One day, she asked if her daughter could send $120 for the money her mother owed the maid for the month of September.

That June, Ivins was in St. Louis faithfully preparing to do one of her monthly ACLU speeches. She had insisted on making good on the promise she had conveyed to John Henry Faulk as he was dying—that she would take on the civil liberties caretaker role. Faulk booked one ACLU speech after another for Ivins. In St. Louis, she agreed to an interview with an alternative paper—and she revisited a theme that she had first written about in 1970: "There is no such thing as objectivity. . . . I actually think it is pernicious as a goal."[25]

That theory, informed by her tenure at the big, mainstream daily newspapers she had worked for as a general assignments reporter, had reached its apotheosis in the marketing and presentation surrounding her books. She was a columnist, of course, and a mainstay of the opinion pages in hundreds of newspapers. But the massive success of her first book underscored her allegiances in bigger, bolder ways—and did it on a unified, national stage. And then, as Republicans made big strides in the 1994 elections, it seemed as if more people than ever before were turning to Ivins as a stalwart of liberal, progressive populism.

In the fall of '94, the paperback version of *Nothin' but Good Times Ahead* was released and she did another national book tour. Comedian Harry Shearer called to ask if she wanted to work with him on a pilot for a news-based quiz show on national TV. Comedian Red Buttons told her he appreciated that Ivins had used some of his material about Michael Jackson.

Dennis Miller was putting together a show for HBO and wanted her in it. Michael Jackson's representatives contacted her, asking if she would write something nice about him.

Even more newspapers were signing up for her column—beyond 300 of them. She was still writing for *The Progressive*, but doing so was harder now and had evolved into a dutiful obligation, something she was reluctant to yield because of what the publication symbolized. There were endless letters from readers that had been sent to her through Creators Syndicate. And Faulk and the other aides shook their heads at some of the vile, howling bile in the envelopes. "You are a fool and I challenge you to call me," said one man in Houston. Someone else said: "Your stars and stripe is for niggers only . . . piss on your kike operation." And, "just in case you are interested in what your face looks like, take a good look at your ass." There were hundreds of letters pouring in every week, most of them positive, ones that lauded her for bringing a reader to tears, to laughter—and also those that accused her of "steamy encounters with Annie Richards." The volume of correspondence escalated throughout the increasingly polarized years of the Clinton administration and Newt Gingrich's Republican Revolution. Some of it hinted at what John Leonard had suggested—that there was a constituency. People were writing from small towns saying that they felt like the only liberals in town, that Ivins was a lifeline to something bigger, some national coalition. That theme was constantly repeated, over and over again, from writers in Oregon, Texas, North Dakota, and elsewhere. The vast majority of letters addressed her simply as "Molly"—and the writers often apologized for the presumption of familiarity, saying that Ivins seemed like someone they knew well enough to address on a first-name basis.

The mug shot on her column, and the book jacket images, suggested that she was always predisposed to laugh. The clear-eyed, wide-open face with the barely contained grin was on the bookstore posters and the billboards touting her column. In their letters to her, readers said that they felt as though she would prefer to be called by her first name. It was the kind of familiarity that politicians spent lifetimes looking for—and in the '90s, it was exceedingly rare for any print journalist to have that kind of coalescing constituency. The kind that engendered a first-name-basis correspondence from people who felt geographically and politically isolated.

While reading a *New Yorker* article about Ralph Ellison she decided to cut out a quote from him: "One of the advantages as a writer I still have is that people usually don't recognize me. . . . One of the mistakes that some good writers make is latching on to celebrity, being fêted wherever they go. That blurs things. You can be lonely in a crowd."[26]

In September, she took a break with Sara Speights to stay at the exclusive Rancho La Puerta health spa in Mexico. It was somewhere friends had recommended she go to try to lose weight, to dry out, to get away, to just get healthy. She had been ordering wine, by the case, especially white port and champagne. And she wrote a letter to her sister-in-law:

> Trying to sort out how much of one's pain is internal and how much is external circumstances is always dicey. I believe it takes some fairly painful work with a good shrink. . . . I used to think that we all had to "grow up" and get over whatever pains our parents left us. That one became a mature person and left all that in the past. Not so. It needs to be worked through carefully and honestly, it's not much fun. One of the dangers that confronts you is the possibility of developing the disease from which I suffer—alcoholism. I know that it is not a disease you can handle by yourself. . . . None of us, you know, ever arrives at having everything all figured out, having it made, sailing through life without fear or hesitation. . . . But all I can do is share with you some of the steps I am learning on my own journey. From your liberal, secular but very affectionate sister-in-law Molly.[27]

Her relationship with alcohol was as complex as the one with her parents—and the relationships seemed intertwined. Her letter suggests that she thought she could just get older and essentially will herself to surmount any of the pains she felt had been inflicted on her by her father. It also suggests that she was aware of how complicated it would be to work through those pains, and through her disease. Her father was eighty-two, and he was trying to stay on the water—yachting with two equally old friends, they called themselves The Ancient Mariners—but it was harder than ever because of age. Her sister Sara wrote her a card:

> Dear Mole, you are too busy! Honey, slow down and take care of yourself. Please get thyself to a health farm . . . my dear Mole, quit worrying about Daddy and start taking care of yourself. You need more self-love and self-care.[28]

⤙⤚

On October 22, 1994, just after his eighty-second birthday, her father sent her some startling news. It was buried toward the end of a letter in which he suggests the controversial book, *The Bell Curve*, supports his own theories that someone's racial background should be considered when analyzing their intelligence. He sent the letter to her home on Alta Vista in Austin:

> Dear Mole: I've been waiting to hear even over here the sound of steam gushing forth from 2000 Alta Vista over the triad of book reviews in the last Sunday's *Times Book Review*: *The Bell Curve*, and the other two pretty much on the same topic, intelligence, race, etc. . . . All this reminded me of the discussions you and I used to engage in when you were a teenager, and you would become so infuriated at the mere suggestion that perhaps race had something to do with intelligence that you would stutter and seethe, unable to find words to express your indignation. Anyway, I am happy to note at this late date my position has been taken up by some eminent academics of impeccable standing, well documented by statistics. . . .
>
> I was in the hospital early this month for a periodic exploration of my bladder and unfortunately one of the biopsies turned up positive. I go back to the doctor in November for further consultation on "where do we go from here."

In the one-page letter, he resurrects some stinging, forty-year-old arguments tied to the heart of their complex relationship—and then he tells her there is new evidence of cancer. He also mentions that he has been reading a book called *In Defense of Elitism*—and that it was a gift from the woman he had gone to live with after he left Molly's mother.[29]

⊰⊱

Bush upset Richards and when he was sworn in, in 1995, it was like a funeral in parts of Austin. There was a true sense in some progressive liberal corners that an era had ended, that an opportunity to spend four more years making the systemic changes that could really make a difference in Texas had been lost. Inside the Richards circle, it was painful, even bitter. The core waited to see who would get dismissed from various boards, commissions, and agencies—and run out of town—once Karl Rove began checking his list and dictating personnel changes from Bush's office at the State Capitol.

Ivins wrote a piece for *The Nation* placing the blame for Bush's win on an anti-Clinton backlash in Texas—and in a column in early 1995, she praised Richards as one of Texas's best governors: "Good on ya' Annie. So now go camping and have some fun." With Richards out of office, she turned her attention to trying to keep the *Observer* afloat—helping form the nonprofit Texas Democracy Foundation, essentially a way for Ronnie Dugger to transfer ownership to a tax-exempt foundation. It meant some serious fundraising, and an intensified reliance on her celebrity capital. There were never-ending, quirky reminders of that celebrity: She was getting letters from a woman in Trinidad, California, telling her that she had named her cats Molly and Ivins. And the kings of polarized talk radio were doing their part to keep her name in the news as a hero to the left and an anathema to conservatives. As Rush Limbaugh continued to beat up on her, she wrote a balled-fist rebuke in *Mother Jones*: "Satire . . . has historically been the weapon of powerless people aimed at the powerful. . . . When you use satire against powerless people . . . it is like kicking a cripple."[30]

Meanwhile, she and her literary agent Dan Green talked about the best way to piggyback on her celebrity. The "big book" seemed elusive. It was something that she lost interest in after Richards ascended. Bob Bullock, the man who taught her to drink hard and who also schooled her in Texas politics, was still there. He was the lieutenant governor—but he was showing an increasing tendency to spend time with the kinds of Republicans that Ivins loathed. He seemed entranced by George W. Bush, more supportive than he should have been. Given his proclivities, there was zero possibility that Ivins could reprise the boozy, imaginative skull sessions that they had locked into together back in the 1970s. Too many things had happened since they were baring their souls to one another over drinks in his office, or on a canoe trip during a river campout. The Ivins he knew best was an earnest, digging reporter who was writing insider accounts of the day-to-day workings of the big political machinery. Back then, she wasn't a columnist with a constituency; she was still more of a gumshoe reporter. Back then, he wasn't committed to an arch-conservative member of the Bush Dynasty; he was guided by strains of populism. One thing was clear: To do the book that she once wanted to do, an explosive one that pulled back several layers hiding things in Texas, she would have to work on it for years and years. It might even have to wait until Bullock decided to walk away. She had enough of his secrets, but for the book to really work, she'd need even more.

Throughout 1995, Bullock continued to align himself even more closely with Bush. To Ivins, his betrayal was like something out of a Greek tragedy. She told people that she, too, was initially inclined to give Bush the benefit of the doubt, to see if he really was some sort of compassionate conservative—not a hammering Gingrichian, not a slave to Limbaugh, not an anemic elitist like the elder George Bush. But Bush and Rove had moved quickly to dismantle many things Richards had set in motion. Bush was surrounded, in many ways, by the same head-hunting, right-wing insiders who had come to dominate the political operative warrens in Austin. Ivins had to wonder why and how Bullock was so swayed—he never seemed like someone who could be seduced.

It was also in 1995, during George W. Bush's first term as an elected official, that she abandoned the Bullock book idea, yet again, and instead toyed with doing one more collection of old stories and columns. Maybe, this time, a rolling chronicle of the Clinton-and-Newt Gingrich years. It was a formula that had struck gold the first time around, and there was no reason to abandon it. It was relatively easy, and it was a way to put out-of-work friends on the payroll—hiring them to comb through and compile her previously published stories for the new book. In the meantime, she had also decided that there was probably going to be a book about Bush—especially if he decided to do what everyone in Austin assumed: run for the White House in 2000.

⋯

That summer, she endured the heaviest blow to her literary career. The writer Florence King accused her of plagiarism in an article King had written in *The American Enterprise*. King, a humorist who wrote about the South, said Ivins had used her material in a piece Ivins had done for *Mother Jones* and that was also reprinted in Ivins's 1991 first book. "She credits me on minor observations, but when the subject is politics—her turf—she plagiarizes me," said King.[31]

Ivins wrote her a letter:

> Dear Ms. King: You are quite right. There are three sentences in my article "Magnolias and Moonshine"—one of them a really good political line—that should have been attributed directly to you and are not. On the third matter you raise in your Author Author! column in *The American Enterprise*, I have no idea how I managed to attribute to you more than you actually said—perhaps a recollection of something somewhere else in one of your books on the South. But I do not think a mistake of excessive attribution can be considered plagiarism.
>
> I owe you an apology and I hereby tender it. I am deeply ashamed. I regret not giving you credit, and devoutly wish the matter had been brought to my attention earlier so it might have been corrected in subsequent editions and the paperback edition of the book. I hope this does not sound too defensive to you, but there was no intention on my part to deceive anyone into thinking I had not read the many funny things you have said about the South. I hope my good faith is evidenced by the fact that I did cite you directly six times in the piece and praise one of your books as "definitive" on the peculiarities of Southerners as well.

> I was inexcusably sloppy about the three sentences in question, with emphasis on the inexcusably. Over the years, I have not only quoted many of your wonderful lines about the South in speeches—always, I believe, giving you credit—but also recommended your books to hundreds of people. I realize this does not excuse my lifting lines of yours without credit, but I did want you to know.
>
> As for the rest of your observations about me and my work in your Author Author! column, boy you really are a mean bitch, aren't you?
>
> Sincerely,
>
> Molly Ivins, plagiarist[32]

The shit hit the fan, in the sense that the story was picked up across the country. The *American Journalism Review* devoted a column to it. She told the AJR that "at first I was so depressed . . . I thought I didn't deserve to live. But King's column was so nasty in tone that frankly I felt better after reading it." Her new editor at the *Star-Telegram*, Paul Harral, launched an investigation and said she didn't intend to lift any words and no disciplinary action was coming.[33] Random House, her book publisher, accused King of trying to capitalize on Ivins's "notoriety."

Ivins told friends that the plagiarism accusation stung; it was like calling someone a molester, the taint stuck around for a while. She really did like to quote Florence King in speeches—Roy Blount, Jr., and King were her favorite funny Southern writers. And Ivins had once met King at a conference in Austin; she had gone up to King and told her how much she liked her.

Her friends knew she was laughing, especially at the way she had responded to King. She apologized, seemed to be writing an almost literary mea culpa, and then simply called the woman a . . . bitch.

In Fort Worth, Texas—home to Billy Bob's, the world's largest honky-tonk, and where the club sold 16,000 bottles of beer during a Hank Williams, Jr., show, and where Merle Haggard once set a "world record" for putting the greatest number of drinks on the house—the *Star-Telegram* was cooking up a new ad campaign: Molly Ivins: "Bettern' a Bottle of Cuervo and a Fine-Tuned Pickup."

CHAPTER TWELVE

You Got to Dance

It was a slow process for me to just crawl out of it, like a snake leaving his skin behind.

—FRANK McCOURT

The younger Bush had called his piss-poor oil company Arbusto—the Spanish word for a bush or a shrub. She liked that and began calling him Shrub. The Newt Gingrich–inspired Republican Revolution was in motion and she wrote about Bush and Texas against the backdrop of what she saw as a wholesale recall and deregulation of government policies that the liberal senators like Yarborough, and even LBJ in his enlightened domestic policy moments, had forged in the '50s and '60s. It wasn't just that she thought the GOP was literally out to dismantle environmental rules, the right to abortion, and the welfare system; it was what she had heard in Patrick Buchanan's speech—what she had seen in his eyes when they debated on TV. It was the anti-Austin-izing of America, the social conservatives not even bothering to lay on the velvet, not even pretending to be compassionate conservatives—but being brimstone-invoking, hard-right, Christian conservatives who would just as soon make Oliver North, G. Gordon

Liddy, and Rush Limbaugh members of the Supreme Court. Maybe it was an outgrowth of seeing Richards tossed out of office, and seeing how many Republicans in Texas were surfing in Bush's wake—and how many formerly faithful Austin Democrats had gone to the dark side. Bullock, her besotted confrere, had done it. So had Mark McKinnon, who had worked for Al Gore, who had once been a promising prospect for the extended liberal wing but now was constantly currying favor with the Bushies and angling for a job making TV commercials suggesting that Bush was a really hip, fun guy.

When Richards lost, some blamed the strategy, the strategists, the Dr. Dirt spinmeisters for it all—they were outwitted by Karl Rove, he had simply worked harder and more cleverly to beat them at their own game. And it suggested that there was no one, really, leading the liberal vanguard. Where was the big-time Democratic machinery? Why hadn't it airlifted aid, the deep opposition research that would have destroyed Bush once and for all—maybe found the people who would say they snorted coke with him at that Midland polo club, maybe found the people who would say that he had paid for an old girlfriend's abortion? The Democrats were in disarray during the Bush-Richards race, and afterward it was like trying to herd cats. Richards eventually segued into the lobbying world, trying to secure her financial future. Her aides took corporate jobs, some of them going to work as public relations flacks for big businesses and TV stations in Austin. In a way, Ivins was the only one holding down the high-profile liberal center. She was the lightning rod, she had the platform, and she had the muscled-up will to continue to rail against Bush, Christian conservatives, and the right wing.

Ivins, for sure, had plenty of material to work with when it came to the Bushes. Most of what she had been writing about the old man she could apply to Junior. The younger Bush had grown up in Midland; it was the city where Clayton Williams, the man Richards had beat to become governor in 1990, was from. She knew about Bush's world out in Midland, and she knew about his world from his high school days in Houston. He was always about the black-and-white, the here-and-now. He was never an expansive, critical thinker. He always seemed to be yet another cocky heir to the gilded tent. Not as lucky as Glenn "Shamrock" McCarthy in the oil business, but lucky enough to be born into the right family. Those people were newly minted around her all the time when she lived on Chevy Chase Drive in River Oaks. She and Bush had also gone to high-end Eastern colleges in the '60s. He was at his fraternity wielding a branding iron and searing the skin of pledges—and getting his name for the first time in the *New York Times*, in stories about wicked hazing rituals at colleges. He was hating the Beatles because they had moved beyond three chords and into sitars and Sgt. Pepper. He despised ambiguity. Ivins cherished it, and said there were a thousand sides to every story.

Tackling Bush—in her columns, but especially in book-form—would be easy. She knew the context of his evolution, she literally knew where he was coming from. With that back story, with her ability to peg the caste system he emerged from, she could begin lopping at each move he made to privatize welfare, to hand over social programs to churches, to derail trial lawyers, to let oil companies skirt pollution provisions.

⋘⋙

John McCain was on the phone, calling Ivins to talk about his resistance to some of what he was seeing set in motion by the Republican Revolutionaries. It was a dangerous dance, calling Ivins. She liked him, and she thought the late-1990s version of McCain was as close to an independent Republican as she wanted to get. There were other calls, from White House staffers and then, ultimately, Bill Clinton. They wanted to talk about ways that Ivins could be a battering ram against the GOP revolution and its screaming imams, especially Limbaugh. He was an unlikely phenomenon and gaining traction, and then leverage, and the Clinton White House didn't want to be surprised, overtaken, the way some people were flummoxed by the political awakening of the Christian right in the late 1980s.

Producers talked to Ivins about getting her own national radio show, something like Limbaugh did. She communicated with other producers who wondered if there was a way to build a national TV show around her. Was there some way to move her beyond her newspapers? No one could ever have predicted that a collection of rehashed stories in *Ms.*, *The*

Progressive, and *The Nation* would have squatted on the bestseller list for more than nine months. It was unheard of, and it suggested to Clinton that Ivins really did have her own constituency that could be mobilized for the Democrats. It was, maybe, the bedrock base of liberal America. And it needed to be shored up in the face of the Republican Revolution, in the face of Clinton administration scandals, in the face of Ann Richards losing to another Bush—who was presumed to be running for the presidency in 2000. She told Clinton and the other people calling her from the White House that she was, essentially, open to all possibilities. "People probably didn't understand how powerful she was," one of her researchers said.

⤛⤜

In February 1996 calls were made all over Austin, alerting people to the fact that Ivins and cowboy poet–singer–river guide Steve Fromholz were going to be camping, with sleeping bags, on downtown Congress Avenue—and trying to get arrested for civil disobedience. It was a protest against Austin laws aimed at "clearing out" the homeless. They were joined by eighty other people with signs and camping gear. She liked hanging out with Fromholz; he was part of the singer-songwriter tradition—people like Lyle Lovett, Townes Van Zandt, Jerry Jeff Walker—that once defined Central Texas. Ivins grew close to Fromholz's daughter Felicity. One time Fromholz heard his daughter say: "Mother? When I grow up I want to know as many adjectives as Molly Ivins does."

At the protest on behalf of the homeless population in Austin, neither Fromholz nor Ivins was arrested, but the publicity they created helped lead to changes in the anti-homeless ordinance. Fromholz said: "Well, we both had celebrity in our lives, and it didn't kill us. We didn't believe our own press much. It's safer that way."[1]

A few weeks after she was camping out on the streets with the homeless, Random House sent Ivins $120,500 in royalties from her first two books. And in the fall her agent Dan Green began negotiations with Random House and secured a $250,000 advance for her next collection of previously published material. Her new editor was going to be Ann Godoff, Random House's editor-in-chief. Her agent suggested titles: *They Dance with Them That Brung Them and Other Cautionary Tales* or *What Do Politicians Want?*

The work was steady and lofty. She entered negotiations with CBS's *60 Minutes* producer Don Hewitt, who had devised a plan to change the format of the show. Ivins, writer Stanley Crouch, and conservative pundit P. J. O'Rourke would take turns doing a point-counterpoint segment in the slot that Andy Rooney occupied. Ivins would be filmed in Austin and her "debate" with Crouch or O'Rourke would be spliced onto their bit of tape. They were told to keep the topics—Medicare, abortion—funny. And they wouldn't be in the same room with each other. No moderator. The segments started in April, with Ivins against Crouch, but the entire experiment was canceled after eight weeks. Critics assailed the segments and Hewitt issued a press release saying, "Our mail suggested the segment was not catching on, and I never argue with our viewers."

⋯

Her father was still battling cancer and she and her siblings talked about how much longer he had to live. He was going on eighty-five and incapable of getting out on the water, and that was almost a death sentence in itself. His letters were not coming as often. They had communicated, a little, about Shrub. He didn't like Clinton, he didn't like Richards, and he didn't necessarily really like Bush either. To her father, Bush seemed thin, flimsy, filled with bluster and fake bravado. A bantam rooster. Her father had rubbed shoulders with some serious ass-kicking oilmen, ones who hadn't inherited shit—but who wound up taking some crazy rides on the top of the Big Oil locomotive as it hurtled from the Permian Basin to the East Texas gushers. They were cowboys, making it up as they went along. Then they somehow grew brains and were able to translate their daring into impenetrable corporate castles. They conquered Texas in their earth-scorching way, and they made billions doing it. Jim Ivins didn't think that Shrub had done that. Shrub couldn't hold his own with the real men at the top of the Petroleum Club. The big leather chairs were reserved for the Big Oil hunters: In Texas, people talked about the Elephant Field—the big score, the big patch, the burst of oil and money that would seriously change a lot of lives. Wildcatters in West Texas still said Bush was that "corner shot" artist, a small player trying to drill his well at the corner of the Elephant Field, hoping that a few barrels would flow his way.

Jim Ivins had sat at the head of Tenneco for a while, had mingled with the people who invented the modern Big Oil oligarchy. Hell, he had his own hand in it—he had found the legal means to get anything done that the Tenneco people wanted done. Shrub didn't have the brains, balls, and luck to do what most of the people he knew had done. But that didn't mean that Jim Ivins was in love with Bill Clinton or Al Gore. He was still a Nixonian Republican, loyal, and he wouldn't bend toward the politicians his daughter supported. The bottom line was that he just didn't like the way Bush had emerged as a public figure. It was almost a rare moment where he and his daughter could concur.

⋞⟷⋟

Ivins had a woman to clean and care for the house, to run some errands, exercise the dog, do some shopping. And she brought things for herself and her family, too. When her friends called and said their children were passing through Austin, she opened her house up. When students, ones who had talked to her for just a few minutes at a function in the city, asked her for a letter of recommendation for law school, she would interview them for five minutes for some material—and then write a persuasively glowing reference. When friends sheepishly told her that they weren't able to find a hotel room in Paris, she would duck into her home office, make some calls, and arrange for them to stay with other friends. If they needed to borrow her car, they had it for the day. She paid for her researcher to fly to Alaska.

When she was in New Orleans for the ACLU banquet honoring Sister Helen Prejean, famous for her *Dead Man Walking* book about death row, Ivins took friends out to dinner. She treated several people to brunch at Commander's Palace, ordered a bottle of Dom Perignon, and made a toast—"You can't have new old friends." She liked taking people to Commander's Palace, she loved to eat, and when she would come to town for literary festivals or ACLU speeches, she would organize a group of a dozen or so—the members of the Brennan family recognized her and sent over an order of one of every dessert, plus some more champagne. The Brennans were not sure what to expect: One day she was introducing people at the restaurant to J. Anthony Lukas, the two-time Pulitzer-winning writer—and Ivins was dressed in a buckskin jacket.

"Molly was exhausting. But she was so much fun. You never knew what would happen. You never knew who would show up," said New Orleans reporter John Pope.[2] And she cooked, something she liked to do more than ever before. It was her Zen, a way to decompress, sometimes surrounded by some of her mother's old utensils—even ones she had a hard time identifying. She liked to cook rich things, French food, and she liked to shop at the quality organic stores in Austin.

Ivins invited people to her house for "orphan holidays"—people who had nowhere else to go, people whose families had splintered. She created her own, instant family at holidays. When people showed up, sometimes bringing a potluck dish, they were almost never surprised that they hadn't brought enough. She had kept inviting more and more people, until it was more than a dinner, it was a party. One time her old colleague from Houston and Dallas, Billy Porterfield, was there—another in a long line of newspaper people, politicians, and writers who had had their children crash at her house, who had been fed by Ivins, who had seen her act like Great Aunt Molly. Porterfield laughed out loud when he realized—as did many others—that she had taken her impressive journalism awards and used them as trivets, as coasters, as serving trays.

It was never unusual for her to stay up as late as she could, making sure that everyone had eaten as much as they wanted. If they wanted to crash on her couch or the floor it was perfectly fine. Her neighbors thought that she was almost the anti-celebrity—especially when she invited them to the gatherings, or she delivered leftovers.

In January 1997, she learned that her mother had died on New Year's Day at a "Hoppin' John" party—a Southern tradition of eating black-eyed peas and rice as a way to kick off the year with good luck. Her mother had just dropped dead. Ivins wrote about her just a few days later: "Margaret Milne Ivins was a gay and gracious lady, and also one of the kindest people I've ever known. In 84 years of living, she never mastered the more practical aspects of life—I believe the clinical term is 'seriously ditzy'—but she was nobody's fool."

Her mother had held the family together in her way—reminding her children to mind their manners, checking on their well-being, and recommending things that they do to feel better, look better, behave better. She had an irrepressible garrulousness. She could "charm the birds from the trees" even though she was lazy, a horrible housekeeper, and prone to depression. "It was like living with a combination of Gracie Allen and Sigmund Freud."[3] She stayed that way, people said, through the moves from Houston to Maryland, and on all those yachting trips.

Molly, meanwhile, had thought, for years, about whether there was something she could have done better to piece the family together. The only thing she could come up with, when she talked to friends, was that her mother would have wanted her to have a spouse and a child—and that her mother would have doted on the baby, because she doted on all babies and somehow that would soften The General.

The new book, *You Got to Dance With Them What Brung You*, was released in the spring of 1998. By now she had received a few death threats—and constant, endless, vicious, ominous missives, many of them written in red ink. In Dallas, as she headed to a book signing, there was a bomb threat. The police were notified. Finally, the all-clear signal was given. Sucking on yet another Marlboro 100, blowing out cigarette smoke, Ivins told her handlers not to call the media—she didn't want free press for the people who were behind the deal.

On April 18, 1998, at 8 P.M., she sat at her computer in her home on Alta Vista in Austin and began writing a column about her father. She knew millions would read her painful assessment. She was fifty-three, still staying up way too late at night. She was arguably the most famous female journalist in America. Now, she had decided to finally put down on paper what she had held back for years. She was going to tell her father exactly what she thought of him. She had started the mini-biography as an act of appeasement—or, at least, as much of a rapprochement as she could muster. She was always so unforgiving, uncompromising, but she wanted to be clear-headed about this; she wanted to write something that he would read before his bladder cancer consumed him and that would make him realize that though she had railed against everything he worshipped, she had some capacity for forgiveness. She began typing on a fine line, trying to capture the man who had had a stranglehold on her life:

> My old man is one of the toughest sons of bitches God ever made. I say that after second thought, and I say it again after third thought.
>
> My father is a throwback. He would have made a great 18th-century sea captain. He has incredible courage, stamina and fortitude. And he is a stoic to the bone. I've known him for 53 years, and I've never heard him whine or complain about anything.

After working for twenty minutes on her column and writing seven sentences, she heard the phone ring. Someone had news: Her father had slipped out into his Florida backyard. His cancer had advanced, he had been told he had to move into a nursing home. In the backyard, he raised a gun to his head and shot himself.

In Austin, she absorbed the news, put the phone down, and turned back to her computer. She continued writing:

> I started this column at approximately 8 P.M. . . . about 8:20, seven sentences into the column, I received a phone call informing me that my father had put a bullet through his brain. I am shocked but not surprised.
>
> And so I continue. . . .
>
> Because my father was a closed man emotionally, there are many things about him I do not know. . . . My father and I had many bitter quarrels about the civil-rights movement and the Vietnam War. . . . So

> what am I supposed to tell you about Big Jim? Am I supposed to tell you that he was a great father and a loving human being? He wasn't. . . .
>
> He blew his brains out six hours ago, and I, as his child who most bitterly disagreed with him, tell you that this was a man.

Some of her closest friends were angry at her father—and at the idea that he had abruptly vanished, as he had during his marriage. He was dying from cancer, couldn't control his bladder, and he was stoic, stubborn. "When he committed suicide, it was just one more asshole thing to do. Don't even bother to say goodbye. Just go out in the yard and shoot your head off," said Speights. She thought that Ivins clearly wanted to remember him at his best.[4]

Ivins flew her brother and sister to Florida and they scattered their father's ashes in Sarasota Bay.

⋯

Karl Rove was in his downtown Austin office, the one with no windows, and he was perhaps thinking about nasty things. He was busy buying up domain names, ones that some slimy operatives on the Democratic side would appropriate so that if voters clicked on a "Bush link," they would automatically be directed to a prank site or a lurid sex site. The George W. Bush campaign for the presidency was in full operation, jackbooting forward with a very crisp precision. Rove wasn't leaving anything to chance.

Ivins's publisher wasn't leaving anything to chance either, especially when it came to Ivins and Bush. Random House wanted another book from Ivins, and it had to be original, campaign-timed work about Bush, not a collection of columns. As always, she gave work to friends, this time to Lou Dubose, a faithful editor at the *Observer* and someone who could bring a calm efficiency to the process. He was an excellent reporter, in tune with Ivins's politics, and an almost obvious choice to co-author the project. Godoff and the editors at Random House hoped that her "constituency" was still there, that the new book, gusted by interest in the election, could get her back on the bestseller list. Dubose began working on chapters.

At her office downtown, in the *Star-Telegram*'s cramped quarters at 10th and Congress, near the governor's mansion where Bush lived, sacks of mail were still being dumped on her desk. In 1999, a trickster started signing her up for subscriptions to magazines she didn't want. *MAD*, *Gun Dog*, *Model Airplane News*, *Wildfowl*. She was signed up for book clubs, record clubs. And not long afterward, there were notices from collection agencies, demanding payment for the subscriptions. There were more overt attacks: an official-looking envelope with the words "PREGNANCY TEST RESULTS" on the outside. Inside was a typed message: "You ain't seen nothin' yet Bitch! The best is yet to come!"

She would gather people in her office and sometimes read the letters out loud. They seemed to increase in vitriol as she wrote more and more about Bush—work, in her columns, that might segue into material for her book. She told her friends that Austin had changed in deep, indelible ways. It was filled with strivers, newcomers, more sophisticated political operatives who had been imported to the city to work for—and against—Bush. It was a far cry from the days when everything she needed to know was gathered over several bourbons with Bob Bullock. As if by design, as if things had finally changed too much even for Bob Bullock, he died that June—just as Ivins was working on something tantamount to her first real book, not a collection of old stories.

Just a few days before Bullock died from cancer—and a soul stretched thin by his personal and political excesses—a writer working on an unauthorized biography of George W. Bush had finally secured an interview with him. Bullock was suspicious of the writer; he wasn't a regular member of the political press corps, and he wrote about poverty more than about lawmakers. Bush and his communications person Karen Hughes desperately tried to frighten the writer away from doing the book—including sending him threatening letters. For some reason, Bullock finally summoned the writer, perhaps because he knew he was dying, and said that if the writer didn't get the fuck to Bullock's house in ten minutes, he wasn't going to talk.

He was in his bed, gaunt, looking at his personal financial statements and flat on his back. He was sweating, hollow-eyed, and would swoon in and out of coherence—demanding to know if the reporter wanted any fried chicken, talking about limousines and even about Dick Tracy. He kept muttering Ivins's name. He'd sit up, say her name, and then fall back down. On his deathbed, the man who essentially delivered Texas to George W. Bush was still obsessing about Molly Ivins . . . the "hairy-legged liberal."

Like him or not, Bullock had been her spirit guide into the netherworld of Texas politics. And she knew better than anyone that he had made many compromises, that he had structured deals with his own homunculus from hell. She liked him nonetheless, and this was probably tied to the simple fact that he was outrageous and anti-authority in his own fevered way. They always got along, even when he buried the hatchet in Ann Richards's back and refused to help her win reelection—even when it became increasingly clear that he was aligning himself ever more deeply with Bush.

She wasn't sure that she could ever invent someone like Bob Bullock. And she wasn't sure that she could ever write about him—given all that he had taught her, shown her.

For relief from the rollercoaster ride, she was still attending her book club. They had chosen to read Sena Naslund's *Ahab's Wife* and Frank McCourt's *'Tis*. Dave Richards, Ann's former husband, had remarried and she went to parties at his house. The Final Friday gatherings that had started up years ago in Austin as First Fridays had shifted around, threatened to be exiled to history, and then found a permanent home at her house. With Bush moving forward, the city was filled with out-of-town reporters from *Newsweek*, *Rolling Stone*, and CBS, and many of them wangled an invite to the Friday parties—or simply showed up. The political reconnaissance people were there, too, including some Bush spies who had been sent to figure out who Ivins was talking to and what she was telling them.

By the summer, she and Dubose had a title for the book—*Shrub: The Short but Happy Political Life of George W. Bush*. She had an ACLU speech in South Carolina and then she'd fly to New York, check into the Waldorf Astoria, and go to the Hugh Hefner First Amendment Awards with Christie Hefner. In New York, her literary agent Dan Green was going to meet her at the Waldorf and walk her to the Random House offices so she could meet the publicity people and then go to lunch with Random House's Ann Godoff and *New York Times* book review editor Eden Lipson, her trusted friend.

An advance copy of *Texas Monthly* had her listed in the Bum Steer awards section under the headline "Ivins The Terrible"—the magazine took her to task for saying the *Observer* was in financial trouble, while Dubose was saying things looked good. And there were some good letters coming in, ones that she took the time to read, rather than letting Faulk or Eckhardt filter them for her in the ninth-floor office. A lawyer in Houston had met her at a party in Austin, and he reminded her that they had gone on a river trip to Big Bend National Park a couple of years ago and that Herradura tequila was involved.

In November, she attended the Texas Book Festival in Austin—an event that was co-founded by Laura Bush—and she found herself face to face with Shrub. It was the Friday-night black-tie gala and Bush was going to be a "surprise reader"—his mouthpiece, Karen Hughes, had written his autobiography for him and when he stepped to the microphone to read it, someone at the Random House table remarked that it seemed like he was hearing about his own life for the very first time. When he saw Ivins, he spontaneously hugged her; they both laughed and people stared. She had been telling people, publicly and privately, that Bush could almost be likable—his policies were flawed, but he could be charming, fun to be around.

Meanwhile, her own speeches, her public appearances, were increasingly crowding her schedule. Faulk had prepared a list of speeches for next year—Texas A&M, the ACLU in Utah, Bowling Green University was offering $12,000, ACLU in Massachusetts, ACLU in Tennessee, and a Caribbean cruise sponsored by *The Nation*. But the carefully prepared schedule was going to change that fall when she was diagnosed with Stage III inflammatory breast cancer. She told only a few people, but then decided to put a short note at the bottom of her syndicated column on December 14, 1999:

> A personal note: I have contracted an outstanding case of breast cancer, from which I fully intend to recover. I don't need get-well cards, but I would like the beloved women readers to do something for me: Go. Get. The. Damn. Mammogram. Done. My friend Maryln Schwartz

> says: "If you have ever wondered what it would feel like to sit in a doctor's office with a lump in your breast trying to remember when you last had a mammogram, I can tell you. You feel like a fool. I'd say 'a damn fool.'" My friend Myra MacPherson says that if you want to prepare a girl for her first mammogram, you should tell her to go lie down on a cold cement slab in the garage and run a tire back and forth across her chest. True, but it sure beats a serious cancer. Please, go get the damn mammogram done. That would be the best Christmas present that anyone could give me.

⟻⟼

Shrub was set for release in early 2000, at almost the exact same time she was beginning her first round of chemotherapy under the direction of Austin oncologist Dr. John Doty. Godoff, the editor-in-chief at Random House, sent a handwritten note about the book: "I think it looks wonderful and the timing couldn't be better. My thoughts and prayers are with you through this difficult period. If there is anything—anything—I can do to lighten your load, just let me know. In the meantime, thanks for all your hard work."[5] Her agent Dan Green sent a note saying: "Let's hope the greater the prospect of President Shrub, the greater the sales of the book."[6]

There was also a letter from The White House:

> THE WHITE HOUSE
> Washington
>
> December 17, 1999
>
> Dear Molly:
>
> Hillary and I were sorry to learn of your illness, and we wanted you to know we're thinking about you and pulling for you.
>
> I'm grateful to you for spreading the word about the necessity of getting mammograms.
>
> You'll be in our prayers. Happy Holidays.

Sincerely,
Bill Clinton

Hang in there—You will cause thousands of women to get mammograms, and your courage will inspire your fans and cause the skeptics to read you more carefully— [7]

⊰⊱

Throughout early 2000, she had chemotherapy treatments in the morning and then she would come home, rest for an hour, and resume work. The Bush media juggernaut was in full-on mode and there were endless demands, along with well-wishes: PBS's *Frontline* wanted to do a series of one-hour interviews with her. Author Anne Lamott was wondering about Ivins doing a joint lecture with her. Ralph Nader called and "would like to talk to [Molly] personally." Michael Moore wrote a letter asking for some publicity and saying "thanks for all the support in the past." And a stranger named Natalie, who described herself as Ivins's C-SPAN psychic buddy—an eighty-seven-year-old mystic and scientist—called from New York saying she had some pointers that would make her journey to a cancer-free existence much easier. Bernard Rapoport, the longtime angel to the *Observer*, sent notes telling her not to worry about the publication, that he was taking care of it. The writer Bud Shrake gave her a copy of his book *The Borderland* and, invoking a nickname for cancer, wrote inside: "I always considered you a formidable and indestructible presence. The Red Queen has picked on the wrong sailor in the saloon. May you be blessed with a quick victory."

Meanwhile, Faulk realized that Ivins's schedule had to be corralled. She began sending notes to Christie Hefner and others telling them Ivins was cutting back in 2000, that she had to deal with her cancer. There was little sympathy for her condition from the people who stalked her via mail and email: Faulk had to send a note to the directors of a triathlon in Austin telling them that someone had prank-signed Ivins up, just like they had prank-signed her up for all those magazines and record clubs. *Shrub* entered the bestseller list that winter and stayed on it for a little over two months. There were mixed reviews. The *New York Times* said the book "reads like a long editorial rant at Mr. Bush's political record, a rant that's sometimes persuasive, sometimes unfair, if almost always entertaining." Another review in the Sunday *New York Times* book section said it was written by the "East Coast's favorite Texas journalist" and that it was a "glorified clip job."

Faulk and her other aides tried to buffer Ivins from any bad news. Dubose thought the criticism in the *Times* was harsh. Either way, the fact that it had floated to the bestseller list seemed to engender more creepy, anonymous attacks. The letters were stamped from locales around the country: "Ivins, you are an ugly, mean, vicious bitch. You are sickening to look at." Meanwhile, at home, doctors told her she needed regular, self-administered shots to keep her white blood cell count up. She asked friends if they knew how to do them. A diabetic neighbor volunteered but Speights sought backups just in case. And as word spread that she was sick, her home was inundated with calls and gifts and cards from friends in New York, Houston, Dallas, San Antonio, San Francisco. Her spirits were boosted when *Time* magazine agreed to print a book excerpt and executive editor Stephen Koepp wrote that "it's so impressive that you are going through such a regimen and still producing such great columns."[8]

On April 13, Al Gore sent her a letter:

> Dear Molly, My sincerest thanks for the inscribed copy of your book, *Shrub*. Please accept my best wishes and profound gratitude. Sincerely, Al.[9]

By May the book had slipped off the bestseller charts but she was in constant demand for TV and radio sound bites. Film crews from most major networks sought her out. When Gail Sheehy came to town to write a piece for *Vanity Fair* about Bush, a meeting was arranged between her and Ivins. Foreign journalists were camping out in Austin and many of them wanted something funny, snappy, irreverent from Ivins. In June, she heard from Roy Blount, Jr., and he reminded her that he had crashed at her house some years ago and had made a racket when somebody came to pick him up early in the morning and Athena started barking. "I was sorry to hear you got cancer. I can't think of anybody who deserves it less. You are one of my heroes, and I wish I could send you something more appreciative than an armadillo picture. At least you can feel relieved that I am not sending you an actual armadillo."[10]

Throughout the spring, the medical news was getting worse. She had been diagnosed with anemia and now was on an even more intense medication routine. There were shots for her white blood cell count. Shots for the anemia. Vitamin B12 and folic acid supplements. She was taking Prozac and Ritalin. She was taking something for acid reflux. And she couldn't eat oranges, salads, or unpeeled apples. She wrote her feelings down in her notebooks:

> Tense. Anxious? Whatever I'm feeling, I'm not letting much through. Will be glad to have it over. That is what I least wanted and still think a bilateral mastectomy would have been preferable. . . . All last week inundated by visitors until I was exhausted with them. All yesterday got phone calls of love and support all day. That was wonderful. . . . It's raining. Took a last look at my breasts—still pretty damn good. I would not mind being flat-chested, but not matching is a bummer. Best call from Marilyn. Told her it was an odd feeling to contemplate, voluntarily walking into a place to be mutilated. Freak, deformed. . . .
>
> Mercy insisted I get in touch with my feelings (Yoo-hoo, anybody there?) . . . Have been sleepless . . . also drinking far too much and smoking. Am learning I cannot take good health for granted. Have been burning candle at both ends for a long time; 55 is not too young to take up moderation and even abstinence. . . . I hope I can remember this for the rest of my life, sitting here in the first light, paying the penalty for years of drinking and smoking and not eating right.[11]

Nadine Eckhardt had developed a habit of trying to respond to the thousands of pieces of mail with the occasional postcard that featured Ralph, the "world famous swimming pig" that dived for tourists at Aquarena Springs south of Austin. It served as comic relief in the wake of the stir when former Texas Republican chairman Tom Pauken had called *Time* in 2000 to complain about a book excerpt that suggested he had endorsed Dan Quayle. The editors and lawyers were worried but the issue blew over. The book, despite the flap and the tepid reception in Ivins's old newspaper, was selling well. The politicos continued to sense that she was a valuable figure in the heartland, someone it was worth staying in touch with: Senator Christopher Dodd sent her a scrawled note in May saying he was a long-distance admirer.

As summer arrived, some friends in Austin sent out invitations to celebrate the end of her chemotherapy sessions. Her medical expenses were skyrocketing. The syndicate was paying her almost $13,000 a month to distribute her column to those 300-plus newspapers. She was on track to make $200,000 a year in speeches. She had her *Star-Telegram* salary, the gushing book royalties. The money was there and the speeches continued to be the ultimate fallback in case there was a financial shortfall. But her best friends were quietly talking about their belief that she hadn't hunkered down to do a deeply personal accounting—not of her finances, but her health. It was the same thing that the blunt women in her world—Faulk and Eckhardt—had been asking: Did she have the capacity for the kind of slow, steady introspection that would lead her to the only logical choice—to give up drinking, smoking, and all the brutal, work-related stress? Would she be as generous to herself as she had been to everyone else? Friends talked about ways to intervene—to get her to finally stop drinking, to finally stop smoking.

Her sister Sara even wrote her a note: "Please take care of yourself and give up those fags. I didn't know you were still smoking. Stop! Stop! Stop! I love you and I want you around for your 'Sexy Sixties.' Please Mole, the medical profession can only do so much, you've got to do the rest."[12]

⁂

Anthony Zurcher had become her editor with the Creators Syndicate, saw the way she was with his son. When his son was born, she gave him three books: In *Alice in Wonderland*, she wrote: "Here's to six impossible things before breakfast." For *The Wind in the Willows*, it was "May you have Toad's zest for life." And in *The Little Prince* she wrote: "May your heart always see clearly."[13] A friend from Houston brought his daughter to see Ivins, and he felt that his daughter had been "blessed" to see her. Ivins bought *The Little Prince* and *The Paper Bag Princess* and wrote careful notes inside them.

She barely slowed down, even with the uncertain news about the exact progress of her cancer.

In the fall, she flew to Marin, California, to do "An Evening with Molly Ivins & Anne Lamott." She consented to yet another round of promotional book tours. She agreed to quickly bat out a piece for *Time*—she would have to produce it as quickly as possible after Election Day. She worked hard to deliver a piece but the editors didn't like it—they said it was "too spiky" and suggested she probe for the bright side of Bush. At the top of her draft, she scrawled "rejected by *Time* magazine." But her agent Dan Green had told her that there was a bright side to Bush's election: She could gather material for yet another book. Some of her friends had secretly hoped Bush would not emerge victorious—not for just the obvious political reasons, but because his election would only lead to more work, more stress, more demands for Ivins. If Bush won, and if he was reelected, she would simply yield to all the energy-sapping interview requests, the pressures of deadlines, the intrusions on the time she needed to heal herself. Liz Faulk, for one, had seen it before: Her husband had to, as she put it, "sing for his supper"—he was hardly ever allowed to step out of character. Ivins's friends in Austin wondered if the "Molly franchise" would ever be granted a rest.

⤛⤚

As a salve for the rejection at *Time*, she left for a cruise to Mexico sponsored by *The Nation*—with writers Eric Alterman, Calvin Trillin, Lawrence Goodwyn, Studs Terkel, and Barbara Kingsolver, activist Tom Hayden, and former Texas agricultural commissioner and *Observer* editor Jim Hightower. When she returned to Austin there was good news waiting for her: a letter from Random House publisher Ann Godoff that left Ivins with the impression she was all but assured of yet another significant six-figure book deal. "In the end, you may have written the core text on George W.—no matter what the political climate, you have my best wishes for a healthy and happy New Year."[14]

Of course, Bush's election ramped up interest in Texas again and she was flooded with more requests to write about him and the state. National Public Radio wanted her to do regular commentaries on *Morning Edition*.

NBA Commissioner David Stern even called and asked her to appear at an All-Star game luncheon. But in April, she was stunned when the editors at the *Fort Worth Star-Telegram* suggested she should move on. The reporters in the Austin press building gossiped that it was purely a money move. The *Star-Telegram* could buy her column from the syndicate for a lot less than paying her salary. Plus they could save on health insurance.

She had lost fifty pounds, her hair had fallen out and grown in again, but now she had a shorter, spiked mane. She had gone through nine months of chemotherapy and radiation therapy, and doctors had finally recommended a radical mastectomy. She was given a 70 percent chance of the cancer being gone by 2006—or, joked her friends, a year or two into the administration of the president who would oust Bush. She told people she had stopped smoking, she was going to write only two columns a week, and she was going to visit France again. She wondered, in an August 2000 column, if after her mastectomy she would gain some deeper meaning or understanding, something that would let her know what drove her father to his death: "The trouble is, I'm not a better person. I was in great hopes that confronting my own mortality would make me deeper, more thoughtful. [But,] there was not a single iota of spiritual improvement or growth." She joked that, on the upside, she no longer had bad hair days.

Vincent Bugliosi asked her to write the foreword for *The Betrayal of America: How the Supreme Court Undermined the Constitution and Chose Our President*. She made plans to fly to San Francisco for a speech to the Center for Gender Equality at the University of California. There were discussions about another Bush book, something that would have to be released before the next election, something perhaps that might influence the outcome. Meanwhile, she was still holding Final Friday parties at her house, and a friend she had met at an ACLU function in Dallas, journalist and food writer Ellen Sweets, was becoming a regular friend and houseguest. Sweets had a long connection, through her family, to Paul Robeson, James Baldwin, and Langston Hughes. And they would talk about John Henry Faulk: "She called him John Henry. She had a photograph of him on top of a stack of his books in her living room. We talked a lot about the blacklist because Paul Robeson was a friend of our family and on the blacklist," says Sweets, one of the few African-Americans in Ivins's circle of closest friends. They would spend hours shopping at local grocery stores, laughing their way down the aisles, and then spending a few more hours cooking together at Ivins's home. Ivins and Sweets would argue over ingredients, portions, presentation. Ivins loved having her visit, loved getting to know Sweets's daughter, a budding chef. Now she had another person for whom she could be Aunt Molly. Cooking was an escape, she needed to gain some of her weight back, she needed to eat and it was good to spend so much time in the kitchen, not on any real deadline, not staring into another television camera, not on stage somewhere channeling Faulk or Ann Richards.

One time, on a visit, Sweets was griping about how the newspaper she worked for in Dallas wouldn't pay her expenses to a festival in France. Ivins went into a backroom and arranged for Sweets to stay with some old college friends from Ivins's days at Smith. "I don't think we will ever know how many people she helped. Her generosity, you hear the term 'largesse' spread around, hers was incredible. She never talked about it, she never told other people," says Sweets.[15]

She learned that Ivins loved the movies, but she never liked going early in the day because there were too many people who would recognize her. She would go to the 10 P.M. show. When they went out to eat, she would ask for a booth in the back, and then not face the room. Some old friends still stopped by the Friday parties. Elliott Naishtat, a state representative who had been raised in a Jewish household in Queens. Sara Speights. Her new assistant, Betsy Moon, who used to work for Jim Hightower. The women in her book club. Marilyn Schultz, the ex-TV producer who was now a college professor. People she had known at the *Houston Chronicle*, Carlton Carl and Dave McNeely. She had stayed close with McNeely—his wife had died a few years earlier after fighting breast cancer for eight years. And Ivins had always been attentive to McNeely and his children. Billy Porterfield, who had his teeth knocked out by Ivins in Dallas, would come. Sometimes her New York friends were in town. And there was a feeling that she still liked telling stories and that she was still trolling for ideas.

But then there were those uninvited tourists who wanted her to entertain them. One Friday night Sweets heard two people asking: "Where is she? I don't see her, she's tall isn't she?" The strangers started peeking into Ivins's bedroom, where Ivins had gone to rest, and as one of them reached for the door handle Sweets challenged them. For some people who showed up at her house, it was like looking for the living heir to the legacy of the old guard of Texas liberals—the link to John Henry Faulk, Willie Morris, and Ralph Yarborough. Some friends wondered if she was ever comfortable in her role as the grey eminence. Some suspected that she would rather be out doing pranks—mooning the KKK, camping out on a downtown street and hoping to get arrested—as opposed to being gingerly treated like a revered icon. And some friends knew that what she really wanted at times was to be under the trees in her yard, sipping on some wine and staying up until 3 A.M. singing old country songs with whoever had brought a guitar.

The American Academy of Arts & Sciences inducted her in October, along with King Juan Carlos of Spain, former Secretary of State Madeleine Albright, musician Quincy Jones, and photographer Richard Avedon. She told people "It's so establishment. I am so anti-establishment."[16] The award, to her, seemed like the kind of thing that is awarded to people who are at the end of their careers, maybe the end of their lives. She talked with a few friends about mortality, about how the people who had an enormous influence on her were gone—her father, John Henry Faulk, Bob Bullock. At the exact same time, she was reading and then reviewing a new work by Studs Terkel, a writer she greatly admired, that examined how ordinary Americans felt about death: "Living in a death-obsessed culture is clearly no better. As Jessica Mitford once remarked about ancient Egypt: 'Now there was a culture where they let the funeral directors get completely out of control.' I've always liked the Mexican tradition of seeing death in life, grinning at you from the oddest places. And the Irish tradition of laughing and drinking at wakes."[17]

CHAPTER THIRTEEN

Dearly Beloveds

Molly,
I am shouting,
With two voices,
Walls come down!

—MAYA ANGELOU

In early 2002, she wrote about her cancer for *Time*. The piece was titled "Who Needs Breasts Anyway?":

> Having breast cancer is massive amounts of no fun. First they mutilate you; then they poison you; then they burn you. I have been on blind dates better than that. One of the first things you notice is that people treat you differently when they know you have it. The hushed tone in which they inquire, "How are you?" is unnerving. If I had answered honestly during 90% of the nine months I spent in treatment, I would have said, "If it weren't for being constipated, I'd be fine." My friend Judy Curtis demanded totally uncritical support from everyone around her. "I smoked and drank through the whole thing," she

> says. "And I hated the lady from the American Cancer Society." My role model. . . .
>
> You don't get through this without friends. Use them. Call them, especially other women who have been through it. People like to help. They like to be able to do something for you. Let them. You will also get sick of talking about cancer. . . .
>
> Losing a part of a breast or all of one or both has, obviously, serious psychological consequences. Your self-image, your sense of yourself as a woman, your sense of your sexual attractiveness are going to be rocked whether or not you have enough sense to realize that tits aren't that important. I am one of those people who are out of touch with their emotions. I tend to treat my emotions like unpleasant relatives—a long-distance call once or twice a year is more than enough. If I got in touch with them, they might come to stay. My friend Mercedes Pena made me get in touch with my emotions just before I had a breast cut off. Just as I suspected, they were awful. "How do you Latinas do this—all the time in touch with your emotions?" I asked her. "That's why we take siestas," she replied. As a final indignity, I have just flunked breast reconstruction. Bad enough that I went through all that pain for the sake of vanity, but then I got a massive infection and had to have both implants taken out. I'm embarrassed about it, although my chief cancer mentor, Maryln Schwartz [who went to the Palm for lunch after every chemo session], has forbidden this particular emotion. So now I'm just a happy, flat-chested woman.[1]

She had been in touch with a documentary film crew that wanted to produce *Dildo Diaries*, based in part on the work she had done in that first column for the *Fort Worth Star-Telegram*—where her editor saw his career flash before his eyes. She eventually appeared in the movie (along with former porn star Annie Sprinkle) and it was released in 2002. Her friends thought it was perfectly ironic and funny as hell that she had tried to sneak the word "dildos" into a story—and now she was in a documentary about them and about how backwards the laws in Texas could be.

It was funny but it only temporarily served as a distraction for the bigger themes that were dominating her life. In the coming years, the main things on her mind were the cancer and the hard right turn toward war, triumphalism, and what she saw as a wholesale disregard for civil liberties by the Bush administration. The bellicosities emerging from the White House, the almost preordained inevitability of America going to war, gave her ample material to work with. So did the expanding belief that Rove, Bush, and Cheney were wickedly empowering the executive branch, creating an imperial presidency—and that Cheney, particularly, had taken on greater powers than any modern American vice president. She was watching Bush's White House Counsel Alberto Gonzales, Justice Department lawyers, and Cheney advisors as they worked hard to "interpret" ways to bypass the usual judicial and investigative methods that had been used against terrorists. They were prosecuting the so-called war on terror in ways that slammed up against the very things that she had been advocating around the country for years—things that she felt duty-bound to argue for, to defend, and not just because she had made a deathbed promise to John Henry Faulk. Gonzales was calling portions of the Geneva Conventions quaint and obsolete; there were whispers that the CIA was waterboarding, torturing people; there were rumors about secret prisons, secret tribunals, and a wholesale suspension of due process. Too, reporters she knew in Washington and New York were chasing down leads on just how extensively the administration had endorsed a domestic spying program, bypassing warrants, eavesdropping on anyone they wanted. It was, to her, a John Henry Faulk issue, a constitutional issue: freedom of expression, freedom of speech, a right to equitable treatment.

In an obvious reflection of the two intense themes that dominated her thinking, she thought about a book that would outline all those assaults on the Constitution—and she also thought about doing a cancer diary. She didn't want the cancer book to be a whimsical Chicken Soup for Breast Cancer Survivors affair, with gentle sermons and upbeat fortune cookie advice. She didn't want it to be a righteously indignant rant—it would be hard to pin her breast cancer on someone or some institution. It would be hard to make any cancer book drop-dead funny from beginning to end. She did know plenty of cancer jokes by now, and when friends were brave enough to start one, she would finish it for them. People who made pilgrimages to Austin, or saw her on her good days, heard the devilish laugh and assumed the best. She would stand close to people, her face cracked into a grin, and talk about what the Democrats needed to do to take back the White House. Final Fridays were still going on, and if she couldn't be there, or had to slip back into her room, her friends would quietly clean up the place, wash the dishes, take out the trash, and lock her front door. She hated it, though, when people tip-toed around her. She liked it when Bryan Woolley, one of her old drinking buddies from the days in Dallas at the *Times Herald*, had sent her a note: "Damn it Molly, every time I turn my back, your tits get in trouble."

Friends said she was in search of quieter patterns, that she appeared to be less fixated on doing everything and on doing it fast. Her book club was still meeting once a month, going into its third decade, and she would show up toting a big sack, a grocery bag, filled with books. She had accumulated thousands of books, including all the sappy autobiographies every politician had sent her. She turned the book bag upside down and dumped paperbacks all over the table and began roaring with laughter: "I know everybody always says what kind of books people read when they're sick, but I'm here to tell you, it isn't true. This is what they're reading about when they have cancer!" On the table were the cheap, paperback bodice-busters and crime thrillers.

She increasingly looked forward to visits from Ellen Sweets, who sometimes put on the ACLU T-shirt that Ivins had given her that said "Alaska, left of everything." Sweets was irreverent and had made a point her whole adult life of seeking out card-carrying members of the ACLU. Ivins liked having her around, because there was no agenda—other than to eat, cook, laugh:

> Molly knew she needed that time just to do nothing. We would cook dinner, get ice cream, and settle down in front of the TV and do on-demand movies, go to Blockbuster, no agenda, no routine, no nothing. I would come down and I would walk in the door on 7 o'clock on Friday, I would bring ribs or chicken from Popeye's and she would say, I forgot, I was supposed to speak out of town and I will be back

tomorrow. I had a key to the house, I would go to the grocery store, and I would cook something she liked so that she would have something to eat when she got home.[2]

—

In November 2002, she took her reporter friend John Pope and his wife to Jeffrey's, one of the best restaurants in Austin. "You want to come to a Thanksgiving dinner?" she asked them.

"Sure, where?" they asked.

"Paris," she answered.

She made arrangements: She knew a San Antonio financier who owned a $10 million penthouse apartment in a building on the Ile St. Louis. It was an old building, but inside there were paintings from Texas and Mexico. Willie Nelson was on the CD player. There were sixteen people for the Parisian dinner and Ivins plucked the turkey with her eyebrow tweezers. She insisted everyone stand up and do what she called The San Antonio Stroll. Pope had no idea what that was so he and his wife did a New Orleans "second line" dance around the table. After dinner, there was a walk along the river.[3]

While she was in France for Thanksgiving, newspapers ran one of her columns—one of the only columns in mainstream papers predicting what might really happen if the United States followed through on an invasion of Iraq: "The greatest risk for us in invading Iraq is probably not war itself, so much as: What happens after we win? . . . There is a batty degree of triumphalism loose in this country right now."[4]

That night in Paris, Pope thought she hadn't lost her sense of spontaneity or the absurd, even with cancer eating away at her. He remembered something else, something else absurd: How she couldn't stop laughing after they had once seen a sign outside a drugstore that read "Generic Prozac Here. God Bless America."[5]

—

The journalism school at Columbia asked her to give the 2003 Henry Pringle lecture, in honor of the former Pulitzer Prize–winner and presidential biographer. She had already been given the William Allen White Award from the University of Kansas; the Smith Medal from Smith College; the American Academy of Arts and Sciences fellowship. She still asked friends if she was being honored because of her cancer, because it was aggressively moving again. Throughout the year, she would fight her second bout with cancer—and friends in New York wanted to make arrangements for her to see oncologists on the East Coast. Some friends in New York also wanted to know if she had written a will and she weighed where to donate her estate. There was *The Texas Observer*, of course. There was the ACLU. There was her network of friends, and the people she had paid, given money to, or loaned money to and never asked for it back. There was her family; she wanted to leave money to her siblings, her nieces and nephews. And there was probably going to be more money coming: She talked to her agent Dan Green and they agreed that she and Lou Dubose should do another Bush book, this one a hard attack on his ruinous policies. They'd call it *Bushwhacked* and publication was set for September.

⋄⋄⋄

She had invested in some land in Marfa, in far West Texas, where some people were escaping to, and putting Austin and anything else behind them. It was remote, almost its own oasis, and she liked being out under the endless skies—looking for the trippy celestial show they called The Marfa Lights. There was also a place in London, Texas, a little farm-ranch house where she and Andy were going to spend more time together on the western edge of the Texas Hill Country, only an hour and change from Austin and close to the magical, crystal-clear Llano River—one of the last wild rivers in the state. She loved going west, following the trail of wildflowers that were Lady Bird Johnson's legacy in Texas—sometimes there were nesting bald eagles along the Llano. And there were common-sense old Germans out there who were as skeptical as she was of most politicians. There were no-bullshit cowboys, fence-post diggers, mesquite-clearing farmers. People who kept their opinions to themselves and worked their asses off when the tornadoes threatened to blow the tin roof off the hay barn and straight down Whiskey Road.

⤛⤜

In March she flew to Atlanta to accept the Ivan Allen Jr. Prize for Progress and Service, which had been given to President Jimmy Carter the year before. In May she spoke at Columbia: "It is the duty, naturally, of all good civil libertarians to stand up for the right of these blue-belly nincompoops to spew whatever vicious drivel they want to, and that is a stand that is about as popular as a whore trying to get into the SMU School of Theology. It's not going to improve your standing with the neighbors, believe me."

Back in Austin, she began work on another significant anti-war column in the summer of 2003: "I opposed the war in Iraq because I thought it would lead to the peace from hell, but I'd rather not see my prediction come true and I don't think we have much time left to avert it. That the occupation is not going well is apparent to everyone but Donald Rumsfeld. . . . We don't need people with credentials as right-wing ideologues and corporate privatizers."

⤛⤜

In August 2003, Ivins traveled to Vermont to deliver another speech on behalf of the ACLU and to do a book signing at Bear Pond Books in Montpelier. She was hurting, in pain from her cancer surgeries—she had just had some surgery on lymph nodes under one of her arms.

On August 8, a Friday night, she signed books and looked up at a tall man standing in line and waiting patiently.

"I'm William Holland," said the man.

It was Hank Holland's brother.

She gave him a big hug. "Sit here by me so I can talk to you," she told him.

They chatted and she looked out at everybody who was standing in line and announced: "This is the brother of Hank Holland, the love of my life."

They talked some more as she signed books. Holland told her he was an educator. "So, you haven't been out in the real world, have you?" she joked.[6]

Holland was worried that the line was too long, that she was distracted by his presence. She insisted that he stay. Hank Holland had died almost forty years earlier. Her oldest friends and some members of her family thought if she had once wanted to be married it would have been to Hank Holland. But after he died, she rarely mentioned him to any of her new friends. Many of them never knew he existed—and were surprised when they heard hints about him. It was, one said, as if it was impossible for many of her friends to imagine that there was once a man like Hank Holland at the center of her life—and that she once contemplated spending the rest of her life with him. Her affairs over the years had been both circumspect and fleeting. To her best friends, she seemed eternally disinclined to surrender to the discipline, maybe confines, of marriage—or, perhaps, the way she viewed marriage through the prism of her parent's union. There were men who would correspond with her for years, hoping that whatever short-term, impermanent relationship they had once had with her would grow into something else. She told friends, and wrote notes to herself, about the fear that as she grew more famous, the men who insisted on being around her were simply there for some frisson of celebrity.

But after she was diagnosed with cancer in the late 1990s, there were other things she was concentrating on—the endless medical rounds and the ebb-and-flow of her lingering alcoholism. She had countless friends who were volunteering to take her to her physicians, who were willing to drop everything and take on the task of being her travel aide and companion. On almost every out-of-town trip she took, there was no shortage of people willing to put her up in their homes, meet her at the airport, prepare meals for her. As a function of the welling, coalescing anti-Bush movement in America, a visit from Molly Ivins in certain places around the nation was like a visit from a familiar, reassuring, rallying figure. Her books, her columns, her national broadcast appearances, solidified her role as a liberal lightning rod—and it served to create an ever-growing sense that Ivins had a tight-knit family wherever she traveled. The assumption that she was as down-home as her writing could sometimes be predisposed her followers to want to make her as welcome as possible—to the point where her schedulers began to worry that Ivins would spend too much time ladling her Southern charm on her hosts instead of resting up for the rigors of another round of speeches and meetings and book signings. There was, really, no time at all for any deeper relationships with those men who wanted to be around her, near her.

In Vermont, on August 9, she also took time out for some sailing on Lake Champlain. It was all so familiar to her. This was where her parents had sent her when she was a teenager, to teach and work at the summer French camp. Her faithful aide Betsy Moon was with her, and Ivins insisted on not slowing down. It was summer in Vermont and it was good to be out of the Texas heat and doing something that reminded her of her childhood. Hank Holland's brother had also reminded her of things in her past.

Some friends had secured a big sailboat and, of course, Ivins insisted on taking her turn guiding the vessel. It was a glorious day. At one point, everyone agreed to stop and take a swim. Everyone jumped into the water, including Ivins. When she heaved herself back aboard the sailboat, pulling herself up the ladder, she felt a pain under her arm.

"Betsy, I think I might have torn my stitches," she said to Moon. She lifted her arm and showed Moon.

"Yes, you did," said Moon, taking a quick glance.

"Well, be quiet," said Ivins.

They told no one. After the boat docked, they got in a car with their driver and then stopped to get some water at a nearby store. While they waited, Moon examined the wound and saw that it was torn apart.

"Molly, there is no way we can leave that," warned Moon. "We have to go get it sewed up again."

Ivins was expected at a dinner and reception for the ACLU in an hour. She and Moon had the driver take them to a nearby hospital. There was a doctor who had read one of her books, loved her, and who took her into a little room and quickly mended the stitches. Ivins and Moon raced back to their hotel, with fifteen minutes to change clothes and attend the reception. The evening was a success, money was raised for the ACLU, and no one knew that she had come straight from the hospital.

The day after their return to Texas, Ivins had both an MRI and a CAT scan. The problems were incessant, mounting: "In addition to the three bouts of cancer she had heart disease," said Moon. "The amount of time I spent at the hospital [with her] was enough for a lifetime."

In meetings with Moon, Ivins insisted that the intimate details of her medical condition be kept confidential. And she insisted on maintaining a full schedule. "She was highly independent. Once she was complaining to me when she was going through chemotherapy that she was so tired, and it really made her mad because she thought she was as strong as an ox and she didn't know what was wrong with her," said Moon.[7]

⋯

The new book, released in September, spent two months on the *New York Times* bestseller list. She started a twenty-city, five-week book tour and a new round of chemotherapy. Arrangements were made to have aides travel with her on the tour, in case of any medical emergencies and to make sure she followed through on her regimen. Betsy Moon traveled with Ivins on the first and last weeks of the tour. Moon and the other assistants found hospitals and clinics where Ivins could get her blood tests and injections that would help her white blood cell count. At one book-signing in Seattle, Ivins was clearly having trouble walking. Moon was worried and she tried to hurry the hundreds of people who had lined up to get their book autographed. Ivins told her that she should leave everyone alone, that they were there to have some fun.[8]

As *Bushwhacked* went up the charts, she wrote another prescient column about the quagmire in Iraq: "Good thing we won the war, because the peace sure looks like a quagmire. . . . I've got an even-money bet out that says more Americans will be killed in the peace than in the war, and more Iraqis will be killed by Americans in the peace than in the war. Not the first time I've had a bet out that I hoped I'd lose."[9]

⋯

Friends were calling her, some of them giving her a hard time. She had endorsed Howard Dean for the Democratic nomination in 2004:

> No one has been waiting with bated breath for me to make up my mind about the Democratic presidential candidates, but I have, and

> you might be interested in how I got there. I'm for Howard Dean—because he's going to win.
>
> It is the bounden duty of bleeding-heart liberals like myself to make our political choices based on purity of heart, nobility of character, depth of compassion, sterling integrity and generosity of spirit. The concept of actually winning a political race does not, traditionally, influence the bleeding-heart liberal one iota—certainly not in the primaries.[10]

Other friends were also calling her, chastising her for not stopping the Friday parties, not giving up making speeches, not dropping down to one column a week, not taking a sabbatical—a year in the Hill Country, maybe out in Marfa, to write her memoirs. The drinking and the chemotherapy were obviously at odds. She had tried to work through it at the Betty Ford Clinic. She had the Hazelden facility booklets and literature at her house. "She had an incredible constitution and seemed to be oblivious to pain. Chemotherapy messes up your body. I don't know how many times she was in Betty Ford," says Northcott, adding "not that many times."[11]

Ivins knew there were going to be those prescribed moments when she was supposed to call her close friends as part of the twelve-step process, maybe even to apologize for backsliding, for lapsing back into a drunken binge. The calls engendered an indelible bond to Ivins for some of her friends. The conversations were often bittersweet and flowing, conversations that touched on the long history Ivins had with the people who had become the cornerstones of her surrogate family. Northcott loved Ivins like a sister. She had known her longer than most people, and she always felt that Ivins was one of the strongest people she had known. Brave, but also physically strong. She hadn't really stopped calling people on their bullshit, in print and in person, since 1970. When Ivins made one of those late-night, confessional calls to her, Northcott always felt "there was nothing she needed to apologize to me for."[12]

She'd suddenly get weary, but when she was in the moment, it was like she was kicking George W. Bush's ass all over again. And she would laugh until the color came back to her cheeks. And when anyone at all brought their young children over, the ones who were impressionable and maybe able to hold a short conversation with an adult, she would get down to their level and walk them through her house, let them pick any book they wanted from her library, let them take anything they wanted in the fridge. And then suggest they go out for ice cream, that she knew a place to get Christmas tamales, that she knew a place for pancakes. "Molly had the metabolism of a daily newspaper reporter. She lived large," says Northcott.

But into 2004, well after Howard Dean had set himself on fire and dropped from the race, she was battling dark moods. "She went into depression and there were times when she was debilitated by alcohol. It was always way too much and I wanted to protect her, and the only way I could do that was not to pass on any requests. To go to dinner with her and talk about silly things. She had girl dinners, and they were good, and they were just anecdotal and absolutely unimportant—but important for all of us, important for her in that there was nobody there revering her. It was absolutely normal," says Northcott.

Of course, the publishing machine wanted another book out before the 2004 conventions, something that it could release in the summer. Betsy Moon helped cull more columns for another collection, *Who Let the Dogs In: Incredible Political Animals I Have Known*, released that July. It spent five weeks on the bestseller list and as it was moving off the list, *Times* columnist Maureen Dowd's collection of pieces about Bush was passing her. The people who had worked for Ivins were convinced that Ivins had paved the way for Dowd, Arianna Huffington, and dozens of other writers or television talking heads. Her huge run on the bestseller list in 1991, the Pulitzer nominations, the parodies of her on *Saturday Night Live*, the gigs on Leno and Letterman, the rumors that someone was set to make a movie of her life—it all had to have influenced *Times* editors to rethink whatever frozen notions they once had about whether it was a good idea to let one of its writers talk about gang plucking. She was steered out for going barefoot, for putting in sexual innuendoes that were now on every other radio and TV show in the nation in 2004. And she paid some heavy dues, not so much because she was sent packing to cover City Hall in lower Manhattan, but because they knew that dulling her style was the worst punishment of all. It was, she had long ago decided, not a giant leap to suggest that she had become her own sawed-off version of a First Amendment issue.

⤛⤜

By 2005, with the help of Betsy Moon, she was trying to cut back on some of the clutter, the cloying sycophants. She routinely turned down offers to make speeches, do TV and radio. Sometimes she stayed up until 4 A.M., not able to sleep. She'd sit at the computer in her home office, the dog nearby, and she would selectively read emails from friends she knew had probably sent funny messages. Other people were insisting on sending her correspondence about cancer. Books about cancer diets. Astrological charts related to Cancer. Testimonials from readers who swore by drinks made from a concoction of pills and vegetables that they had thrown in a blender. There were religious texts—"Steps to The Savior."[13] Hundreds of cards, letters, and emails from cancer patients and survivors. Reporters were calling, wanting to write "profiles" of her, and she knew they were gathering material for a possible obituary. She had a stock recommendation for them. She would offer a free headline: "Molly Ivins Still Not Dead."

A certain détente emerged among some of the compartmentalized factions in her life. Various friends had called one another, even the ones who disliked each other and who wondered who was really closer, really helping Ivins. Her drinking was especially bad in early 2005, and it finally spilled out in public: "She was mean to Nancy Pelosi. Right after that we had an intervention for her. Molly was not putting her best foot forward at a fundraiser . . . she had already been told that if she didn't stop drinking, that it was going to kill her," said Northcott. "She went into depression and there were times when she was debilitated by alcohol."[14]

This time, though, she finally went sober in the summer of 2005—and some of her friends saw a clarity, a zesty kick to her laughter that reminded them of a much younger Molly. Some friends felt she was speaking, thinking, with a clarity that they hadn't seen in years. The late-night phone calls asking for help, for consolation, for forgiveness, had all but ended. There was a solidity to her, said one old friend, someone who felt as though Molly had helped to raise him—as if she was restoring things that had been lost and filling up the room with that strong, purposeful voice, and with peals of laughter. Her friends in the dedicated circles hoped that things would return, as best they could, to the way they had once been—her infectious energy carrying the party, the dinner, or the campout for hours and hours.

Thirty years ago she had written a letter to herself and carefully saved it. It was essentially a time capsule. She had written, back then, about what it would be like to be healthy and free in the future. What it would be like to be free of whatever was haunting her thirty years down the road. She wrote: "I wonder how much one forgets? About the way one feels or felt. If I'm not hung over on my 60th birthday, I should like to do some comparisons."

Now, it was thirty years later and she could revisit that challenge she had written down and stored away. She could make the comparisons and know that she had finally achieved some peace. The people who knew her best said she looked radiant, that she had a glow.

In a bittersweet way, the alcoholic nadir had led to her being reacquainted with people she hadn't had time for while her workload and commitments escalated. "She was more at peace with herself. I think she was finally able to rid herself of the demons she had always felt. I think she had a lot of peace during this time," said Betsy Moon.[15]

Ivins and Dubose talked about the next book. She wanted to take a look at the Bill of Rights and see what the Bushes and Republicans had done to stymie the ACLU, to reinterpret the Constitution, to create loopholes where there shouldn't be any. She was toying with the idea of calling it *The Chicken Snake in the Hen House*—a cautionary parable about lawmakers being so afraid of their own shadow, of perceived bogeymen, that they shit in their pants and began hammering the windows shut until no one could breathe or get out.

After Hurricane Katrina, journalist John Pope came to see her in Austin. He gave her a shirt that said "Screw Fallujah, Save New Orleans" and she roared with laughter. A few weeks later, she made plans to go to her little house in the Hill Country to spend Thanksgiving with her brother. She once told Betsy Moon that Andy was the funniest person she had ever known. They seemed to be growing closer later in life, especially when he began his own battles with cancer.

In the days building up to Thanksgiving, she developed a lingering, dry cough. She was short of breath. During Thanksgiving weekend, her brother and sister-in-law decided it was an emergency and took her to a rural hospital in Junction, Texas. Betsy Moon then made arrangements for Ivins to be taken back to Seton Hospital in Austin. On the Monday after Thanksgiving, tests showed that there was fluid around her heart—and that the cancer was spreading for a third time. As she had done with her second recurrence, she decided to keep the news muted. But word filtered through the Austin network. She appeared at a fundraiser for the *Observer*, and whipped off her wig before her speech. It was, she announced with a grin, "a shameless exploitation for sympathy for cancer. We might as well do something useful, because God knows I don't need another casserole."

She never missed a column deadline. She would talk to Moon at 10 in the morning, ask her to do some research for a particular topic, and then try to have the piece done by 2 or 3 in the afternoon. Then, Moon and the Austin-based editor for Creators Syndicate, Anthony Zurcher, would edit the pieces. Meanwhile, more reporters came to see her, to gather some string for a possible obituary, and now she openly talked about what was in her will and what she was going to give to the ACLU and the *Observer*. It was a struggle for Moon, Sara Speights, Marilyn Schultz, and the other friends in Austin who watched over her; they were trying to find the balance between encouraging her to stay busy and trying to get her to slow down. The Final Friday parties were put on hold. Ellen Sweets came and cooked soups. Ivins wrote her columns, sometimes relying on Moon and others to do the heavier research or editing or phone calling.

Into the New Year, after articles about her medical condition had appeared in Texas publications, almost everyone who was part of her enormous orbit knew that her health had worsened. Her friends took turns shuttling her to various medical specialists. Moon and others worried about her traveling anywhere: When Ivins was on her way to the Aspen Institute, she tried to ignore the pains in her chest. It wasn't quite a full-blown heart attack but something else was wracking her body—she had a welling heart condition. And, compounding the unrest, there were horrible tragedies in her family that arrived in unyielding fashion throughout the year: Her niece's 4-year-old son was battling a cancerous tumor in his abdomen. And, her treasured nephew Dax, Andy's son, had committed suicide—yet another family member who had taken his own life.

She was very close to Dax, and it broke her heart that she couldn't have stopped it. "A lot of bad stuff happened . . . family-wise. I mean horrible, horrible sad things," said Northcott.[16]

⋺⋻

In August, she was getting radiation treatment at Seton Hospital in Austin. One day she called Dave Richards and told him that a friend was arranging a ten-day rafting trip through the Grand Canyon.

"Will you promise to go with me if I am still alive in September?" she asked.

"Of course," said Richards.[17]

People at Seton who heard her talk about the trip said it was something that was giving her some energy, some hope. Friends wondered if she was up for the very intense run on the river. Sara Speights thought that Ivins had come to a conclusion about cancer—that it was a recurring beast, and that each time it comes you treat it. You treat it and it goes away. It goes away and you live. That theory was the way she was coping with it, telling herself that she just had to keep taking her treatments, to go back for new rounds of chemotherapy and each time she did, she would just keep beating it back.

Home from the hospital, she wrote a note to herself:

> So I talked to the doc. He says the shit is back, under my right arm, down in my left hip, in the upper quadrant of my left lung. Six months . . . but there is something liberating about knowing you are

> dying. A curiously emancipatory effect. "Nothing left to lose" turns out to be a strong slogan, in the sense of promoting bravery. I would like to think that I have never pulled a punch in my life. But in fact, I have. Several. Always thought it was in the cause of being a more effective communicator.[18]

In September, she completed the last round of twenty radiation treatments in Austin. The next day she flew to Flagstaff, Arizona, for the Grand Canyon trip. Some people in Austin wondered whether the trip would literally kill her. Some told her that she shouldn't go, that it was beyond reckless. She had talked about it with her aide Betsy Moon, and Moon had told her that she needed to get on the river, she needed to be there.

Dave Richards was waiting. She was weak, unsteady, and people helped to lift her in and out of the raft. People clutched her over the rough rapids, and made sure she stayed out of the water, and that her glasses didn't fly away. For ten days, the weather was fine, people brought her something warm to drink or some food from the grill. She sat in a special chair in the shade while other people hiked. There were songs around the campfire and she organized a talent show one evening.

For a while it was like coming to live in Austin for the first time in 1970, when the Texas rivers shined like emerald glass, the water almost seemed to heal you, and people were turning to see where the laughter was coming from.[19]

On September 13, Ann Richards died at her home of esophageal cancer. Her four children were there. Richards had told people it was some sort of cosmic irony that she had gained her acclaim by talking, and now she had cancer of the esophagus. Betsy Moon pondered the irony of Molly Ivins's gaining her acclaim through her intellect, and now cancer had invaded her brain. Richards and Ivins had converged at a particular moment in Texas history, and they brushed against so many similar things as they became public figures. Ivins had told people that Richards had been exhausted by being in the public eye—and when Richards left it, she was much happier. "She was free to say what she wanted, and she got to do a bunch of stuff that she'd always wanted to do," said Ivins.[20]

John Pope came back to Ivins's home in South Austin at the end of 2006. Pope had always thought that there were constellations of people around her, bringing her food, telling her stories, singing "The Wind Cries Mariah" to her while she tried to sleep. There were a half-dozen people there that night. The food was good, as always. She told some stories. Someone had a "Cheney and Satan 2008" T-shirt. She laughed but she was clearly weak. Pope held her hand and they talked about John Henry Faulk. There was an ice storm coming, bearing down through the Hill Country and the farmhouse in London, Texas, that she and Andy had grown to love. That night there was yet another *Observer* fundraiser. It was at a music club and she really wanted to go. Pope helped wrap her in several layers of clothing and walked her to her wheelchair.

Heading to the car, Pope told her: "Molly, it's just wonderful that you have so many friends."

She looked up at him with a big smile. Pope thought it could light up all of East Texas. "It's magic," she said.[21]

Speights listened as the oncologists went on for almost twenty minutes. Ivins was in bed. The family was nearby. There had been some hope in October that the cancer was in remission. By November, it had spread to her liver, brain, and spine. And finally Speights heard a doctor say: "We have now reached the point where the chemo is doing way more damage. It's not doing any good and so I think the best thing to do is just go home. What do you think?"

Speights heard Ivins say: "Well, I think we just need to give it our best go. Let's give it a try."

The doctors walked out of the hospital room, the family followed, and Speights stayed behind. She offered Ivins some chocolate pudding and Ivins ate some.

"There are just so many choices. It's so confusing," she said to Speights.

"Molly," said Speights. "I don't think you have many choices."

Ivins looked at her.

"Oh well . . . maybe not," she said. "What are we having for dinner?"[22]

⟵⟶

She wrote a New Year's letter to her closest friends:

> Dearly Beloveds,
>
> Two zero zero seven and I'm stayin' alive, that's the main thing. The doctors continue to find new ways to torture me. I'm in pretty weak shape now but planning to get better. A round of physical therapy may help me get my strength back. I've certainly kept up my weight. For that I owe a considerable debt and countless pounds to Blue Bell Cookies and Cream and a better than average appetite.
>
> Being an invalid means you can almost always have your way when it comes to daily desires. That's why I invited almost 50 people to help trim my Christmas tree in early December.
>
> For Christmas, I hauled out many cookbooks and made a menu with Sara Speights and Marilyn Schultz. This included . . . my sister-in-law Carla's unsurpassed pecan pie. In addition to Carla, my sister Sara, brother Andy, niece Darby and nephew Drew were on hand—a seated dinner for 12.
>
> This might seem like a big whup until you understand that my stove was on the blink and couldn't be fixed in time because all of NASA's engineers were otherwise occupied for the holiday.
>
> Lo, came the miracle of Alta Vista Avenue. Ovens to the left of me, ovens across the street, as well as their owners, opened up their doors to the elves. Andy said he liked carting things from house to house. It put him in the holiday spirit.
>
> I visited some and rested some as the preparers prepared. It was lovely hearing the bustle of my friends and family getting a great meal together. My only regret is that I couldn't smell the prime rib as it roasted across the street.
>
> Meanwhile, I have taken up a new sport—shooting BBs from my lounge chair at the squirrels trying to rob the bird feeders in my back yard.

> So now it's the New Year and I want to give each and every one of you a hug and wishes for some good news on the political front. May the D's avoid making bigger fools of themselves than the R's, which seems like a doable deal.
>
> From your as yet Unsinkable Molly.[23]

In January she was dictating her columns to Betsy Moon, who would sit by her, sometimes on the bed. Moon knew that the words were all in Ivins's head, but they were not emerging in the usual, seamlessly cohesive way. The cancer was in her brain. Ivins's fingers were numb, her voice erratic. The last column she dictated to Moon said: "We are the people who run this country. We are the deciders. And every single day, every single one of us needs to step outside and take some action to help stop this war. Raise hell. Think of something to make the ridiculous look ridiculous. . . . We need people in the streets, banging pots and pans and demanding, 'Stop it, now!'"[24]

She had been brought home from the hospital on the last Monday of the month. Her brother and sister were told that Molly wouldn't live much longer and they needed to be at her side.

The home hospice nurse was administering morphine. Sara thought Molly's life was flashing before her eyes, that her sister was floating and reliving good times and bad times.

Andy said: "She can't die, she can't die."

The nurse and Betsy told him that he should tell Molly that it was okay to let go. He did. So did Sara. She whispered to Molly: "Sail on little sis, sail on, sail on over, just let go. . . . "

Molly Ivins died in her bed at her tree-lined home on the last Wednesday of January 2007. Message boards lit up around the country. Impromptu memorial services were held in different cities. Flowers were placed outside her home. It was the anniversary date of Congress passing an amendment to the U.S. Constitution to abolish slavery.

ACKNOWLEDGMENTS

Andy Ivins was extremely kind to spend so much time sharing so many insights about his sister, her life, and her family. It was clear that revisiting the memory of his sister was sometimes painful, so his graciousness and generosity are especially appreciated—he corrected several key details that had filtered into various profiles and tributes. He was, perhaps, the one person in the Ivins family closest to her. He spends time at the Texas Hill Country home he and his sister shared late in life. A special thank you, as well, to Molly's sister, Sara Maley. Her affection for her sister is apparent, as evidenced by the many letters she sent to Molly Ivins over the decades, letters encouraging her sister, supporting her, urging her to fight through particular physical or mental valleys.

A special thanks to these very close friends, acquaintances, and colleagues of Molly who willingly offered their time and memories: The very wise Kaye Northcott spent several hours in Austin talking about her comrade-in-journalism; Liz Faulk, her take no bullshit personal assistant for years and wife of one of her most influential mentors, invited us to her home for several hours and used her influence to open doors; the wonderful Nadine Eckhardt, another personal assistant and someone who can decipher inscrutable Texas better than most, also talked with us for many hours at her home; Sara Speights spent years as one of Molly's faithful friends and confidants and was there at the end of Molly's life. These women saw firsthand the birth of the public figure known as Molly Ivins deep in the heart of Texas.

There were many other friends who helped: Betsy Moon, her "chief of stuff" and faithful friend who worked tirelessly with Ivins and was with her through some of the most challenging moments in her life, literally helping to keep Molly Ivins alive; Carlton Carl, a friend since the mid-1960s, and someone who saw her first fascination with journalism. Terry O'Rourke, who knew Ivins well before most people. Margaret Sher Elliston, who grew up with Ivins and stayed close to her for decades. Marcia W. Carter, who also grew up with Ivins and remained good friends. Ann Holland Dow, who lived near Ivins and especially bonded with her around a particular tragedy; Anne Seifert, who was part of a close circle in college and years after.

Here is a small sampling of the many other people who were also kind enough to offer insights, memories, vignettes, advice, pointers, suggestions, and even good cheer: Dave Richards, Dan Green, Jan Demetri, David Broder, Charles Kaiser, Maya Angelou, Dan Rather, Ronnie Dugger, Dave McNeely, Sam and Lilas Kinch, Sissy Farenthold, John Pope, Billy Porterfield, Anthony Zurcher, Charlotte McCann, Bob Loomis, Doug Zabel, Jack Cox, LeAnne McComsey, Clyde Haberman, Ross Ramsey, Michael Berryhill, Ellen Sweets, Jack Cann, Ken Bunting, Mike Blackman, Steve Fromholz, Paul Stekler, Terry O'Rourke, Rusty Todd, Bob Compton, Paula Poindexter, Gene Burd, Don Carlton, Steve Davis, Alan Pogue, Jay Root, David McHam, Ann Heinzerling Kelsey, Louie Canelakes and his beautiful family.

An appreciation to the people who captured her so eloquently through their work, memorials, tributes: Eden Lipson, John Leonard, Roy Blount, Jr., Lou Dubose, Adam Clymer, Myra MacPherson, Bud Shrake, Lisa Sandberg, Ben Sargent, Paul Krugman, Calvin Trillin. An appreciation to the countless publications that featured some of the better profiles, packages, and analyses of her, particularly the *Houston Press* and the *Texas Monthly*.

A special thank you to the *Texas Observer* and its staff (including Carlton Carl, who granted important interviews and provided key help on the Ivins archives) for the generous assistance. The *Observer* was kind enough to provide materials, insight, and guidance on a variety of matters. The *Observer* has a justifiably long and proud tradition of independent journalism in Texas and anyone seeking to understand the often inscrutable Lone Star State would be well-served to read and support the publication.

Many thanks to Ivins's colleagues from her Final Friday gatherings. Their insights, suggestions, and support were key to the writing of this book.

A thank you to The Dolph Briscoe Center for American History at the University of Texas at Austin. A special thank you to Ian Stade with the Special Collections staff at the Hennepin County Library for his aid. Thanks to the Houston Public Library for its work, its collections. Thanks to various staff members at Smith College for fielding inquiries and offering key insights.

Thank you to several wonderful researchers who offered their talents: Karie Meltzer, Patrick Brendel, and Wendy Grossman. Their work was crucial to the project and they gave their time willingly and frequently. In addition, special thanks to Vanessa Valencia, Haleen Sue Smith, Robert Buck, Heather Bishop, Andrea Ludden, and Stacy Christman, who assisted in innumerable ways to help bring the book to a close.

Thanks, as well, to Roderick Hart, dean of the College of Communications at the University of Texas at Austin, and to Tracy Dahlby, director of the School of Journalism at the University of Texas at Austin. A nod of thanks to all the wonderful members of the journalism faculty at the University of Texas at Austin. It is difficult to envision a more brilliant and good-natured group of colleagues.

We would like to thank our PublicAffairs editors Peter Osnos and Lisa Kaufman; we are extremely lucky to be working with such brilliant literary minds. They were patient, visionary, and simply among the finest folks in publishing—any writer would be blessed to work with them. A very important note of appreciation to Melissa Raymond for her calm, steady hand. Many thanks to the fine publicity and marketing people at PublicAffairs, especially Tessa Shanks and Lindsay Goodman, as well as publisher Susan Weinberg and all the hard-working, behind-the scenes heroes who do so much—copy editor Christine Arden, designer Timm Bryson, proofer Jeff Georgeson, and indexer Kate Bowman. A thank you to Julie Ford and Mark Lawless for their expert counsel. Thanks to David Hale Smith.

W. Michael Smith would like to thank his father, William F. Smith, who passed away during the making of this book. His love, support, and pride in me has been a driving force in my life.

Bill Minutaglio offers love and thanks to his mother Tessie Minutaglio, who was born in 1917 and nobly endured so many things. He offers love and thanks to his wife Holly Williams, and his children Nicholas Xavier and Rose Angelina.

NOTES

Chapter 1

1. Hunter Thompson, "Fear and Loathing, Campaign 2004," *Rolling Stone*, October 20, 2004. Thompson was a person Ivins counted as a friend, one who had obviously, gleefully, abandoned what she had deemed to be the shackles of neutrality in journalism.

2. Letter to the Editor, *Time*, September 29, 1959. Copyright Time Inc. Reprinted by permission. *Time* is a registered trademark of Time Inc. All rights reserved.

3. Interview with Margaret Sher Elliston, July 15, 2008.

4. Molly Ivins, "A Mighty Oak of a Man, Fallen in His Winter," *Fort Worth Star-Telegram*, April 26, 1998.

5. Ibid.

6. Ibid.

7. Ibid.

8. Ibid.

9. Ibid.

10. "Former Chaplain Becomes Bishop on Friend's Death," *Milwaukee Sentinel*, January 16, 1933.

11. Interview with Andy Ivins, June 29, 2008.

12. Molly Ivins, "The Good Mother Who Put a Shoe in the Icebox," *Fort Worth Star-Telegram*, January 9, 1997.

13. Ibid.

14. Ibid.

15. Ibid.

16. Molly Ivins Papers, The Dolph Briscoe Center for American History, University of Texas at Austin.

17. Ibid.

18. Ibid.

19. Ibid.

20. Ibid.

21. Molly Ivins, "A Mighty Oak," *Fort Worth Star-Telegram*.

22. Ibid.

23. Andy Ivins.

24. Bill Minutaglio, *City on Fire* (New York: HarperCollins, 2003), p. 7.

25. Quoted in Fay Jones, *Outside The Pale: The Architecture of Fay Jones* (Fayetteville: University of Arkansas Press, 1999).

26. Sigman Byrd, *Sig Byrd's Houston* (New York: Viking Press, 1953), pp. 12–13.

27. Andy Ivins.

28. Ibid.

29. "The Price of Being Molly," *Texas Monthly*, November 1992.

30. Quoted in "Molly Ivins, Queen of Liberal Commentary, Dies," *Austin American-Statesman*, January 31, 2007.

31. Quoted in "Iconic Texas Columnist Loses Cancer Fight at 62," *Houston Chronicle*, February 1, 2007.

32. Andy Ivins.

33. Ibid.

34. Interviews with Ann Holland Dow, October, 2008.

35. Ibid.

36. Molly Ivins Papers.

37. Ibid.

38. "How Does Your ZIP Code Rank?," Forbes.com, July 10, 2003.

39. Text of speech given on Rally Day at Smith College, *Smith Alumnae Quarterly*, Summer 1993.

40. Molly Ivins Papers.

41. Ibid.

42. Ibid.

43. Ibid.

44. Ibid.

Chapter 2

1. Molly Ivins, "South Toward Home," *The Texas Observer*, August 21, 1970.

2. "Mr. Moore's Opus," *Houston Press*, May 20, 1999. This excellent article is the source of much information about Mr. Moore.

3. Molly Ivins, *Molly Ivins Can't Say That, Can She?* (New York: Random House, 1991).

4. "Molly Ivins," *Texas Monthly*, October 2003.

5. Ibid.

6. Molly Ivins Papers, The Dolph Briscoe Center for American History, University of Texas at Austin.

7. Interview with Margaret Sher Elliston, July 15, 2008.

8. *Smith Alumnae Quarterly*, Summer 1993.

9. Margaret Sher Elliston.

10. Interview with Ann Heinzerling Kelsey, July 23, 2008.

11. Interviews with Ann Holland Dow, October 2008.

12. Ibid.

13. Margaret Sher Elliston.

14. Interview with Marcia W. Carter, July 30, 2008.

15. Ibid.

16. Ibid.

17. Ibid.

18. Kaye Northcott, "The Molly Days," *The Texas Observer*, February 9, 2007.

19. Margaret Sher Elliston.

20. Ibid.

21. Ibid.

22. Ibid.

23. Ibid.

24. Ibid.

25. Ibid.

26. Molly Ivins Papers.

27. Molly Ivins, "The Observer goes to the Big Bend," *The Texas Observer*, May 24, 1974.

28. Molly Ivins Papers.

29. Interview with Andy Ivins, June 29, 2008.

30. "Rough Ride on a Sea of Troubles," *Sports Illustrated*, August 5, 1963.

31. Interviews with Kaye Northcott, August 2008.

32. Molly Ivins Papers.

33. Andy Ivins.

34. Molly Ivins Papers.

35. Ibid.

36. Ibid.

37. Ibid.

38. Ibid.

39. Ibid.

40. Ibid.

41. Ibid.

42. Ibid.

43. Ibid.

44. "Molly Ivins," NACUBO (National Association of College and University Business Officers), *Business Officer*, July 2000.

45. Margaret Sher Elliston.

46. Ibid.

47. "Molly Ivins," NACUBO, *Business Officer*, July 2000.

48. Molly Ivins's commencement address, Scripps College, 2003.

49. "Sassy, Brassy, Unarguably Classy, Molly Ivins '66 Comes to Town," *Scripps Magazine*, Fall 2001.

50. Margaret Sher Elliston.

51. "Molly Ivins," NACUBO, *Business Officer*, July 2000.

52. Ibid.

53. Interviews with Anne Seifert, September 2008.

54. *Smith Alumnae Quarterly*, Summer 1993.

55. "Molly Ivins," NACUBO, *Business Officer*, July 2000.

56. "The Price of Being Molly," *Texas Monthly*, November 1992.

57. Anne Seifert.

58. Ibid.

59. Ibid.

60. Ibid.

61. Ann Holland Dow.

Chapter 3

1. Arthur Schlesinger, Jr., *A Thousand Days: John F. Kennedy in the White House* (Boston: Houghton Mifflin, 1965).

2. Interviews with Ann Holland Dow, October 2008.

3. Letter: "From: Baxter Holland" provided to authors by Ann Holland Dow.

4. Ann Holland Dow.

5. Ibid.

6. Ibid.

7. Ibid.

8. Ibid.

9. Ibid.

10. Ibid.

11. Interviews with Anne Seifert, September 2008.

12. Interview with Andy Ivins, June 29, 2008.

13. Interviews with Jack Cann, January 2009.

14. Ann Holland Dow.

15. Anne Seifert.

16. "The Unsinkable Molly Ivins," *Fort Worth Star-Telegram*, May 27, 2001.

17. Anne Seifert.
18. Story provided by Ann Holland Dow during interviews, October 2008.
19. Ibid.
20. Anne Seifert.
21. Ibid.
22. Ann Holland Dow.
23. Anne Seifert.
24. Ben Bagdikian, "Houston's Shackled Press," *The Atlantic*, August 1966.
25. Ibid.
26. Ibid.
27. Molly Ivins Papers, The Dolph Briscoe Center for American History, University of Texas at Austin.
28. Ibid.
29. Nathanael West, *Miss Lonelyhearts & Day of the Locust* (New York: New Directions, 1962), p. 26.
30. Molly Ivins Papers.
31. Ibid.
32. Conversations with Jan Demetri, August 2008.

Chapter 4

1. Interviews with Carlton Carl, August 2008.
2. Ibid.
3. Dave McNeely, "A Tribute to Molly Ivins," *The Texas Observer*, February 9, 2007.
4. "Molly Ivins," NACUBO, *Business Officer*, July 2000.
5. Ibid.
6. Interviews with Anne Seifert, September 2008.
7. "Molly Ivins," NACUBO, *Business Officer*, July 2000.
8. Interviews with Terry O'Rourke, August–September 2008.
9. "Remembering Molly," *Houston Press*, February 15, 2007.
10. Terry O'Rourke.
11. Ibid.
12. "Molly Ivins," NACUBO, *Business Officer*, July 2000.
13. Terry O'Rourke.
14. Ibid.
15. Molly Ivins Papers.
16. Ben Bagdikian, "Houston's Shackled Press," *The Atlantic*, August 1966.
17. University of Colorado at Boulder, *Bylines*, Fall 2002.
18. "Molly Ivins," NACUBO, *Business Officer*, July 2000.
19. Molly Ivins Papers.

20. Ibid.

21. Robert Ardrey, *The Social Contract: A Personal Inquiry into the Evolutionary Sources of Order and Disorder* (New York: Athenaeum, 1970).

22. Molly Ivins Papers.

23. *Journal of the Columbia Journalism Alumni*, Summer 2007.

Chapter 5

1. Molly Ivins Papers, The Dolph Briscoe Center for American History, University of Texas at Austin.

2. James Boylan, *Pulitzer's School: Columbia University's School of Journalism, 1903–2003* (New York: Columbia University Press, 2003), p.167.

3. Molly Ivins, "A Tale of Two J-Schools," *The Texas Observer*, November 28, 1975.

4. Molly Ivins, "Maureen Reagan Visits City," *Minneapolis Star-Tribune*, May 28, 1968.

5. Interviews with Jack Cox, January 2009.

6. "The *Minneapolis Tribune* Is a Stone Wall Drag," *Twin Citian*, August 1970.

7. Molly Ivins Papers.

8. Ibid.

9. Molly Ivins Papers

10. Molly Ivins Papers; interview with Jack Cann, January 13, 2009.

11. Editor's Note, "Young Radicals," *Minneapolis Star-Tribune*, March 12, 1969.

12. Molly Ivins Papers.

13. Ibid.

14. Ibid.

15. Ibid.

16. Ibid.

17. Ibid.

18. Ibid.

19. Ibid.

20. Ibid.

21. Interviews with Kaye Northcott, August 2008.

22. Ibid.

23. Molly Ivins Papers.

24. Ibid.

25. "The *Minneapolis Tribune* Is a Stone Wall Drag," *Twin Citian*, August 1970.

26. Molly Ivins Papers.

27. "The *Minneapolis Tribune* Is a Stone Wall Drag," *Twin Citian*, August 1970.

28. Molly Ivins Papers.

29. Ibid.

30. Molly Ivins, "South Toward Home," *The Texas Observer*, August 21, 1970.
31. Molly Ivins Papers.
32. Interviews with Ronnie Dugger, May 2009.
33. *Time*, September 9, 1974. Copyright Time Inc. Reprinted by permission. *Time* is a registered trademark of Time Inc. All rights reserved.

Chapter 6

1. Interviews with Kaye Northcott, August 2008.
2. "Jack Newfield, 66, Proud Muckraker, Dies," *New York Times*, December 22, 2004.
3. Ibid.
4. Kaye Northcott.
5. Willie Morris, *North Toward Home* (New York: Vintage, 2000), p. 198.
6. Kaye Northcott.
7. "The National Politician of Texas," *Fort Worth Star-Telegram*, June 8, 1997.
8. "Special Session: Episode 214: Remembering Molly Ivins," KLRU-TV, May 13, 2007.
9. Kaye Northcott.
10. Ibid.
11. "Special Session," KLRU-TV, May 13, 2007.
12. Kaye Northcott.
13. Ibid.
14. Ibid.
15. Ibid.
16. Ibid.
17. Interview with Liz Faulk, August 29, 2008.
18. Ibid.
19. Ibid.
20. Ibid.
21. Ibid.
22. Molly Ivins, "Notes from a Rookie," *The Texas Observer*, March 26, 1971.
23. Molly Ivins, "No Villains, Just Asses," *The Texas Observer*, June 18, 1971.
24. Interview with David Broder, December 12, 2008.
25. Molly Ivins Papers, The Dolph Briscoe Center for American History, University of Texas at Austin.

Chapter 7

1. Interviews with Sara Speights, July 15, 2008.
2. Interviews with Kaye Northcott, August 2008.
3. Sara Speights.
4. Molly Ivins, "Notes from a Rookie," *The Texas Observer*, March 26, 1971.

5. Molly Ivins Papers, The Dolph Briscoe Center for American History, University of Texas at Austin.
6. Ibid.
7. Molly Ivins, "Lib in Longhorn Country," *New York Times*, October 18, 1971.
8. Molly Ivins, "No Bull Bullock," *The Texas Observer*, March 3, 1972.
9. Molly Ivins, "The Trial of the Abilene Three," *The Texas Observer*, March 31, 1972.
10. *Penney Press*, March 1972.
11. Molly Ivins, "John Berryman," *The Texas Observer*, January 21, 1972.
12. *The Texas Observer*, December 25, 1970.
13. Kaye Northcott.
14. Molly Ivins, "The Joe Louis Addition," *The Texas Observer*, December 25, 1970.
15. Interview with David Broder, December 12, 2008.
16. Kaye Northcott.
17. Ibid.
18. Sara Speights.
19. Ibid.
20. Molly Ivins Papers.
21. Ibid.
22. Sara Speights.
23. "The Long and Happy Life of a Political Columnist," *Information Outlook*, May 1, 2001.
24. Interview with Sissy Farenthold, August 21, 2008.
25. Sara Speights.
26. Ibid.
27. Molly Ivins Papers.
28. Ibid.
29. Kaye Northcott.
30. Ibid.
31. Molly Ivins, "A Tale of Two J-Schools," *The Texas Observer*, November 28, 1975.
32. *Oakland Tribune*, December 21, 1975.
33. Kaye Northcott.
34. Molly Ivins Papers.
35. Ibid.

Chapter 8

1. "Molly Ivins: Balancing humor and passion, the proudly partisan Texas pundit elevates a profession dominated by mediocrity and received ideas," Salon.com, December 12, 2000.

2. Molly Ivins, "Drive to Contain Seaway Oil Spill," *New York Times*, June 25, 1976.

3. Molly Ivins, "Professor Asserts F.B.I. Covered Up Typewriter Evidence Helpful to Hiss," *New York Times*, June 28, 1976.

4. Molly Ivins, "Milan's La Scala Makes U.S. Debut; La Scala Opera Has U.S Debut in Washington," *New York Times*, September 8, 1976.

5. *Editor & Publisher*, August 21, 1976.

6. Molly Ivins, "Atlantic City Sees Itself Basking in the Sun Again," *New York Times*, November 8, 1976.

7. "A Tribute to Molly Ivins," *The Texas Observer*, February 9, 2007.

8. Molly Ivins Papers, The Dolph Briscoe Center for American History, University of Texas at Austin.

9. Ibid.

10. Molly Ivins, "Why They Mourned for Elvis Presley," *New York Times*, August 24, 1977.

11. Molly Ivins Papers.

12. Ibid.

13. E-mail from Joe Lelyveld, September 11, 2008.

14. "Molly Ivins," Salon.com, December 12, 2000.

15. "With cancer treatment behind her, Molly Ivins Is as Controversial as Ever," *Fort Worth Star-Telegram*, July 3, 2001.

16. Interview with Charles Kaiser, August 10, 2008.

17. Ibid.

18. Ibid.

19. Interviews with Kaye Northcott, August 2008.

20. Ibid.

21. "Big Apple Cry: Texas our Texas," *Austin American-Statesman*, September 9, 1977.

22. Myra MacPherson, "Living It Loud," *The Texas Observer*, February 9, 2007.

23. Interview with Clyde Haberman, August 31, 2008.

24. *Englewood Sentinel*, August 1, 1979.

25. Molly Ivins, "Colorful Texas Beer Hall Makes History, Officially; Scholars and Schemers," *New York Times*, August 17, 1979.

26. Molly Ivins Papers.

Chapter 9

1. Remarks made by Eden Lipson at Memorial Service for Molly Ivins, New York, September 2007.

2. "Low-key River Trip Impresses High-powered Women Rafters," *Idaho Statesman*, August 14, 1980.

3. Interviews with Kaye Northcott, August 2008.

4. Interview with Clyde Haberman, August 31, 2008.

5. Kaye Northcott.

6. Clyde Haberman.

7. Ibid.

8. Ibid.

9. Ibid.

10. Molly Ivins, "To Find Success Amid the Stress of New York," *New York Times*, December 8, 1981.

11. Interview with Billy Porterfield, August 21, 2008.

12. "Last Day for *Dallas Times Herald*," *New York Times*, December 9, 1991.

13. "Columnist, Author Molly Ivins Dies," *Dallas Morning News*, February 1, 2007.

14. Molly Ivins Papers, The Dolph Briscoe Center for American History, University of Texas at Austin.

15. Billy Porterfield.

16. Molly Ivins, "Uptight Dallas: Sophisticated but Self-conscious," *Milwaukee Sentinel*, August 19, 1984.

17. Molly Ivins Papers.

18. Ibid.

19. Ibid.

20. Molly Ivins, "Sobran Column on Gays was Wicked and Irresponsible," *Dallas Times Herald*, September 19, 1986.

21. "The Price of Being Molly," *Texas Monthly*, November 1992.

22. Kaye Northcott.

Chapter 10

1. Interview with Ross Ramsey, September 12, 2008.

2. Ibid.

3. Ibid.

4. Ibid.

5. Ibid.

6. Ibid.

7. Molly Ivins Papers, The Dolph Briscoe Center for American History, University of Texas at Austin.

8. Ibid.

9. Ibid.

10. Molly Ivins, "Remembering Ann Richards," www.AlterNet.org, September 15, 2006.

11. Remarks made by Eden Lipson at Memorial to Molly Ivins, New York, September 2007.

12. Molly Ivins Papers.
13. Interview with Dan Green, June 2, 2009.
14. Molly Ivins Papers.
15. Ibid.
16. Ibid.
17. Dan Green.
18. Ibid.
19. Interviews with Ken Bunting and Mike Blackman, August 12 and 16, 2008.
20. "A Fond Remembrance," Star-Telegram.com, February 2, 2007.
21. Ken Bunting and Mike Blackman.
22. Ibid.; Molly Ivins Papers.
23. Ibid.; Molly Ivins Papers.
24. Ken Bunting.

Chapter 11

1. Interview with Peter Osnos, June 1, 2009.
2. Ibid.
3. Interviews with Kaye Northcott, August 2008.
4. Ibid.
5. Ibid.
6. Ibid.
7. Ibid.
8. Interviews with Nadine Eckhardt, August 21, 2008.
9. Ibid.
10. Ibid.
11. Interviews with Liz Faulk, August 29, 2008.
12. Ibid.
13. Ibid.
14. Ibid.
15. Interviews with Sara Speights, July 15, 2008.
16. Ibid.
17. Interviews with Andy Ivins, June 29, 2008.
18. Ibid.
19. *Houston Press*, July 15, 1993.
20. Molly Ivins Papers, The Dolph Briscoe Center for American History, University of Texas at Austin.
21. Kaye Northcott.
22. Molly Ivins Papers.
23. Ibid.
24. Ibid.

25. *Riverfront Times*, June 8, 1994.
26. "Seeing Ralph Ellison," *The New Yorker*, May 2, 1999.
27. Molly Ivins Papers.
28. Ibid.
29. Molly Ivins Papers.
30. Molly Ivins, "Bustin' Rush," *Mother Jones*, May/June 1995.
31. "Molly Ivins, Plagiarist," *The American Enterprise*, September 1995.
32. "Fighting Words," *The American Enterprise*, November 1995.
33. "Dueling Divas," *American Journalism Review*, October 1995.

Chapter 12

1. Interview with Steve Fromholz, August 14, 2008.
2. Interview with John Pope, August 18, 2008.
3. Molly Ivins, "The Good Mother Who Put a Shoe in the Icebox," *Fort Worth Star-Telegram*, January 9, 1997.
4. Interview with Sara Speights, July 15, 2008.
5. Molly Ivins Papers, The Dolph Briscoe Center for American History, University of Texas at Austin.
6. Ibid.
7. Ibid.
8. Ibid.
9. Ibid.
10. Ibid.
11. Ibid.
12. Ibid.
13. Interview with Anthony Zurcher, September 22, 2008.
14. Molly Ivins Papers.
15. Interviews with Ellen Sweets, September 2008.
16. "With Cancer Treatment Behind Her, Molly Ivins Is as Controversial as Ever," *Fort Worth Star-Telegram*, July 3, 2001.
17. Molly Ivins, "Living with Death," *The American Prospect*, December 2001.

Chapter 13

1. Molly Ivins, "Who Needs Breasts, Anyway?," *Time*, February 10, 2002. Copyright Time Inc. Reprinted by permission. *Time* is a registered trademark of Time Inc. All rights reserved.
2. Interviews with Ellen Sweets, September 2008.
3. Interview with John Pope, August 18, 2008.
4. Molly Ivins, "Blast from the Past," *The Free Press*, November 19, 2002.
5. John Pope.

6. Interviews with Bill Holland, June 2009.

7. Interview with Betsy Moon, May 21, 2009.

8. Ibid.

9. Molly Ivins, "Why Did We Invade Iraq?," *The Free Press*, October 7, 2003.

10. Molly Ivins, "Picking a Winner," *Naples Daily News*, December 4, 2003.

11. Interviews with Kaye Northcott, August 2008.

12. Ibid.

13. Molly Ivins Papers, The Dolph Briscoe Center for American History, University of Texas at Austin.

14. Kaye Northcott.

15. Betsy Moon.

16. Kaye Northcott.

17. Interviews with Dave Richards, July 2008; Tribute to Molly Ivins, *The Texas Observer*, February 7, 2007.

18. Molly Ivins Papers.

19. Interviews with Dave Richards, July 2008.

20. "Molly Ivins," *Texas Monthly*, November 2006.

21. John Pope.

22. Interview with Sara Speights, July 15, 2008.

23. Molly Ivins Papers.

24. Molly Ivins, "Stand Up Against the Surge," *The Free Press*, January 11, 2007.

INDEX

ABOUT THE AUTHORS

Bill Minutaglio is a professor of journalism at the University of Texas and author of several critically acclaimed books, including the first unauthorized biography of George W. Bush, *First Son: George W. Bush & the Bush Family Dynasty*.

Journalist **W. Michael Smith** was Molly Ivins's researcher and assistant for six years. He has worked with the *Fort Worth Star-Telegram*, writer Gail Sheehy, staffers from the *New York Times*, the BBC, PBS *Frontline*, and ARD-Germany.

PublicAffairs is a publishing house founded in 1997. It is a tribute to the standards, values, and flair of three persons who have served as mentors to countless reporters, writers, editors, and book people of all kinds, including me.

I. F. STONE, proprietor of *I. F. Stone's Weekly*, combined a commitment to the First Amendment with entrepreneurial zeal and reporting skill and became one of the great independent journalists in American history. At the age of eighty, Izzy published *The Trial of Socrates*, which was a national bestseller. He wrote the book after he taught himself ancient Greek.

BENJAMIN C. BRADLEE was for nearly thirty years the charismatic editorial leader of *The Washington Post*. It was Ben who gave the *Post* the range and courage to pursue such historic issues as Watergate. He supported his reporters with a tenacity that made them fearless and it is no accident that so many became authors of influential, best-selling books.

ROBERT L. BERNSTEIN, the chief executive of Random House for more than a quarter century, guided one of the nation's premier publishing houses. Bob was personally responsible for many books of political dissent and argument that challenged tyranny around the globe. He is also the founder and longtime chair of Human Rights Watch, one of the most respected human rights organizations in the world.

• • •

For fifty years, the banner of Public Affairs Press was carried by its owner Morris B. Schnapper, who published Gandhi, Nasser, Toynbee, Truman, and about 1,500 other authors. In 1983, Schnapper was described by *The Washington Post* as "a redoubtable gadfly." His legacy will endure in the books to come.

Peter Osnos, *Founder and Editor-at-Large*